THE GREEN TRAVEL SOURCEBOOK

A Guide for the Physically Active,
the Intellectually Curious,
or the Socially Aware

▼ ▼ ▼

Daniel Grotta
Sally Wiener Grotta

John Wiley & Sons, Inc.
New York • Chichester • Brisbane • Toronto • Singapore

In recognition of the importance of preserving what has been
written, it is a policy of John Wiley & Sons, Inc., to have books
of enduring value published in the United States printed on acid-
free paper, and we exert our best efforts to that end.

Text printed on recycled paper.

This publication is designed to provide accurate and
authoritative information in regard to the subject
matter covered. It is sold with the understanding that
the publisher is not engaged in rendering legal, accounting,
or other professional services. If legal advice or other
expert assistance is required, the services of a competent
professional person should be sought. *From a Declaration
of Principles jointly adopted by a Committee of the
American Bar Association and a Committee of Publishers.*

Library of Congress Cataloging in Publication Data:

Grotta, Daniel, 1944–
    The green travel sourcebook : a guide for the physically active, the
    intellectually curious, or the socially aware / Daniel Grotta & Sally
    Wiener Grotta.
        p.   cm.
    Includes index.
    ISBN 0-471-53911-2 (paper)
    1. Tourist trade—Environmental aspects.   Grotta, Sally
Wiener, 1949–   . II. Title.
    G155.A1G79   1991
    338.4'791—dc20   91-19353

Printed in the United States of America

10 9 8 7 6 5 4 3 2 1

Printed and bound by the Courier Companies, Inc.

For Noel & Edith Wiener,
the best researchers money can't buy

CONTENTS

▼ ▼ ▼

CONTENTS

INTRODUCTION

▼ ▼ ▼

Ah, vacations. For many millions of Americans, the annual two or three weeks away from the office, store, or factory are what life is really about. Vacation is the one time of year to relax, unwind, and decompress from the accumulated pressures of the daily grind. It's also our best opportunity to recharge spiritual batteries and enjoy a well-deserved rest, and to reacquaint oneself with the spouse and kids. We lounge on hot, sandy beaches, enjoy shamelessly sybaritic island cruises, schuss down well-manicured ski slopes, stand in line with the kids to meet Mickey, Minnie, and Goofy at crowded theme parks, or even, perhaps, experience the excitement and wonderment that come from visiting one of those long-dreamed-of, faraway places with strange-sounding names.

Traditionally, we mark our vacations by collecting seashells and passport stamps, buying hokey souvenirs and sending alluring picture postcards, and acquiring sunburns and summer friendships. But in the end, virtually the only things of value we have to show for our vacations are snapshots and unpaid credit card charges.

For almost a century, the annual vacation has been—along with motherhood and apple pie—an ironclad American institution. Until relatively recently, most of us were content with passive vacations amidst familiar surroundings. We rented cottages at the beach and bought into time-share condos at the mountains, played at Club Med-type, subtropical resorts, or gambled at Vegas or Atlantic City. And when we were adventurous enough to travel abroad, we viewed European capitals or the Indonesian countryside out of oversized windows in air-conditioned coaches, dined in three- or four-star restaurants, and stayed in American-style, luxury hotels. Rarely, if ever, did we get to meet the natives— the people who create and define the culture simply by residing there—or to explore and experience the place like a native.

At least, that's how it used to be.

Nowadays, many of us are searching for more meaningful leisure time experiences. We have grown weary of spoon-fed, hand-held trips and tours that whisk us from place to place in insulated bubbles of transported Americana and leave us with little or no contact with the people, the culture, or the environment of the places we visit. Nor are we satisfied any longer with laid-back, do-nothing vacations in which we become transplanted couch potatoes.

Instead, we're longing for gung-ho, do-something, learn-something, give-back-something vacations that will exhilarate us and leave us feeling good. We want vacations that will allow us to experience intimately the people and places we visit while not inadvertently polluting the environment or contributing to an oppressive political regime, and perhaps make the world a little better place. What we're really looking for is an adventure, an experience, a happening that will linger long in our hearts and minds after we return home and make us look forward to more of the same next year.

If that's how you feel, if this is what you've been searching for, then you are indeed a Green Traveler.

Back in the mid-1970s, the Europeans appropriated the word *Green* to describe those of us who are vitally concerned about the environment, world peace, cultural integrity, and a generally higher, gentler quality of life, and are willing to sacrifice something in order to bring about favorable changes. Since then, the fledgling Green Movement has exploded into a veritable worldwide crusade. There's a Green Party in Germany, a Green government in Australia, New Zealand is officially referred to as Green country, and numerous political and social movements and organizations have sprung up around the globe that claim to be one shade or another of Green. Even industry has adapted Green as its favorite color, and Green labels touting claims of ecological accountability or social sensitivity are showing up on supermarket shelves in ever-greater numbers.

The origins of the international Green Movement can be traced back to President Kennedy's creation of the Peace Corps in the early 1960s, as well as his quest to bring about The New Frontier. Since then, many of us have sympathized with or participated in Civil Rights marches, antiwar demonstrations, pro-education teach-ins, grape and tuna boycotts, women's rights issues, Save the Whales campaigns, antiapartheid protests, and a plethora of other consciousness-raising efforts. We've supported Earth Day and trash recycling, alternative fuels and the outlawing of DDT, organically grown foods and natural mineral waters, weapons ban treaties and Amnesty International efforts, as well as a long list of other causes and crusades whose purpose is to help better humanity while making the earth a more wholesome place to live. All that accumulated energy and concern helped create the Green Movement.

Today, living Green means that we select our foods with an eye toward what is environmentally prudent as well as nutritionally sound, purchase biodegradable and recyclable products whenever possible, try to invest primarily in companies that don't exploit Third World countries, and vote for candidates who promise tough environmental laws and humanitarian aid to the poor. Living Green also signifies that we are conscious and concerned about a variety of community, national, and international causes, such as saving the rain forests, protecting wilderness areas, preserving primitive cultures and tribal homelands, and rescuing endangered species from the brink of extinction.

Taking our cue from the Green Movement, we define Green Travel as travel that encourages and promotes personal, intellectual, and spiritual growth and satisfaction through intimate interaction and involvement with nature, people, and/or culture. In other words, a Green Traveler is anyone who opts for more meaningful, challenging, or adventuresome experiences of one sort or another on their vacations, while practicing a certain sensitivity and responsibility to the environment and the local culture.

Green Travel has many different and diverse incarnations. It consists of everyone, from the Indiana Jones-type adventurer who uses his or her vacation to go on an ecologically sound African tent safari to the socially conscious volunteer who staffs a charity clinic for AIDS victims in Port-au-Prince, from the enthusiastic whale watcher on a Baja California cruise to an unpaid assistant helping scientists count giant turtles in Micronesia. What's more, it includes people like the Francophile brushing up on French while leisurely biking through the Loire Valley and the culture vulture who attends seminars at the great museums or takes minicourses at famous universities.

Green Travel also means visiting exotic, out-of-the-way places and peoples unspoiled by tourism, observing wildlife in natural surroundings, challenging oneself to the very fullest by rafting down a wild river or trekking through desolate mountains, or learning more about our global village firsthand by participating in people-to-people programs.

Although a relatively new phenomenon, Green Travel has quickly grown into a $2-billion-a-year business. True, that seemingly significant figure pales when compared to the $200-billion-a-year mainstream travel industry, but it does indicate that Green Travel is a healthy market with a growing audience. At last count, there are well over 500 tour operators and travel organizations scattered throughout the world that specialize in Green Travel.

Unfortunately for the average consumer, uncovering information about the various Green Travel programs and tours has not been easy. As a practical matter, most travel agents can help book you only into a handful of commercially oriented Green Travel programs offered by a few large tour operators like Abercrombie & Kent, Mountain Travel, or Society Expeditions. What's more, no Good Housekeeping Seal of Approval, watchdog-type agency exists that oversees whether or not a tour operator is truly Green or just claims to be in order to garner business. Many legitimate Green Travel companies are either nonprofit organizations that pay no commissions, or are too small and hence not profitable enough to attract travel agents' attention.

And that's the *raison d'être* for this sourcebook: to introduce readers to over 80 Green Travel organizations and programs, many of which you are not likely to discover on your own without doing considerable research. While we make no claim to be encyclopedic in coverage—such a directory would probably run over a thousand pages of small print and cost more than most readers can easily afford—we have attempted to include as many of the important and interesting tour operators and companies as possible. In addition to the main listings, we have also included many other organizations, contacts, references, and supplementary sources of information that may be valuable to the reader (see Part Three). Our criteria for inclusion aren't necessarily size or dollar volume. Indeed, a few listings are shoestring operations that have less than a dozen employees. But, we selected them according to how firmly committed they are to ecological and societal responsibilities, how unique or unusual their programs or challenges are, and how vital and useful the services they perform.

Of course, despite our efforts to be current and accurate, there are certain to be omissions and errors. For these we apologize in advance. We tried to be as accurate as possible, but changes in prices, schedules, and programs are unavoidable and frequent. Therefore, we urge you to double-check all prices, destinations, dates, and conditions with any tour operator or organization before making any firm commitment. We hope to increase the number of companies profiled, as well as fine-tune our coverage, in subsequent editions. If you do come across any errors, or if you know of worthy programs, tour operators, or organizations we've somehow missed and should include in the next edition, we would like to hear from you. More than anything else Green Travel is based on networking and sharing information and experiences.

In the meantime, we're confident that you, Green Traveler, will find this sourcebook both useful and entertaining. Happy Travels!

PART ONE

GOING GREEN

▼ ▼ ▼

Chapter One

THE GREEN
TRAVELER

▼ ▼ ▼

You've made the commitment, at least in your mind. This year, you're going to do something radically different on your vacation. It may be that you will be going away to a foreign university to learn more about the history and the culture of a particular country, or having the adventure of a lifetime in the wilderness, or seeing for yourself what they're talking about when they warn that the equatorial rain forests are vanishing, or perhaps volunteering to help out on a scientific project or a humanitarian endeavor.

Whatever it is, you'd really prefer not putting your hard-earned money into the pockets of anonymous multinational corporations but would rather patronize local hotels, restaurants, and tour operators. Also, you want to make certain that you're not disturbing the environment, upsetting the local culture, or helping prop up a repressive regime. You may be looking forward to seeing wildlife up close, to participating in some sort of people-to-people program, or to intimately experiencing what it is really like to live as a native in another country or culture, if only for a few days or weeks.

In short, you want to be a Green Traveler.

SO, WHAT IS A GREEN TRAVELER
ANYWAY?

▼ ▼ ▼

Bandwagons and buzzwords aside, just who or what are Green Travelers, and how are they different from ordinary tourists or sightseers?

Green Travelers are ordinary people who have decided to do extraordinary things on their vacations. For instance:

▶ Green Travelers may be individuals who are dissatisfied with passive, sybaritic, numbing vacations, and instead crave more zest, meaning, and satisfaction.

▶ Green Travelers may be particularly sensitive to the environment and culture, and want to learn how not to encroach, change, or spoil things, so they may be enjoyed by future generations.

▶ Green Travelers may be lovers of nature, of beautiful, unspoiled, pristine places where they can discover a new intimacy with the variety and beauty of a wilderness.

▶ Green Travelers may be people who actively seek to develop a better understanding of who we are and where we are going, or crave new knowledge and insight about themselves by learning about the world.

▶ Green Travelers may want to meet people on a personal, one-to-one level and enjoy the differences as well as the similarities between our many and diverse cultures.

▶ Green Travelers could be latter-day Shackletons and Burtons saddened that there are no more frontiers or unexplored regions but still eager to visit exotic or remote places few have seen before.

▶ Green Travelers may be Walter Mittys who secretly (and not-so-secretly) crave adventures and personal challenges, albeit within a relatively safe and comfortable framework.

▶ Green Travelers may also be infused with the spirit of an Albert Schweitzer or a Louis Pasteur, wishing to donate time and talent to healing the sick, helping the poor, or contributing to the advancement of science.

▶ Green Travelers may be armchair scholars or perennial students who want to continue learning in an academic or on-location environment long after leaving school.

In short, there's no particular profile of a typical Green Traveler. Green Travelers come from all ages, educational backgrounds, ethnic groups, and occupations. They may be youngsters or octogenarians, lawyers, carpenters, or assembly-line workers, college-educated or high-school dropouts. There are families, couples, and singles, North Americans, Europeans, and most other nationalities among Green Travelers.

What distinguishes Green Travelers from ordinary vacationers is their frame of mind, a sense of purpose and caring, and a degree of commitment to make the most out of their vacations. As a rule, they tend to be just a little more courteous and respectful of people, wildlife, and the environment, less complaining about local conditions, and interested in historical or cultural points of reference.

THE GREEN TRAVEL NETWORK
▼ ▼ ▼

A strange and wonderful thing happens when you join a Green Travel-related organization or sign up for a Green Travel trip or program: You instantly become part of a network of kindred spirits. Taking that first step to express your confirmation of the organization's or tour operator's philosophy, program, or trip often automatically qualifies you as part of the group. It doesn't particularly matter if you are an expert or novice, single or part of a family, or even whether the tour operator is a nonprofit institution or a for-profit corporation.

Another refreshing difference is that in most Green Travel operations, including the more commercialized profit-making enterprises, the distinction between staff and guest often blurs. There's virtually no sense of staffers being disinterested employees or dictatorial leaders, or of guests being treated as sheep or worse. In most instances, staffers and guests eat, sleep, work, and play together. And at the end of the trip, the usual form of reward is a handshake and a "well done!" rather than a gratuity. In some instances, gratuities are accepted by service personnel or local guides but never by staff naturalists, historians, or other experts and associates.

Unlike conventional tours, which are over the moment you reach the airport, Green Travel programs tend to live on long after you've returned home. Often, you are automatically enrolled as a member of the sponsoring organization and will receive its newsletter or regular mailings. In larger cities, there may be small, informal get-togethers, not only of people who were with you on your particular trip but with others from previous, similar trips. Also, once you have participated in one program, you will undoubtedly receive invitations for future programs or trips. A few organizations even offer local tours, nearby outings, weekend trips, and the like. You may also receive mailings from organizations you've never heard of, since it's fairly common for Green Travel tour operators and organizations to rent or trade their computerized membership lists to similar organizations.

In other words, it's fair to say that once you have traveled Green, you need never again be alone if you don't want to be. You become a member of a growing, popular network of interested and interesting people.

Chapter Two

TYPES AND STYLES OF GREEN TRAVEL PROGRAMS

▼ ▼ ▼

Green Travel programs are quite diverse. Essentially, there are six major types of programs and tours: (1) nature field trips, (2) physically challenging endeavors, (3) intellectually satisfying tours, (4) people-to-people encounters, (5) volunteer programs, and (6) reality tours. However, the distinctions usually are not clearly delineated; indeed, it's possible to spend your vacation combining several types into one cohesive trip.

DOLPHINS, WHALES, AND NATURE TRAILS
▼ ▼ ▼

Nature—wild, wonderful, and endangered—is the inspiration for many Green Travel programs. Anywhere animals roam, birds nest, or plants grow, if it is beautiful, interesting, on the verge of extinction, or simply romantic, then there will be a Green tour or field trip highlighting it. Such trips might be treks into Rwanda to interact with the late Dian Fosse's mountain gorillas (the ones portrayed in the film *Gorillas in the Mist*); swimming with dolphins who seem to enjoy playing with their human toys; whale watching from cruise ships and small boats; birdwatching, of course, one of the largest and fastest-growing pastimes in the world; or hiking in one of the world's many and diverse rain forests.

Green nature programs are as inexpensive and accessible as your nearest state park (see page 79) and as exotic and expensive as tiger safaris in India. The one thing they all have in common is that participants seek not just to collect photographs (the way their big-game hunter predecessors displayed stuffed and skinned animals as trophies), but they come to learn and to be inspired.

On a Green nature trip, expert naturalists share their considerable knowledge and insights in lectures, with discussion groups, and on field trips. The best way to describe a Green field trip is to imagine being dropped into the middle of a *National Geographic* television documentary. Treading softly, so as not to disturb any flora or fauna nearby, you'll inch close to koalas or seals or albatross or whatever creature you are studying, while the naturalist will, in hushed tones, point out various distinctive markings or displayed behavior. The learning experience is more than exhilarating, it's an intimate and awe-inspiring firsthand encounter with nature in all its glory.

In some programs you can get as close to the wildlife as Jacques Cousteau or Jane Goodall do in their nature documentaries. For instance, in Kaikoura, New Zealand (which is the Down Under whale-watching capital) (see page 107) if you jump in the water in a certain cove, before you can swim more than two strokes, dozens of fur seals on the surrounding rocks will slip into the surf to play with you. A Green Traveler who is well versed in nature's etiquette (see pages 39–40) doesn't approach a wild creature unless the accompanying naturalist assures him that the animal will not be "stressed" and that it isn't dangerous. And even then, you should watch for signs of an animal's anxiety or discomfort. It's best to just sit down or, in this case, float about, waiting for the creature to come to you. In many instances, if you exhibit nonthreatening behavior, they will approach you.

Many of the Green nature programs focus on rain forests, not just because they are a fashionable cause or because their pristine beauty and profusion of life offer unforgettably vivid vacation memories but also because they are vital to the whole earth's ecosystem. As stated by International Expeditions,

> Though tropical forests cover less than eight percent of the Earth's surface, they support more than half the Earth's known plant and animal species. Rain forests are, in a very real sense, global life support systems, as they perform a variety of essential environmental functions including the regulation of global carbon dioxide levels. . . . Scientists believe there are more unidentified species of plants and animals in the Amazon jungle than there are classified species in the entire Northern Hemisphere.

Just as recent pharmaceutical and industrial breakthroughs often come directly from newly identified rain forest plants and animals, it's possible that the answer to some of our most perplexing problems or intractable diseases might be locked away in the makeup of an unknown plant on the verge of extinction.

Green nature trips may involve camping out in the wilderness in order to be as close to nature as possible, or they may be quite indulgent, even luxurious, including stays in country inns or grand hotels. Some are conducted from cruise ships or boats for the simple reason that certain wilderness areas (such as the Galapagos and Antarctica) or certain animals (such as whales) are otherwise inaccessible. Besides, ships and boats have little or no negative impact on local cultures and ecosystems, and they are a very comfortable way to travel. Whatever your preference, whether you are a backpacking individualist, a creature of comfort, or a curious but not gung-ho nature lover, there are Green nature programs that will suit your personality.

LET'S GET PHYSICAL
▼ ▼ ▼

Another variety of Green Travel is a physically active, adventure-type vacation that meets some sort of challenge or fulfills a fantasy. It may be learning about or performing a sport that brings you closer to nature, such as scuba diving or whitewater rafting. Or it may mean using alternative transportation in order to slow down the pace of life, as well as to see the world about you more intimately; these include backpacking, trekking, bicycling, walking, and horseback riding.

Some physical Green Travel programs look to challenge your abilities and push you to your limits. These include Outward Bound-type programs, mountain climbing, or cross-country skiing expeditions, Arctic treks or other feats of endurance. Such "Yes, I can do it!" experiences help build confidence and a sense of self-worth that reverberate long after you return home.

Then, there are the programs and trips for explorers and thrill seekers. The more unusual, exotic, or offbeat the destination, the better. They shun towns, roads, and tourist attractions in favor of open plains, dense forests, wild rivers, thick ice fields, tall mountains, or other empty, unpeopled terrains. Such Green Travelers are often searching for authentic, unstructured experiences—adventures in which the outcome may be uncertain.

Why do people crave the kind of vacation that involves some degree of physical exertion and discomfort, and perhaps even pain and a little danger? More often than not there is the feeling that the only way to get close to nature is to slough off all trappings of mechanical and technological civilization. Can you imagine the difference between studying a pair of eagles from a mountain trail vantage point overlooking their nest as opposed to hoping for a glance of them from a roadside where the bus is parked? For those who choose the more rugged, or even dangerous, journeys, there's a bit of machismo mixed in, the desire to do something extraordinary and then be able to brag about it for the rest of their lives.

But a more common motivation is self-testing. Many individuals need, at one time or another, to find out what their limits are and then push themselves even further; for such people, vacations are times to explore their own internal landscape along with that of the world.

But while many of these programs require physical fitness and, perhaps, a bit of courage, even if you aren't in top condition, you still can choose from a variety of physically active Green Travel programs that will bring you close to nature. There are a variety of programs designed specifically for senior citizens, for the physically handicapped, for children, and, yes, even for terminal couch potatoes who want to see just how far they can go.

THE WORLD IS MY CLASSROOM PROGRAMS
▼ ▼ ▼

Less taxing to the body but challenging to the mind are the many enlightening, learn-something-new, explore-possibilities-type programs tailored for cerebral or intellectually curious Green Travelers. Among them are tours and cruises conducted by naturalists, historians, academicians, and other recognized authorities, in which participants learn about nature and the environment, history, foreign cultures, and so on. Such tours are often sponsored by museums, universities, college alumni associations, and other nonprofit special-interest groups. (See pages 173–176 for a listing of some of the museums and universities that offer tours on a regular basis.) Usually, they combine several hours of lectures each day, intermingled with field trips and free time.

For instance, you may take a tour to Greece and Turkey accompanied by professors of classics or other experts of ancient civilizations. They usually not only lecture on pre-Christian Hellenic culture and history, but they help make an otherwise sterile recitation of facts and dates come alive by sparking an infectious enthusiasm among the participants. They may accomplish this during walks, say, through the magnificent ruins of Ephesus, where they translate some of the ancient graffiti and explain the social and political situations that fueled it.

Generally, the main purpose of these tours isn't to prepare participants for further academic study. Rather, it's to inflame the mind, provide fuel for thought, and entertain via information. Most Green Travelers enjoy learning and appreciate the opportunity to learn more about the subject or region for their own personal pleasure or enlightenment.

Another form of cultural Green Travel is attending a school or university for a few days or weeks. It's a wonderful opportunity to visit, however briefly, famous institutions like Oxford University or the Sorbonne, or unique milieus like a venerable grand hotel, rain forest research center, or isolated mountain lodge. These programs usually have a specific semiacademic or cultural purpose, such as learning a language, exploring an artist's work, or learning about a particular endangered species. Others are socially slanted, such as observing the poverty and politics of Third World nations, or delving into the economic and environmental impact of drag-net tuna fishing in Peru, or slash-and-burn farming in the Amazon.

Most of these programs are fairly sophisticated, concentrating many weeks or even months of normal course and field work into days or a few weeks. While they're designed for college-educated individuals who have been out of school for some years, the overwhelming majority do not require any background knowledge or degree achievement.

Incidentally, study programs usually devote a substantial amount of time to field trips, sightseeing, and other recreation, so you needn't worry about spending your entire vacation in a classroom. Depending on the program, scholarships or financial assistance may be available. And if you're a student, your school may accept some of these programs for college credit; check with your school counselor and the tour organizer before leaving home.

PEOPLE-TO-PEOPLE OUTREACH
▼ ▼ ▼

Over the past several decades, tourism has become a major force for peace in the world and is credited in part for opening up China (despite the 1989 crackdown), liberalizing Eastern Europe, and reducing international tensions. And, for better or worse, tourism is the economic mainstay of many countries. The most basic and intimate form of tourism is when strangers from one nation or region have an opportunity to meet, talk to, eat with, and even host citizens from another country. The better we understand our neighbors, the smaller and more peaceful the global village becomes.

Green Travel tour operators and nonprofit organizations take this concept a step further by providing programs that arrange people-to-people encounters according to common interests. Such interests range from a mutual concern for protecting the environment to helping eradicate hunger or disease, from saving endangered species to a common love of tramping through the countryside. Often, there's a shared goal or purpose, such as groups of Green Travelers from one country getting together with their counterparts from another country for study programs, research projects, or rallies for world peace or environmental action.

Many people-to-people programs are arranged by religious organizations, educational institutions, and action groups. Depending on the locale and the sponsoring organization, these programs may involve swapping students, being hosted in a member's house, or sharing barracks-like accommodations. Shorter stays of one or two nights, arranged within a tour or other group program, are common. Lifelong friendships often evolve from such encounters.

On a more informal basis, it is often possible to arrange your own people-to-people encounter, just for the pleasure of it. (See pages 55–57.)

CARING AND SHARING
▼ ▼ ▼

About the only point on which philosophers and theologians agree is that the two main concerns of humanity are death and immortality. Since no one has successfully evaded the former, much of human endeavor is devoted to ways of leaving lasting monuments of our existence. If we can't engrave our names in history books by heroic acts or public exploits, then the next best way might be doing good works that will leave a lasting legacy.

Of course, that's the orthodox psychoanalytical explanation for why many people feel compelled to help feed the hungry, heal the sick, and assist the poor. However, as card-carrying idealists, we would like to believe that we help others simply because it's the right and noble thing to do. Besides, it can be extremely satisfying, even fun.

Whatever the reasons, a groundswell of goodwill and a spirit of volunteerism compels many individuals to dedicate their vacations to helping others. There are many Green Travel programs available that make use of volunteers. It's a mutually advantageous exchange: The programs profit from donated manpower and skills, and the participants feel enriched by giving of themselves in a new kind of learning environment.

Different types of volunteer programs attract different kinds of volunteers. One type deals primarily with the environment. For example, there are programs that use volunteers to track and count rare wildlife, rescue injured animals, work with a cleanup crew on an oil-covered beach, or plant trees in a reforestation campaign. Volunteers for such programs frequently (but not always) sleep in tents or huts and cook on a campfire.

Then there are programs that allow volunteers to reach out and help those less fortunate than themselves. These involve helping to build low-income houses in depressed inner-city areas, staffing a Third World health clinic, assisting with relief supplies distribution, giving cholera injections in an area devastated by a natural disaster, teaching good nutrition to nursing mothers, digging water wells in rural villages, or many other specific long-term, temporary, or emergency projects. Volunteers should be prepared to live communally and eat cafeteria-style, or to be housed with local residents.

A number of programs are more ideological than idealistic in nature, and the sponsoring organization may have a particular political or philosophical agenda. Typical programs of this type might deal with monitoring an election to insure that it remains fair or taking testimony chronicling human rights abuses.

Then there are scientific and cultural projects. Often, universities and museums stretch their research grants by inviting paying volunteers to assist on projects. Such projects vary from archeological digs to dolphin studies, recording tribal folk songs to analyzing soil samples. Accommodations range from camping out to spartan huts to comfortable private or semiprivate apartments.

The last type of volunteer program isn't really for vacationers but for those who are so infused by their brief experiences and committed to helping others that they want to go back into the field for months or even years at a time. The Peace Corps is the best example of long-term volunteerism, and it requires a minimum commitment of two years. (In some instances, if you have certain needed skills, the Peace Corps may consider a stint as short as three months.) Another example is Harvard University's World Teach, which sponsors a volunteer teaching program for those willing to give a summer or a year. Other charities, institutions, and church or synagogue groups have comparable (but private) programs that use both skilled and unskilled volunteers willing to work hard under primitive conditions for little or no pay. What's more, many of these programs are so strapped for cash that they require that volunteers pay their own transportation costs and most of their living expenses.

(Although this book does not focus on these long-term volunteer programs, we have listed a few of them on pages 217–218 for readers interested in obtaining further information.)

The cost for volunteering can range from nothing to thousands of dollars. Typically, the volunteer must pay to join the organization and pay for air fare or other transportation to the site, and, sometimes, food and lodging. There are some programs that provide expenses and a small stipend to qualified volunteers. Scholarships or grants may be available. Most of the programs are either partially or wholly tax deductible. Also, you may be able to earn college credits.

Volunteer programs run a wide gamut of times, places, and prices. Some last only a few days, while others go on for months or years. Some programs call for working from the moment of arrival to the time you leave for home, while others alternate between work and sightseeing or other leisure-time activities. Usually, however, the evenings are your own. Some programs require specific qualifications, and the most desirable ones fill up early, so check as far in advance as possible on any that might interest you.

REALITY TOURS
▼ ▼ ▼

Reality tours are designed to impart to their participants a firsthand knowledge of political, social, environmental, or economic conditions of a region, country, or culture, in such a way that they will be motivated to do something when they return home. They differ from volunteer programs in that the participants are there primarily to learn and observe and not to work or achieve a specific result.

Many reality tours are political in nature, usually left-leaning. For instance, some of the more popular reality tours take small groups of semicommitted people (that is, participants who are predisposed to reinforce their already established views and opinions) to visit war-torn El Salvador, post-Sandinista Nicaragua, black townships in South Africa, slums in Calcutta, military regimes in South America, or other controversial spots. Some tours are not open to the general public but require that you be a member of a particular group or organization first. However, membership can usually be arranged.

Reality tours can be quite grim and shocking. Depending on the organization and the locale, you may be quite closely exposed to starvation and disease, war and violence, repression and death. Conditions may be primitive, and while participants rarely, if ever, risk danger or death, their viewpoints and their lives may be fundamentally affected.

VARIOUS SHADES OF GREEN TRAVEL: RUGGED, SOFT ADVENTURE, AND SYBARITIC
▼ ▼ ▼

By now, you may have conjured up an image of Green Travelers as gung-ho, Goody-Two-Shoes wearing L.L. Bean clothes, shouldering high-tech backpacks and sleeping bags, and slogging through the wilds far from civilization. Yes, certainly, some Green Travelers love the great outdoors and dress and pack accordingly. And yes, some Green Travel programs and trips involve varying degrees of physical exertion and entail enduring primitive conditions. But Green Travelers may just as likely be wearing fashions from Bloomingdale's as Bean's, may opt for charming *pensiones* or even grand hotels as opposed to tents and cots, and may do nothing more strenuous than walk the corridors of a museum or the halls of a university.

Green Travel does *not* automatically imply rugged hardships and rudimentary amenities, deprivations, and sacrifices. True, some programs project a spartan, back-to-nature pioneer spirit, something like Crocodile Dundee shaving with his Bowie knife, but others allow for human nature and local conditions by offering varying degrees of comfort. Also, while some programs require physical exertion, others are really quite tame. It all depends on the program and the tour organizer's philosophy.

Basically, there are three styles of Green Travel: rugged, soft adventure, and sybaritic.

Rugged Green Travel involves a lack of comforts and amenities. You may be camping out in the wild or trekking for hours up mountain trails. Or, you may be living communally, dormitory-style while on volunteer programs. On some trips, you may be able to actually live with natives, stay in their huts, bathe in the nearby streams, and eat whatever food is in the communal fire. On most rugged programs, hot showers are few and far between, and, in some cases, toilets are outhouses or a spot behind an isolated bush. You are often expected to share in the responsibilities of cooking, cleaning, and setting up camp. Rugged is the way to go if you are a gung-ho, up-and-at-'em type of outdoorsperson, adventurer, or volunteer. But this is an extreme form of Green Travel that represents only a small percentage of programs that are available.

Soft adventure Green Travel is far less strenuous and depriving. Rather than trekking the entire distance by foot, raft, horse, or skis, participants are bussed, flown in, or ferried over by boat to remote sites. Accommodations, meals, and amenities are usually on board a ship or in a lodge or hotel. And if you are camping out, it is the staff that puts up and breaks camps, cooks and serves the meals, cleans up, and so on. (Some African safari companies actually offer air-conditioned tents replete with *ensuite* private toilet and shower!)

Soft adventure is an ideal choice for those who want or need basic creature comforts, or who, for one reason or another, may have difficulty keeping up with a rugged program. Incidentally, soft adventure via cruise ships or bush planes is sometimes the only practical way that Green Travelers can visit certain remote areas, such as the Galapagos Islands, Antarctica, or the Arctic Northwest Passage.

Sybaritic Green Travel is the term we use to describe those tours and programs in which participants can expect moderate to luxurious accommodations and amenities. In most cases, you will have your own private bathroom with a hot shower or bath every evening. Some diehard Green Travelers cringe and scoff at the very thought of air conditioning or other comforts, as if it somehow compromises the authenticity of the experience. According to Ann Waigand, editor of *The Educated Traveler*, these are ''purists who always use recycled paper and don't want anyone to use a Jacuzzi in the jungle.'' But many Green Travel programs, especially museum tours and university seminars, feature facilities comparable or even identical to those on ordinary commercial tours.

There are even some Green Travel tour operators who cater to individuals who demand, and are willing to pay for, the very best available. These are the people who book the suites on adventure ships, fly first class to assembly points when everybody else is in economy, sleep in chateaux and fine hotels while others stay in small hotels and *pensiones*, and eat at the top restaurants instead of always taking group meals. Is there, or should there be, a moral dilemma about trying to travel Green while living an unabashedly sybaritic life style? So long as there is no overt exploitation of the locals or destruction of the ecosystem, such decisions are yours and your wallet's to decide. The sense of purpose that defines Green Travel doesn't require deprivations and hardships, unless they add to the experience for you. Many a day, we have basked in the pleasure of a big bed, hot bath, and room service after a long, hot day traipsing through the wilds.

ECOTOURISM AND GREEN TRAVEL: IS THERE A DIFFERENCE?

▼ ▼ ▼

A new term gaining rapid acceptance in the travel industry is *ecotourism*. As its name implies, ecotourism is concerned primarily in one way or another with environmentally responsible travel. It covers everything from jungle treks to birdwatching, naturalist projects to river rafting. It also involves such things as patronizing locally owned hotels and restaurants, using native guides (and paying them decent wages), buying food and supplies locally, adhering to published guidelines regarding correct behavior around wild animals, properly disposing of refuse, walking only where your footsteps won't destroy fragile plant life, tying scuba dive boats up to buoys rather than dragging your anchor over easily damaged reefs, and so on.

Ecotourists are, by definition, Green Travelers. However, Green Travelers are not necessarily ecotourists. Green Travelers include, in addition to those interested primarily in nature and the environment, individuals concerned with humanitarian matters, cultural interchange, and intellectual enrichment. Often, such activities have little or nothing to do with flora or fauna.

Some purists will argue that ecotourism has been around for decades, if not centuries. After all, it's claimed that John Muir, Theodore Roosevelt, and Richard Halliburton, just to name a few, were ecotourists long before the word was ever invented. However, the large-scale commitment to respect and preserve the environment is relatively new. New Zealand's Sir Edmund Hillary, the first person in history to scale Mount Everest and a renowned conservationist, confesses that he developed ''a sense of preservation over a period of time. When we first went into the Himalayas in 1951, we had no awareness of conservation at all. We just left our rubbish in heaps. All this environmental business is very recent. As I spent more time in these areas and saw much more of the carelessness people were displaying, then I became more and more aware of the environment. But initially, I was as careless as anybody else, but I learned.''

Ecotourism is already a vital part of responsible tourism, and experts predict that it will be one of the fastest-growing segments of the travel industry throughout the 1990s. Unfortunately, because the profits from ecotourism (as with Green Travel) are projected to be quite sizeable, inevitably there will be some unprincipled tour organizers who will put on the patina of responsible tourism just to garner extra income. (See page 44 for a discussion on how to determine just how Green a tour organizer really is.) If you suspect that a company is Green in name only, either investigate further or select another tour operator.

Chapter Three

STRANGERS WHEN WE MEET

▼ ▼ ▼

The mark of an ordinary vacation is that everybody is a stranger when they first arrive, and unfortunately, most remain strangers when they depart. Couples rarely have anything to do with singles, families avoid the old folks, and the physically disabled are shunned by almost everybody. Green Travel is almost the opposite: Everybody may be a stranger when they first arrive, but by the time they leave for home, most people are on a first-name basis and often become lifelong friends.

There are several good reasons why this happens. For one thing, most groups are small so it's impossible to be ignored or lost in the shuffle. Also, Green Travelers tend to be more sensitive and caring, not only about the environment, world peace, and other ''cosmic'' issues but about people. But more to the point, Green Travelers share a common interest and, probably, a similar philosophy. The more the points of reference coincide, the more likely bonds will form.

What is remarkable is how well all groups—couples, singles, seniors, families, physically disabled—mesh. Age is of little consequence when everyone participates on a more or less equal footing. Since Green Travel programs are not known as pick-up opportunities, there's little or no sexual pressure on the single traveler. Families tend to be on their best behavior when away from home, and if couples wanted to be aloof and alone, they would have stayed home or gone to a resort that caters to that kind of activity. Seniors are valued for their wisdom and experience. Green Travelers go to great lengths to make the physically disabled welcome rather than pitied or ignored.

Yet, each class of Green Traveler has its own special problems and considerations. A family with kids requires very different planning from that of a carefree single. A physically disabled individual must be much more aware of the potential limitations that a program might present than an on-the-go couple.

However, there's no reason why anyone could not enjoy a Green Travel trip or tour.

GREEN TRAVEL FOR FAMILIES
▼ ▼ ▼

One of the pleasant byproducts of Green Travel is that it offers something of a return to innocence and the wide-eyed wonder we all felt about the unknown and the beautiful when we were young. For instance, a nature tour through the Amazon rain forest harks back to a time when we, as children, might have explored a backyard or city park, getting muddy knees, playing with insects, capturing frogs, or picking wildflowers. Memories of playing "king of the mountain" resound during an adventure trek up the Himalayas. Educational tours are an idealized version of long gone, never fully realized school days.

Green vacations allow adults to become naive, open, and playful again, relearning the basic principle of childhood: that the world is our playground where the truly important lessons of life are learned. It could even be argued that children are the original Green Travelers, because everything is new and possible to them and because their minds and spirits haven't yet been shackled by adulthood limitations.

Therefore, it should come as no surprise that taking the kids along is one of the most rewarding aspects of Green Travel. A tramp through rural England to retrace the footsteps of beloved Dickens characters releases the child in every parent and the mentor in every child. A study tour of Native American traditions in the American Southwest allows each member of the family to reevaluate his or her own attitudes and way of life against an unexpected and fascinating cultural counterpoint. A whitewater rafting trip in British Columbia tests each person's abilities and, at the same time, becomes a fertile ground for a new kind of mutual respect and cooperation.

Unlike traditional tourism, Green Travel is not simply an extension of home life away from home. Rather, it puts the family into an entirely different milieu where new and magical things can and will happen. Family members become so focused on interesting, intriguing events and ideas outside themselves that they don't have the time, opportunity, or desire to fall into old routines and bad habits. In the process, they can begin to see each other in a new light. The ordinary father/mother/child roles metamorphose into friendships, interdependency, and an awareness of each other as people.

Of course, the best reason to take the kids with you on your next Green trip is that it adds to the fun. Their excitement at seeing a tropical reef for the first time heightens your own sense of thrill and wonder. Sharing an evening around the campfire or the heart-thumping sight of a breeching whale with your loved ones increases the exhilaration of the moment. Green Travel offers opportunities for really splendid new experiences, which become all the more wonderful when they happen to the entire family.

Incidentally, some Green Travel programs and tours may be of particular interest to parents of college-bound children. In today's intensely competitive struggle to get into prestigious institutions of higher learning, admissions departments are giving more and more weight to nonacademic activities, experiences that indicate the student is well-rounded and well-traveled. Quite candidly, a resume showing that your son or daughter trekked the Himalayas, attended summer school at Oxford University, went on an Antarctic adventure cruise, helped build low-income houses in Mississippi, or participated in any research program is bound to be looked upon favorably.

Numerous Green Travel organizers offer programs for families and for individual kids. But it is an unevenly developed field. While certain kinds of programs are appropriate for all ages, others have age restrictions. (Most notable are certain adventure tours that require stamina or skill and some reality or volunteer programs that are considered too trying, upsetting, or confusing to youngsters or even adolescents.) Some tours and projects are open to families and children only at certain times of the month or of the year. Others become available on a custom-design basis—that is, when there is enough demand to justify adding counselors and other kids-oriented services. A growing number have family tours all year round.

Even more noteworthy are the vast majority of programs that fascinate and entertain anyone, regardless of their age. Green Travel has more to do with a state of mind, a curiosity about the world and a desire to experience life to the fullest, than any other artificial criteria, such as age.

WHEN ARE YOUR KIDS OLD ENOUGH TO GO ON A GREEN TRIP?

▼ ▼ ▼

As any parent knows, age has little to do with a person's ability to function well in new surroundings. We have known youngsters who were so ready to go out and explore the world at five years old that their parents had to learn new skills just to keep up with them. Conversely, we've known kids of 13 who were so distressed by new things that they were unable to walk around the corner without first being shown the way. Of course, both kinds of children can benefit from and enjoy a Green trip, but you must carefully assess their flexibility and maturity when choosing what kind of program to share with them. There are two very basic questions you must ask yourself:

▶ Is your child able to function well with groups, both of other children and of adults, with and without you? If not, perhaps you should consider a shorter program that helps them learn how to enjoy being part of a team. Excellent programs are available that directly address this drawback, such as Outward Bound (page 132), School for Field Research (page 161), and certain Sierra Club (page 136) and Audubon Society (page 84) workshops and camps.

▶ Is your child flexible enough to accept unexpected changes or new experiences as part of the adventure of travel? Or does he or she still need familiar surroundings to be comfortable and happy? Of course, the antidote to this problem is exposing the child to new things little by little while still reassuring them and helping build their confidence. Try starting out with one-day trips to a nearby park or museum. Then take them away for a weekend, and if you think your child is ready for it, stay in a nontraditional establishment rather than a typical hotel room. Eventually, as you add to your kid's new experience vocabulary, he'll begin to look forward to new environments and wonder what you have up your sleeve for his next adventure. Just remember to go slowly, telling them what to expect and helping them to feel safe wherever they go.

HOW TO DETERMINE IF A TOUR OR PROGRAM IS RIGHT FOR YOUR FAMILY
▼ ▼ ▼

The annual family vacation can be an extraordinary opportunity for sharing, learning together, exploring new horizons, and seeing each other in a new light. And, certainly, it can be a great deal of fun . . . or it can be a disaster of disappointments, unpleasant surprises, and unhappy tots.

Unfortunately, most people spend less time shopping around for their vacation than they do picking out a new washing machine. This, despite the fact that the vacation represents a much greater investment in money and dreams than any appliance ever could. If you take the time to do some research and a bit of planning, you can almost guarantee a wonderful trip.

After you have narrowed your choices of possible trips down to about a half-dozen, look more closely into the programs offered by talking directly with the people who run the trips. Any tour organizer worth considering is willing to spend some time with you on the phone answering your questions. Don't just settle for "yes" or "no," but explore the "whys" and "hows" to help you get a better idea of just who these people are and how well they will handle your family.

▶ What will be the most memorable part of the trip for the kids, for the adults, for the family as a whole? How the tour organizer focuses the answer will give you a good idea of just how the trip program itself will be slanted. For instance, if you are told that the most memorable experience you will have will be sitting around a campfire with other families toasting marshmallows and learning about astrology, you can expect that outdoors trip to focus on teaching in an informal, relaxed atmosphere.

▶ What exactly is involved in the advertised "family" tour? Will there be supervised activities for the kids, separate from adults, or are the adult programs given in such a way that kids will enjoy it? Does that mean that adults might not be challenged or excited? Many programs are appropriate for any age group, especially the ones that explore nature. For instance, the only requirements for fun snorkeling trips to study coral formations off the Yucatan Peninsula are being able to swim and using lots of water-proof sunblock. On the other hand, some children may be bored by an adult program that involves sitting for hours on a windy bluff, watching and hoping that the resident albatross might display their famous mating dance.

▶ Are there any special programs designed specifically for families? What are they, and how do they differ from the regular adult programs or the typical kids' activities?

▶ What will the kids learn, and how? What is the focus of the children's program and how flexible or regimented is it? As a rule, a trip that is fixed week in and week out to the same schedule is less fun and less responsive to individual needs and interests than one that is relaxed and flexible. (This is true for adult programs, too.)

▶ Will the kids and parents have private time away from each other? Are periods put aside for the parents and kids to share quality experiences together? How much time do the kids spend away from the adults? During what part of the day? Are all meals taken together? Are there supervised rest periods for younger children during the day? Are babysitters available in the evening when the kids go to sleep or other times when the parents may wish to go off on their own? How much extra should you expect to spend per hour on a babysitter? Who are the babysitters?

▶ Single parents should be very direct and honest in their questions. Ask the tour organizer what in their program is going to help you work on your relationship with the child with whom you may not have the opportunity to spend quality time at home.

▶ Ask them to describe a typical day. Ask to see a representative week's schedule of activities to get an idea of the timing of programs as well as what kind of things your children may be doing.

▶ Ask for the names, addresses, and phone numbers of families with kids of about the same age as yours that have traveled with the tour organizer. Then call them, talk to them about what was good and what wasn't so good about their trip—and what they would have done differently if they had it to do over again.

▶ Who are the counselors that run the kids' programs? What are their backgrounds and training?

▶ What is the ratio of counselors to kids? Obviously, the fewer children that each counselor is responsible for, the more personal attention each child will receive.

▶ How many kids do they handle during any one program? Though small groups tend to be preferable in certain kinds of nature tours, most children prefer to have enough playmates about so they can pick their friends from the right age group and sex.

▶ Do they break up children according to age groups? Most twelve-year-olds that we know would rather "die" than be thrown in with a bunch of "babies" for hours on end.

▶ Will there be opportunities for your children to meet local children? What are they? If the youngsters enjoy it, can it be repeated throughout the trip so they can develop friendships? For example, on some of Rascals in Paradise's trips (see page 143), they will arrange for your kids to be picked up to go to the local school and meet native children their own age.

▶ What kind of equipment do they have for the kids' programs? What is provided for free and what must be rented or brought with you? For instance, if there is a snorkeling program, will they outfit your children with snorkel, mask, fins, and flotation vest? Are kids' bicycles available? Do they use workbooks or other materials that help to make a learning experience fun and vice versa? How?

▶ How do the counselors handle children who are frightened or confused?

▶ Do they have printed guidelines that they give their counselors? If so, ask for a copy. If not, ask them to explain how they instruct their counselors about handling children (and parents).

▶ Is the tour organizer associated with any educational or conservation group? Did they seek any advice from such associations in planning their children's programs? What were their objectives in designing their children's programs and how did they achieve them?

▶ Will a pretrip package be sent to the kids to help them prepare for their upcoming adventure? Is any follow-up provided after the vacation, such as a trip log or a subscription to a kids-only newsletter?

▶ Do any of the children's programs cost extra? Which ones, and how much?

▶ What kind of discount or special pricing is available for families? Such discounts are not always published, and you may have to ask for them to get them. If your family is large enough, you might even qualify for a group discount. (This is especially appropriate for family reunion travel.)

▶ Will the children have rooms of their own or will they have to share with you? In a camping situation, will they have a separate tent, or, for smaller children who might be frightened, will there be room for them to crawl into your tent in the middle of the night?

▶ If your children are picky eaters, ask what kinds of food and drink are served. It would be a shame to let the want of a jar of peanut butter ruin your vacation. However, if your kids are willing to try new tastes, don't bother asking about the food. After all, experiencing other cultures' cuisines is part of the adventure of travel.

▶ Be sure to note the name of the person to whom you speak, so you can ask for them again with any further questions you may have. Also, ask that person their own personal advice about whether they think the particular trip you are considering would be appropriate for your family.

PREPARING FOR YOUR GREEN TRIP WITH THE KIDS

▼ ▼ ▼

Vacation fun begins long before your trip. It starts with the build-up of anticipation that comes from planning your adventure. Where will we go? What will we do? What kinds of wild animals will we see? What new experiences will we have? With each question asked and tentatively answered, the fantasy builds momentum.

Unfortunately, too many parents take on all the responsibilities of planning and preparing for family vacations, leaving the kids out of the process. That means that the youngsters not only don't know what to expect, they are cheated out of the fun and excitement that comes from dreaming about the upcoming trip. A family trip should be just that, something that is done for, with, and by the family. Neither the burdens nor the pleasures should belong to any one person.

There are several steps in planning for your trip, all of which are opportunities to involve the entire family: selecting your trip, learning about your destination and what to expect, packing for your trip.

SELECTING YOUR TRIP

► Once you have narrowed down your choice of trips to ones that fit your budget, schedule, and your family's individual interests, it's time to take your selection to the family council. Show the brochures to the kids, explain what each trip offers, and ask them which ones they think they would like.

► If the tour organizers have promotional videotapes, borrow them. Or, you may be able to get documentary tapes from the library on the various destinations you are considering. Watch the tapes with the whole family to get a better idea of what the trips would be like.

► Listen carefully to what your children have to say, not just the words but the fears and confusion behind them. For instance, a youngster might rule out a trip that seems very inviting to you for what may appear whimsical reasons, but their concerns are very real to them. Perhaps they aren't sure what it means to hike on a mountain trail and think that it's the same as mountain climbing. Similarly, they might be frightened about getting close to wild animals. Many fears, once recognized, can be easily and gently dispensed with by just answering questions, whether or not they are asked. Try to think like a child, and take nothing for granted. For instance, one young boy we know, whose parents wanted to go on a luxury Alaskan cruise, had never been at sea. But he had sailed on a small Sunfish, and he knew he didn't want to go on a boat for a whole week. It turned out that he didn't know where he would be able to go to the bathroom and how he could sleep without rolling over into the water.

► Explain why you prefer any one trip over another, and detail what each member of the family could do on the trip you would choose. Then, listen to their reasons why they think they'd enjoy certain trips and not others.

► If you can't answer them immediately, make a list of everyone's questions and uncertainties. Then find answers before deciding what trip to take.

► After the family has narrowed down the field to one or two choices, let the matter rest a while. Leave the brochures where everyone can look at them whenever they want. Let impressions percolate for a while, and discuss any further questions that come up. Eventually, without any pressure, the family will probably come to an agreement for a trip that excites everyone.

LEARNING ABOUT YOUR DESTINATION AND WHAT TO EXPECT

► The more you and your family know about your destination, the more enlightening and enjoyable your trip will be. Consider taking the family to the zoo or a museum that specializes in artifacts related to your trip. For instance, if you are going on an archeological dig together, visit your local historical museum to see pottery shards and other items that have been unearthed by archeologists. Or if you are planning a birdwatching trek, visit the aviary at the local zoo and learn how to identify birds that you might see on your trip.

▶ Subscribe to magazines that relate to your upcoming trip and read them together. For instance, the National Geographic Society, the Cousteau Society, and the World Wildlife Fund have magazines specifically written for kids.

▶ Public television and some cable channels air a large number of documentaries about different cultures, endangered animals, historic sites, etc. Keep an eye out for listings in the TV program and have the whole family watch shows that are related to your trip.

▶ Talk to your child's teacher (if it's okay with your child). Perhaps, when you return from the trip, you and your kid might put on a slide show or prepare a special "show and tell" that could relate to something they are studying. Since Green Travel is often involved in very important contemporary issues, such as conservation, natural history, or international relationships, the school would probably appreciate a presentation. It would also give your kids a special project to pursue and enjoy during the trip, and it might even earn them a higher grade.

▶ Try to find out if other families with children the same age as yours have already signed up for the program. If any live near you, it might be a good idea to try to arrange a meeting so the kids can get to know each other before the trip.

▶ Learn how to use a camera. Each child should have his or her own camera, even if it is just an Instamatic or "film in the box." Taking pictures is an important part of the pleasure of travel, and it helps them to focus their minds on the experience of the trip. Several weeks before leaving, have each member of the family shoot at least one roll of film, have it developed, and then examine the results. That way, they can better understand how to control and enjoy their photography.

▶ Spend some time with the kids discussing how to relate to people from different cultures, handle themselves among wild animals, and what it means to respect the environment. Study the Guidelines on page 39 with them. Help them understand what they mean by describing possible scenarios and discussing how to react.

▶ Find out what the bathroom situation will be from the tour operator. While most trips will offer the same kind of flushing toilets with which kids are familiar, others may involve using latrines or bushes. It's best to explain how to use them before your trip. That way, your children won't be confused or frightened by an unusual situation at a most inopportune time.

▶ Similarly, find out about fresh water, any food precautions, or adverse weather, and discuss them before the trip.

▶ Just before you leave on your trip, teach your children how to make collect phone calls home and whatever else you want them to know in the event of an emergency or if they get separated from you. Give them emergency money, perhaps in a special pouch they can always wear around their necks.

▶ As wonderful as traveling with kids can be, it can add work to your vacation. To make sure you don't feel cheated, reserve a weekend sometime before or soon after your family trip during which you can spend some quiet time alone or with your significant other in pleasant surroundings.

PACKING FOR YOUR TRIP

▶ Try involving the entire family in packing for your trip, even though it can mean that it will take much longer than if you did it all yourself.

▶ Whenever we travel with our young niece or nephew, we tell them they can bring whatever they want—so long as they can carry their own suitcase. That automatically cuts down on how much extraneous stuff they'll ask to bring along. Once the suitcase is packed, have them test carry it up and down the stairs and through the house for at least 15 minutes. (Of course, we usually end up carrying all the suitcases anyway, especially at the end of a long day.)

▶ Each child should have a couple of items, such as a favorite book, travel-size game, or doll, but give them a number limit of such items and stick to it. Discourage them from bringing hand-held video games or other noisy solo devices, if only because they can't share them with other kids. You may wish to give each child a small backpack for carrying personal items.

▶ Consider buying a couple of sets of small FM walkie talkies—all on the same wavelength. (Radio Shack has some inexpensive ones.) Give one to each member of the family. That way, if anyone is ever out of sight, they can use their walkie talkie to help you find them.

▶ If you are traveling where you hope to be involved in people-to-people encounters, have the kids pack a couple of gifts to be given to local kids (see page 43).

▶ Though you can put your kids on your passport, it is really better for each child to have his or her own. Make sure everyone has the required visas, inoculations, etc. And if you are not the parent of the child with whom you plan to travel, be sure to have a notarized statement from the parent giving you *loco parentis*.

WHILE ON YOUR FAMILY TRIP

▶ When you first arrive, take a walk around with the children so they can understand the lay of the land and where everything is.

▶ Give yourself and your children a vacation from too many rules. However, discuss and agree on a few rules that the kids promise to try to obey. When we went on a cruise with our ten-year-old niece, we gave her only three rules, which she could remember easily: (1) Don't go out on the open decks without an adult when the ship is at sea (and we showed her what we meant by open decks); (2) Don't leave the ship without us; (3) Be courteous to everyone. With only a few rules governing her, she was obedient, had a good time, and could win adult approval easily. Try to explain your reasons for whatever rules you make, and base them on the physical layout of your surroundings.

▶ Try to schedule a time for the entire family to be together every day. That way, you can share what you have learned and enjoy telling each other stories. If you spend a lot of time involved in separate activities, you might want to get into a routine of having a soda together before dinner, or taking a swim together before breakfast.

▶ Consider working on a family project together, such as putting together a scrapbook. A scrapbook is a vehicle for sharing what each person has done during the day and a nice memento of the trip when it is over. One family we know takes a Polaroid camera on all their trips to take pictures of people they meet, both to give away and to put in their scrapbook. Then, they write notes in the scrapbook next to the pictures to remind themselves about how and where they met. They also note the person's name and address. Another project might be a family log book or diary.

▶ Relax, enjoy the kids, and let them enjoy you. Take for granted that most things won't go as planned. That's why they call travel an adventure.

THE FAMILY REUNION
▼ ▼ ▼

Most families no longer live near each other. Sisters and brothers can be separated from each other and their parents by hundreds or thousands of miles. For that reason, more and more families are looking to the annual family vacation as a possible family reunion.

Green Travel programs are often limited to small groups, so it may be possible to book an entire tour just for your family. Naturally, there would be a discount for such a volume purchase. For instance, the Foothills Safari Camp at Fossil Rim in Texas (see page 91) offers an African-like safari in a wildlife reserve. The small camp of luxury tents (with private *ensuite* bathrooms) holds no more than 12 people. Can you imagine three or four generations of your family sitting together in the evening twilight watching the animals congregate at a nearby watering hole?

Sometimes, you might want to consider having your family reunion as part of a larger tour so each member can enjoy meeting new people, too. Again, you may well qualify for a volume discount. We once met a family of about 26 individuals from all over the world who had gotten together to take a Clipper Cruise (page 230) of the Virgin Islands. There was enough to do so that the various generations and individuals could go off on their own whenever they wanted, but they were together for an entire week, dining together, playing bridge, gossiping, and meeting each other's children and new spouses.

Green Travel is especially suited for family reunions because it offers an unusual environment in which to rediscover each other while you rediscover the world. (See page 24 for a discussion of what makes family Green Travel so rewarding.)

GREEN TRAVEL FOR SINGLES
▼ ▼ ▼

Most of the traditional purposes and problems of singles vacations simply have no place in Green Travel. As we stated previously, it doesn't really matter to Green Travelers whether or not a person is married or single, rich or poor, college-educated or a high-school dropout. You'll be judged instead on your sense of companionship, whether or not you are first to spot a storm petrel or some other creature, how interested and interesting you are, and other rather esoteric abilities that will add to the general group's fun.

It's quite pleasant to travel as a single among Green Travelers, because you no longer feel like an outcast within a society based on couples and families. Besides, if there is someone on the trip who catches your eye, both of you are involved in a common activity within a very congenial group. So, even shy individuals can enjoy meeting new people.

Conversely, if you are looking to find a partner (either temporarily or a relationship that will outlast the vacation), you would probably be disappointed in a

Green trip. The groups tend to be quite small, so the probability of finding a compatible companion of the opposite sex and in the right age bracket is limited. (But then, how probable is it on traditional tours or, even, in singles bars? Not very.)

Women generally outnumber men in any kind of travel. However, certain kinds of Green tours do tend to have large numbers of men. In fact, physically adventurous travel may be one of the few types of vacation where a woman could meet an interesting man without really trying. It is certainly more comfortable to simply fall into a friendly banter when whitewater rafting or scuba diving than while laying about on a beach of an oceanfront resort or some other more traditional vacation spot.

Singles who travel alone usually must pay a surcharge for taking up an entire double room by themselves, unless they are willing to bunk with a stranger. Most tour operators and travel agents will make an effort to find someone of the same sex for you to share a room. Otherwise, expect to pay a surcharge of 125 percent to 200 percent over the normal rate (which invariably is based upon double occupancy). Of course, that applies only to those trips in which you will be staying in hotels, on cruise ships, or other such establishments. Camping trips usually don't involve singles surcharges.

GREEN TRAVEL FOR SENIOR CITIZENS
▼ ▼ ▼

Not surprisingly, a high percentage of Green Travelers are senior citizens. That's because retired individuals have the time to take long trips and the inclination to do something meaningful with their remaining years. Frequently, a couple will spend decades close to home, going on conventional vacations only, unable to indulge their fantasies and desires because of the relentless pressures of everyday responsibilities. But once the kids are married, the mortgage paid off, and the pets gone, there's nothing holding them back from that long-dreamed-of safari or trek or journey.

Green Travel has few age limitations, so long as Green Travelers remain physically fit and mentally alert. We have seldom been on a Green trip anywhere that didn't include at least one grandmother or grandfather. Certainly, some trips and tours are more strenuous than others, but unless elderly individuals are completely unrealistic about their capabilities, common sense will prevent serious errors of judgment. Before committing to a particular trip or program, seniors should follow the guidelines below:

▶   Read the brochures carefully. Do they, as many do, list levels of difficulty? If not, ask the tour operator what physical exertion is involved. Assess yourself carefully, and decide if it's something you not only can do but want to do. If the description sounds like more than you can handle, pass it up and consider another, less strenuous trip.

▶ Have a complete physical examination, and inform your doctor that you want a realistic evaluation of whether or not you are fit enough to participate in a particular program.

▶ If you are considering having surgery or some other medical procedure, you would probably be advised to have it before going on any trip. A medical crisis might just blow up at the point you are furthest from civilization.

▶ What will the weather be like? If you are particularly sensitive to heat, humidity, or cold, avoid trips that travel to those extremes. Also, if it's likely to be rainy or windy, come prepared so you won't catch a chill or a cold.

▶ Take out trip insurance and supplemental medical insurance, just in case. Also, although the chances of dying on vacation are small, make certain, if possible, that your financial and legal affairs are in order and someone knows what to do if you fail to return home.

It would be a mistake to associate only, or even primarily, with fellow Green Travelers of your own age. What makes Green Travel so compelling is that everyone shares common, but extraordinary, interests, so 18-year-olds can mix and mingle as equals with 80-year-olds. Senior citizens will find that they fit in comfortably and are more than welcome by all members of their group.

One of the many benefits of being a senior citizen is that, frequently, airlines, hotels, and even tour organizers offer special rates for seniors. Often, you'll read about discounts in the brochures, but, if not, always ask if you are entitled to them. Even if a particular program has no discount available, you might be able to save money anyway when on vacation by eating at restaurants, taking public transportation, or attending theaters or movie houses that have special senior rates.

GREEN TRAVEL FOR PEOPLE WITH DISABILITIES
▼ ▼ ▼

A number of Green Travel programs are accessible to the physically disabled. The rule of thumb, though, is that if no restrictions are specifically mentioned in the brochures, check with the organization and tour operator before signing up. What is very heartening is that when queried, many, if not most, of the tour organizers with whom we spoke said they would work with anyone who was interested in participating to make their programs as accessible as possible. It's another indication of how Green Travel is different and more open than traditional tourism.

When you talk to a tour organizer, be very frank about your limitations and honest about your abilities. Ask in detail what activities and areas would be accessible and which ones wouldn't. For instance, some nature tour operators are very willing to work with you to make their trips accessible to individuals in wheelchairs. However, there is no way that they can build ramps or smooth over rough trails in the wild. Adventure cruise ships, too, are not equipped to handle wheelchair-bound, disabled passengers because of the difficulty of getting in and out of the small Zodiac boats, especially during wet landings.

There's a book that lists a variety of specific programs for the physically disabled, titled *A World of Options for the 90s: A Guide to International Educations Exchange, Community Service, and Travel for Persons with Disabilities*. It costs $16 (postage and handling included), and may be obtained from *Mobility International*, P.O. Box 3551, Eugene, OR 97403, tel. (503) 343-1284 (Voice or TDD).

One company that specializes in outings and wilderness access for persons with disabilities are: *Environmental Traveling Companions*, Fort Mason Center, Building C, San Francisco, CA 94123, tel. (415) 474-7662.

Another organization of note is *Whole Access*, 517 Lincoln Ave, Redwood City, CA 94061, tel. (415) 363-2647. They provide information and assistance to persons with disabilities and their families and friends, who are seeking recreation activities in parks and wilderness areas. They also provide advice on how to best ascertain whether a program is truly accessible.

Chapter Four

TAKE NOTHING BUT PHOTOGRAPHS, LEAVE NOTHING BUT FOOTPRINTS

Guidelines for Responsible Travel

▼ ▼ ▼

One of the definitive aspects of Green Travel is the guidelines by which Green Travelers agree to abide. In fact, an important measure of a tour operator's commitment to responsible tourism is the quality of the printed guidelines for proper behavior that they provide their clients, volunteers, and staff and, of course, the degree to which they adhere to their own standards.

Though the guidelines will vary depending upon the purpose, method, and destination of the program, the best all have these three basic concepts in common:

▶ Take nothing but photographs, leave nothing but footprints (or, if you are scuba diving, leave nothing but bubbles). This often stated rule is simply asking you to not leave any mark of your having ever passed that way. In other words, don't pick the flowers, walk through easily damaged bushes, trample on delicate turf, litter, or otherwise change the natural status quo of the place you are visiting. Future visitors have the right to expect that anywhere you have been will be as beautiful and pristine for them as it was for you.

▶ Be sensitive to local cultures and attitudes. Take the time to learn about and understand their expectations and taboos, and, if possible, learn a few words of their language. Don't ignore them or be shy to the point of avoiding any interaction. The golden rule of cultural sensitivity is to always respect and treat other people (your fellow travelers as well as the locals) as you would have them respect you. Honor everyone's inherent right to human dignity.

▶   Be sensitive to how your presence and actions might affect animals. Listen to the experts in order to learn how to properly read the behavior of wild creatures, so that you can know when you might be frightening or stressing them. Then behave accordingly. Be especially careful not to do anything that would inhibit an animal from properly taking care of its young. Remain calm and quiet around animals, trying not to tower over them or crowd them. If they're passive or uncooperative, don't charge or frighten them, or ask your driver or guide to make noise, just to get an action photo. Give them the respect that is due them as living creatures.

THE UGLY TOURIST SYNDROME
▼ ▼ ▼

Suppose you were out gardening in your front yard and a busload of tourists from a distant land suddenly stopped, everybody got out, and started jabbering at you in an incomprehensible language, all the while pointing their cameras and clicking away. Or let's say you were attending church on Sunday when a group of African animists came in and started fingering their bones and amulets. Farfetched? Not really, if you think about it. We travel to faraway, exotic lands, and in our enthusiasm to absorb or record on film or tape the appearance, life styles, or rituals of the natives, we may intrude on their privacy or inadvertently mock or make fun of their customs and practices.

There used to be a phrase for aggressive, selfish individuals who were insensitive and ignorant of foreign cultures: The Ugly American. Nowadays, The Ugly American syndrome isn't restricted to any particular nationality, so he's now known as The Ugly Tourist.

The last thing that a Green Traveler wants to be is The Ugly Tourist. Unfortunately, many tourists from America and Western Europe, among others, share an unenviable reputation around the world as boorish, insensitive, demanding, and often unruly visitors. In many places, foreign tourists are tolerated only because they bring in vital dollars, but at the same time they are disliked because of their unconscious arrogance, sense of superiority, and insular behavior.

It's not hard to be an Ugly Tourist, regardless of your nationality. Just demand that everything be up to your hometown standards. For example, to complain because the air conditioning isn't cold enough, the bus is noisy and dusty, the rafting equipment old, or there's no artificial sweetener with the tea is to ignore the probability that the lack of money or precious foreign exchange prevents more modern, comfortable, convenient, or up-to-date equipment and facilities. Similarly, it's bad form—as well as potentially dangerous—to flaunt what to impoverished peoples is extreme wealth. This might include wearing flashy jewelry or watches, spending large amounts of money, throwing away half-eaten food, handing out coins to children, offering to buy everything in sight, etc. Ugly Tourists also refuse to patronize local businesses, transportation, and restaurants; won't shake hands or have any physical contact with the locals; or use insect sprays or antiseptics in such a way that it gives an impression that the area is unhealthy and the natives diseased. What bad manners!

The best way to avoid becoming an Ugly Tourist is to try to become friends with the locals—on their terms. Talk to them, and, if possible, try conversing in their language. You might know only a few words, but the effort will be appreciated. Don't complain or whine about less than perfect conditions, or knock the government, or ridicule any local customs or institutions, and be sensitive and circumspect about appearing to be wealthy. (Though you may not be among the rich in your country, you are certainly ranked among the privileged of the world if your income is more than, say, $5,000 per year.) Above all, don't be a caricature of yourself by appearing stiff or ill at ease or taking issue with things that do not really matter.

Also, arm yourself with as much knowledge of the culture and region as you can read or study before leaving on your vacation. Many Green Travel tour operators and organizations will send out a fact sheet or booklet outlining what to expect on your trip shortly after you book the tour or program. It may include a list of do's and don't's, local customs and taboos, and tips on how to best get along without offending. If such information is not provided, you can always pop down to your local library or write to the country's embassy in order to obtain background data.

As mentioned earlier, the other important thing to keep in mind when dealing with different cultures is to practice your own personal version of the Golden Rule. You may not specifically know or understand what is acceptable or not, but you'll probably do the right thing if you trust your instincts and proceed on the principle that you won't do or say anything that you would find offensive yourself. This includes such things as not staring, ridiculing, or criticizing, being overly familiar with strangers, touching anyone or anything without first asking for permission, disturbing the normal rhythm of life, ignoring the presence of locals, dressing immodestly in areas in which the religious practices are overtly conservative, expressing obvious dislike for local food or drink, or acting in an offensive or aggressive manner.

In other words, be a considerate and gracious guest whenever visiting another culture.

MEMENTOS
▼ ▼ ▼

Plowshares International, a nonprofit organization that conducts reality tours, suggests that you take no more than $100 in discretionary spending money with you when you travel to a foreign country. (That doesn't include the money needed for your basic travel and living expenses.) That way, they reason, you won't fall into the tourist stereotype of simply wandering through a culture buying up souvenirs but never seeing, learning, or understanding anything beyond the shops and markets.

Most Green Travelers, unlike traditional tourists, are generally not shoppers or souvenir hunters. What they take away most from their vacations are vivid memories of incredible experiences, new friendships, a sense of achievement and satisfaction, and other intangible, transcendental feelings.

But let's be realistic. Green Travelers are not immune to the desire to bring home souvenirs of an exciting vacation. Almost every Green Traveler we know appreciates small physical tokens and mementos of their trips, such as tee shirts, sweatshirts, patches, and other articles of clothing. In response to this interest, many tour organizers will give you one or two (or more) gifts: paid-up memberships to nonprofit organizations, arctic parkas, tee shirts or sweatshirts, backpacks, passport wallets, flight bags, notebooks, patches, mugs, reference books, newsletter subscriptions, trip logbooks, etc. These tangible souvenirs of your trip may be prestigious mementos, such as windbreakers with the name of the expedition silkscreened on the front, or simply token reminders that can produce pleasurable memories. Keep in mind that such souvenirs aren't always included, and when they are, you are paying for them in the cost of your trip. Many Green Travel enterprises, especially nonprofit organizations, simply do not have the budget to supply souvenirs to everyone *gratis*. Even so, it's rare indeed not to find any souvenirs available for sale at a nominal cost.

In addition, the Green Traveler may be in a unique position to obtain more than run-of-the-mill commercial souvenirs. For instance, a few days before we went on an adventure trek through part of the upper Amazon, we obtained a half-dozen inexpensive hammers at our local hardware store. (The tour operator told us in advance that they would be extremely desirable trade items.) These we traded with a remote Indian tribe for an authentic blowgun and a pictographically decorated tree bark skirt, two of our most highly prized aboriginal artifacts.

On the other hand, if you buy certain souvenirs, you might inadvertently encourage and subsidize poachers and killers of endangered species. Please don't buy sea turtle products (such as items made of beautiful tortoise shell), elephant ivory, the furs or pelts of protected species, and any other forbidden artifact of murdered wildlife. Not only will you not be allowed to bring them home because of customs laws, but by buying them you are encouraging the sellers to go out and destroy more endangered animals. If you're not certain whether or not to buy a specific souvenir, ask your tour organizer and the accompanying naturalist, not the shopkeeper. Your best bet would be to arm yourself with information before traveling. Find out what native animals are endangered and the kinds of products that poachers may offer to sell you. That way, you'll recognize what souvenirs will be happy mementos and which ones will be embarrassing reminders of a mistake made through ignorance.

You probably already know that it is illegal to bring back into your own country or take into another country any organic items, such as fruit, nuts, meat, plants, etc. This isn't just a bureaucratic barrier to protect marketplaces. Rather, it is a very necessary safeguard against transmitting any parasites that can destroy entire crops across borders.

Another consideration that most tourists overlook is that souvenirs are a two-way street. Just as you wouldn't dream of going to a friend's mother's house for dinner without some small gift in hand, we have learned that you never visit another culture empty-handed. Giving or exchanging gifts is not only an internationally recognized gesture of goodwill, it's one sure-fire way to break the ice. One thing we try to carry with us are postcards of our home state, which we hand out to those who ask where we're from and what it's like there. It's better not to give out candy, gum, or money to children, because it makes beggars out of them. But local schools in impoverished regions appreciate pens or small pads that they can distribute to the students. (Of course, you might give these directly to the parents, indicating that they are for the children.) For the adults, we sometimes bring small souvenir pins from our home state. We even occasionally give away the very souvenirs we were given by the tour organization, such as patches or tee shirts. We've discovered that one of the most prized gifts is a series of commemorative stamps that you can get from the post office at a fraction of the price of any other souvenir. You'd be amazed how many people from diverse (and not necessarily sophisticated) cultures collect stamps. When we visit research stations or other remote sites where scientists, teachers, or others live and work in isolation for months on end, we try to bring a couple of magazines and paperback books. When we're really far from civilization, there are times when we even bring trade goods, like hammers or cosmetics. By the way, Polaroid pictures are still a big hit around the world, and, when you give them away, it makes people more agreeable to being photographed.

Ask yourself: What might visitors to my hometown buy as an inexpensive souvenir if they were on a tour here? That is probably what would interest your interculture hosts.

DETERMINING JUST HOW GREEN
A TOUR ORGANIZER IS
▼ ▼ ▼

Just because a travel brochure has the word "Green" or "Ecotourism" embla-zoned in a banner across the front does not necessarily mean that the trip is offered by a socially and environmentally responsible organization. Nor does it guarantee that you will have the meaningful adventure that you seek. The tour organizer could just as easily be a sleazy operation that's trying to cash in on a new buzzword. Until the industry sets standards for itself, and establishes an authority for determining—and certifying—how well an organization conforms to those standards, Green Travel is essentially a *caveat emptor* marketplace.

On the other hand, there are quite a few socially and environmentally conscientious organizations whose sense of responsibility is much more than skin deep. For instance, the maverick Virgin Atlantic Airways supports and implements important humanistic and ecologically oriented, non-profit programs. When they inaugurated their service to Boston, their Fair Share program donated money for every Boston passenger to local homeless programs. The inaugural celebration of Los Angeles included planting a tree for every passenger originat-ing from that airport for several months. They also attempt to recycle waste and limit their use of plastic whenever possible. Other Virgin programs are done so quietly that you'll hear about them only if you ask the right people on the executive board. They do this even though it costs them more than they receive back in good public relations. They are simply a company with a conscience.

Nations, of course, have varying levels of institutionalized conscientious-ness. Costa Rica is probably the prototypical Green nation. Over a half-century ago, Costa Rica abolished its own army, choosing instead to invest in peace and human welfare. Today, it has one of the highest literacy rates in the world, and it provides advanced social and health-care services for all its citizens. Costa Rica is also at the forefront of Green Travel, balancing carefully conservation of its profuse wildlife and tropical ecosystem (supported by tourism) with the need for economic development.

Other countries have embraced Green as the national color. New Zealand is officially Green, having banned all heavy industry and nuclear power. (This decision cost them dearly; the United States won't give most favored nation status to any ally that won't allow their warships to come into port.) In addition, New Zealand is the world capital for outdoors vacations, in which the great majority of the citizens take a trek at least once a year.

It is possible to apply similar gauges to tour organizers to determine just how Green they really are. Ask the following questions about any company with which you are thinking of traveling. If the answers aren't in their brochures, call them up and ask directly. A truly Green company will be happy to answer your questions; they may even volunteer further details about matters that we didn't even think to ask. A free and open exchange of information, too, is part of being Green. Only those who have something to hide will sidestep your questions.

▶ *What is the company's stated philosophy?* You can learn much about a company from their published credo or philosophy. Is it a superficial statement that is designed to sound good, without making any real commitments? Or is it substantial and well supported by their established track record?

▶ *To what organizations does the company belong? What institutes use their services for travel programs? What projects are they involved in or support in one way or another?* While just about any company can bandy about big names in an attempt to puff up their own reputation, it's easy to check on their claims by simply calling some of the organizations they name. Also, if a very reputable group, such as the World Wildlife Fund or the National Audubon Society, has used a certain travel company for more than one year, it is a rather good indicator that the company stacks up to that group's criteria for responsible tourism. Just as important are the small groups, whose names you've never heard, that a tour organizer might support. For instance, a number of Green Travel operators have assisted in establishing self-help groups in the villages that their tours visit. This they do as a matter of course, with little or no publicity, but they will be delighted to tell you about what they are achieving in these projects if you ask about them.

▶ *Do they put aside part of their money for conservation, environmental, or social causes?* A simple "yes" should not suffice here. Ask how much they give to what organizations or projects and why. Their explanations will tell you a lot more about how they do business and what they consider important, rather than just knowing that they have a conscience. However, if the underlying reasons are not easy to get to, ask yourself: Does it really matter why they do something good, so long as they do it?

▶ *Who are the people involved? How long have they been working in Green Travel? What are their credentials?* Green Travel organizations are very personal and personable. The guiding force behind how most do business is usually a very direct, hands-on personality. The employees and executives' backgrounds usually tell a great deal about how committed the company is to the Green philosophy, rather than simply being a money-making enterprise. Are they themselves avid backpackers, experienced outdoors people, skilled rafters, etc.? Have they been published in conservation or scholarly journals? Have they been involved in some of the many symposia around the world that convene to study the effects of tourism on local cultures and environments?

▶ *What nonprofit organizations does the staff of the tour organizer belong to personally?* If the staff itself supports programs such as Amnesty International, the Sierra Club, World Wildlife Fund, etc., then their stand for a better, Greener world is a personal commitment and not just profit motivated. (The best Green tour brochures will give you biographical data on the naturalists and lecturers who will lead the tour.)

▶ *What support infrastructure do they use? Where do they buy their supplies?* Travel to exotic, undeveloped regions can help the local economies considerably if the tour organizers use local hotels, restaurants, staff, etc. But if they use only large, multinationally owned hotels, import all their staff, and ship in all their supplies, very little of the money you spend will stay in the country. On the other hand, it is not always possible to get all that is needed from within the region and may even represent a drain on local supplies. In addition, certain things should be brought in, such as wood for campfires. Too many virgin forests have been cut down to fuel tourists' desires to camp out in the very forests that are thus eventually destroyed.

▶ *How do they handle their waste and refuse? Do they recycle?* Is it simply collected in plastic bags and hastily buried so animals can easily dig it up later? Or does the company take it with them, or bury it deep in accordance with good conservation practices? Are the latrines covered properly? Is the campsite struck so there's little evidence of having spent the night?

▶ *How many participants will be with you on the trip?* Generally, the smaller the group, the higher the quality of experience you will have. For instance, on a wildlife tour, if you are one of only 8 or 12 people who will be walking through the Australian outback in search of, say, koalas, it will be a quieter, more beautiful experience than being one of 50 participants. On the other hand, a manageable group size varies with the kind of program. On some types of programs, such as adventure cruises, 100 would be considered a relatively small group. Then there are times, such as in people-to-people rallies, that you may actually want as large a group as possible, to increase the diversity of possible relationships.

▶ *Do they guarantee wildlife sightings?* No one can be 100 percent accurate about predicting the behavior of wild animals. That's what makes them wild. If a tour organizer guarantees sightings, ask what makes them so certain. Are they controlling wildlife habitat or behavior in some manner, such as using beaters to flush the game toward camera-bearing tourists?

Such attempts to control or inhibit wild creatures can indicate a lack of respect for the animals' rights and may represent a stressful or even dangerous situation for the animals.

▶ *What guidelines do they give their staff?* While the published guidelines given to participants by tour operators may be all based upon similar concepts (see page 39), those that they give their employees are much more telling about how committed they are to their public posture. For instance, are drivers told to turn off motors while waiting for passengers in order to reduce pollution? How much authority does the staff have in changing itineraries if wildlife would be stressed by another visit? How strongly worded are the taboos against littering, disturbing visited ecosystems, or disrupting local cultures? Ask for the social or ecological guidelines given to the tour organizer's staff, and read them with a critical eye. Then call the tour operator to ask any questions you may have.

▶ *What follow-ups to the trip do they provide?* Many Green tour organizers consider their former participants members of a family. The best not only send out newsletters informing about future trips and discounts for repeaters (as would any travel business for the sake of better profits), but they also send you a log of your trip and keep you informed about what has happened with the animals, wildernesses, and people you learned to care about in your travels. Some also provide memberships for you in nonprofit organizations involved in conservation or other worthy causes in the area you visited.

The above questions are general guidelines intended only to help you make your own personal judgment about the commitment and intentions of a trip organizer. Please don't dismiss a company because it doesn't answer every question with the ideal answers. For instance, a tour may be entirely Green, except that in certain areas they have to arrange accommodations in a large chain hotel, for the simple reason there is no other place available. Or, they may use gas-guzzling old buses rather than energy efficient ones, because it is impossible to import the newer models under the restrictive currency laws in certain countries. Another consideration is that a number of tour companies that are working to be Green are quite small, and their profit margin is such that they can only afford to make changes slowly. Temper your idealism with common sense and patience, while working for changes by asking for them.

Making Choices

Being a Green Traveler includes recognizing that our choice of a vacation destination can have greater ramifications beyond simply satisfying our personal whims.

The dollars we spend can help support a region's economic or political system. Does that mean that by going to certain countries, we are also supporting the status quo? Should we boycott a repressive regime to express solidarity with the people of that country? Or does our avoidance of their homeland also mean that there will be fewer jobs, less money to feed their children, and a greater restriction on the freedom of information about the world outside their borders?

Economic sanctions do tend to work, when and if they are directed toward a clear-cut purpose, uniformly enforced. A good case in point is South Africa, which has had to change over the past decade in order to appear more appealing to the rest of the world. On the other hand, the isolation that such sanctions create can be a fertile breeding ground for further repression and injustice, especially since there are no outside witnesses to report it.

We do not claim to have the answers to these questions. Each time we plan a trip to a certain area, we evaluate it based upon the purpose and effect of our travel.

For instance, many people have decided to boycott travel to China in reaction to the Tiananmen Square massacre and its aftermath, because they don't wish to indirectly support such a bloody regime with their tourist dollars. On the other hand, there is no doubt that tourism to China over the past decade was one of the principal influences that led to the movement for liberalization. Only a truly closed society can remain intolerant and dogmatic. Outside influences, especially tourism, open up otherwise closed communities to the possibility that there are other ways to live and be governed. Each traveler must make his or her own decision about whether it's morally correct to either boycott China or visit the country in the hope that every contact with the West will hasten the end of the current regime.

Similarly, there is unquestionable value in programs such as the International Peace Walks (see page 192), which bring people together from opposing sides of political and sometimes even military disagreements to learn about each other.

We would never consider going into war zones—not any more, at least. Daniel's war correspondence days ended in 1973. Nor would we travel where the State Department advises that it is currently dangerous. However, we might go where the State Department prohibits Americans from visiting certain areas for political rather than safety reasons, such as Cuba or Vietnam, if the purpose of our travel was important enough to give such a visit meaning.

Some readers may feel that these are questions that don't or shouldn't have any relationship to your vacation plans. But if you are thinking of traveling to some of the more remote or adventurous destinations—Rwanda, Burma, Tanzania, Fiji, Paraguay, Thailand, Indonesia, or Algeria, just to name a handful at random—you will probably be heading toward regions that are ruled by military cliques, totalitarian regimes, or governments that routinely trample over basic human rights. In fact, some Green tour operators' catalogs of trips and tours read like a ''Who's Who'' of tribal strife, insurrection, starvation, revolution, or civil war. The reason why is simple. Nature still reigns supreme in Third World countries that have not yet felt the full brunt of modern civilization and where mass tourism has not polluted the local cultures. These developing nations are, quite frankly, among the most beautiful and exciting in the world. But many are also beset by large social and economic problems of the kind that lead to—and are caused by—dogmatic, repressive governments.

How you handle yourself in those countries, on an interpersonal level, can effect the people more deeply than you can imagine. That is why thoughtful individuals tend to ask themselves soul-searching questions more and more before deciding on where to go for their next vacation. In fact, numerous symposia are being convened throughout the world to discuss just how the traveler and the travel industry influence local cultures, politics, and environments. And various organizations, such as the Center for Responsible Tourism (see page 254), are working to try to increase travelers' awareness of how their vacation choices affect local societies.

As the world shrinks, and people embrace each other in a Green movement toward recognition, mutual respect, and friendship, governments will not necessarily keep up with us. Dictators will remain stubbornly repressive. Tribal prejudices will continue to affect domestic and foreign policy. And Green Travelers will end up voting with their feet and their dollars to try and change the world for the better.

Chapter Five

PRACTICALITIES

▼ ▼ ▼

HEALTH PRECAUTIONS

▼ ▼ ▼

On most Green Travel programs to industrialized areas, the normal health precautions associated with traditional tourism should suffice. For instance, you probably wouldn't be particularly concerned about health issues when preparing to fly off to France or Italy on a relatively sedate museum tour or to cruise up the St. Lawrence Seaway.

It's another matter entirely if you plan to take off for isolated areas, far from the nearest medical center, or intend to exert yourself on a strenuous trek through the Appalachians. The farther away you get from civilization and the more you push your body to the limit, the greater the risks become. People can and will get sick or break bones in remote areas, and a small number *do* die on expeditions.

First and foremost, be sure you are healthy. Have a checkup in order to have your doctor ascertain your level of fitness before signing up for a trip. In fact, it would be useful to show the trip brochure to your physician. Most Green Travel brochures and catalogs give some indication of the degree of difficulty involved in their trips and programs. If your physician isn't comfortable with you participating in certain activities, consider reasonable alternatives. For instance, if your doctor says that you're not in shape to join a mountain bike rally through the Grand Canyon, ask your doctor about a less strenuous rafting trip down the Colorado River, or a leisurely paced tour of the southwest deserts that includes some moderate walking.

Travel to exotic places may require advance precautions. For instance, check on whether you will be entering a malarial zone and therefore must build up immunity, or should have gamma globulin shots because of a high incidence of hepatitis. The Green Travel tour organizer should provide you with this information, but, if not, check for yourself.

Don't rely on the tour operator to look after your well-being. Almost all require that participants sign an intimidating-sounding waiver absolving them of all responsibility and liability in the case of accident, sickness, local strife, etc. Whether or not it's legally binding is a matter for lawyers and courts to decide, but the prudent Green Traveler should always assume that he or she is personally responsible for any and all health matters.

Ask your insurance carrier if your normal medical coverage will protect you in case of illness or accident in foreign countries. If not, it may be prudent to buy a temporary supplemental health insurance policy or even sign up in advance for air evacuation service insurance that would whisk you back to civilization by helicopter or jet, if necessary. You might also consider buying trip insurance (see page 59) that will reimburse you in case a serious illness or accident prevents you from going on your trip or forces you to drop out before completion. Such policies are available through travel agents as well as insurance agents.

We highly recommend contacting IAMAT (International Association of Medical Assistance for Travelers) at 417 Center St., Lewiston, NY 14092, tel. (716) 754-4883, or 40 Regal Rd., Guelph, ONT, N1K 1B5, Canada, tel. (519) 836-0102. IAMAT will provide you with invaluable advice about staying healthy when you travel and getting medical assistance abroad. Especially valuable is their referral service to English- or French-speaking physicians who were trained in the United States, Canada, or Western Europe, and who agree to a fixed fee schedule. There is no charge for joining IAMAT, but tax-deductible contributions are always welcome.

Once you are on the trip, try to remember that you don't have to do absolutely everything. We have seen otherwise sensible individuals push themselves past the breaking point, caught up in the excitement of the trip and the realization that if they don't do it now, they won't have the chance next month. While such reasoning may seem understandable, it is also foolish. In the early 1980s, we were on a China tour with one of our publishers, a robust, athletic 70-year-old man. While we gave up climbing to the top of a particularly steep portion of the Great Wall, he insisted on achieving the pinnacle. That evening, he died suddenly of a heart attack.

It is prudent to assess your level of health and physical fitness long before leaving home. Then, stick to your guns about limiting yourself to what you can safely do.

Although it shouldn't be necessary, let us briefly remind you of a few basic rules that all travelers should adhere to. Always take enough prescription medicine for your entire trip, and, if possible, bring along a doctor's prescription in case you must obtain refills (and to reassure customs officers). Take all medicines with you in your carry-on. Be sure to take an appropriate kit of over-the-counter drugs and accessories, such as aspirin, adhesive bandages, antacid, tweezers, sunblock, tissues, etc. Also, pack at least one spare pair of prescription glasses. Women headed for exotic (noncommercial) destinations or the wilds should consider packing a supply of sanitary napkins or tampons, since it may be difficult to obtain your favorite brand (or any).

If you are prone to motion illness and plan to be on a boat or riding over rocky terrain, either get some Dramamine or ask your doctor to prescribe antinausea medicine patches that you stick behind your ear.

GOING GREEN ON YOUR OWN
▼ ▼ ▼

If you prefer to travel independently, rather than with a tour (or if you tend to go off on your own from a tour group, if only for a few hours), then your vacation instincts have probably taken you off the beaten track, setting your own pace, making contact with local people. You have probably discovered the pleasures of small bed and breakfast inns, public transportation, picnic foods bought at local markets, leisurely walks or hikes through parklands, and so on.

In other words, you have gone Green on your own already, at least to a certain extent.

Going off on your own is an adventure of possibilities, filled with confusion and mistakes as well as new friends and unexpected discoveries. For instance, when we were with a tour in Australia recently, instead of staying with the group for a bus tour of Tasmania, we rented a car with another photographer. We got lost, of course—that's part of the adventure—and ended up going around one mountain about three times, following the same dirt road, before we finally found the right turn off for the national park. On that thrice-circumnavigated dirt road, we met and chatted with several remarkable characters and happened upon a country fair. We also found a roadside stand selling the largest, most delicious boysenberries we had ever eaten, and because we had as much time as we wanted at the park, we discovered and photographed up close a marsupial and other wild creatures that would have been scared off by a group. None of that would have happened if we had stayed with the tour group.

If you do go on a packaged tour, even a Green tour, learn as much as you can about your destination, so you can choose when you want to stay with the group and when you want a more personal experience off on your own.

Perhaps the purest form of Green Traveler is the person who completely forsakes tours and sets off for an unstructured vacation of discovery. If you're Hawaii-bound, for example, instead of spending a week in a high rise hotel on Waikiki Beach, you might consider renting a bungalow in the village of Maunaloa on the infrequently visited Hawaiian island of Molokai. Because there's not much tourism there, the people are quite accessible and friendly. Molokai has the highest percentage of native Hawaiians and an awesome natural beauty. The tallest sea cliffs in the world are here, and some of the rain forest is still unexplored. In short, things are much closer to what life on the islands was like back in the 1950s, before mass tourism to the area began.

Or you might pass up packaged tours and resort stays to tramp steamer your way through Polynesia. These ubiquitous small ships carry pigs, passengers, and all sorts of cargo from island to island, sometimes on a fixed schedule, sometimes whichever way the wind blows. You may sleep out on deck or in the cargo hold with a dozen natives, sharing food and friendship as you roam from island to island. They're cheap, romantic, and filled with the promise of adventure.

A similar escape, much closer to home and less primitive, are the ferries in Alaska's Inside Passage. Officially designated as part of the United States' Interstate Highway system—there is no other transportation connecting most of the towns in the area—the Alaska Marine Highway is an exciting way to see what the more expensive cruise ships see but more in-depth and at your own pace.

Of course, independent travel can be quite civilized, such as a stroll through the English countryside in search of ancient Celtic monuments or a birdwatching jaunt through Oregon.

Pretravel Tips to Make the Most of Your Trips
▼ ▼ ▼

Over the years, we have developed some rather unorthodox ways to prepare for our trips, whether we are taking off on our own or traveling with a group tour. Before we leave home, we try to find out about the special places and events that we wouldn't want to miss. More importantly, we try to arrange introductions so we can be plugged into an interesting network of people wherever we travel.

Here are a few hints, based upon what we've learned. We would appreciate receiving stories about how you go about it, to possibly include in our next edition.

Tourist Boards, Embassies, and Visitors Centers

Travel agents can be useful for booking trips but mostly *after* you have already decided where you want to go and what you want to do. While travel agents can make things easier, and sometimes save some money by knowing where the bargains are, they're motivated primarily by the lure of commissions and want to book you into those places that they know will pay them. Few are able or willing to provide you information about events and places that offer them no commission, or about which they know next to nothing.

A better approach is to contact the tourist board or embassy of the country you will be visiting. States, cities, and regions also have tourist boards or visitors bureaus. From them you can get all kinds of material on museums, parks, historical sites, or local attractions, plus calendars of special events. They may also have listings of private individuals who are willing to accept paying visitors in noncommercial (and usually delightful) home stays or farm stays. Other material and information they might provide include brochures and booklets listing airlines, trains, car rentals, hotels, wildlife refuges, places of natural beauty, details on local flora and fauna, historic sites, the names and addresses of local conservation organizations, universities, museums, restaurants, native activities, etc., and information on trekking, backpacking, mountain climbing, or other activities. Plus they can provide free maps and suggestions of what there is to do.

Also the tourist boards or visitors centers will inform you about such things as a lecture series in a local museum on the native arts, walking tours through the wilds being conducted by the curator of the zoo, or small boat owners who take paying guests out on marine mammal watches. Similarly, if there is a festival of dance or a celebration of a regional hero that sounds particularly interesting, you may want to schedule your itinerary to coincide with it.

Some tourist boards also work with people-to-people associations to help introduce travelers to locals on a more personal basis than the typical tourist encounter.

It would take an entire book to list all the addresses and phone numbers for various governmental divisions that could help you. But once you know where you are going, it is a simple matter to find the right numbers through directory assistance and make a few phone calls to zero in on the information you want. Tourist boards for scores of countries and regions are located in New York City, Los Angeles, and Toronto, among many other cities in North America. The embassies are in Washington, DC, and Ottawa; many have consulates in New York City, Chicago, Miami, and other international gateways. In addition, hundreds of cities, states, countries, and regions throughout the world maintain a convention and visitors center or tourist boards in their central tourist area.

When you call a tourist board, try to give them some specific idea of the kinds of things that interest you. Otherwise, you may receive only commonplace suggestions and materials from them. Also, once you get to your destination, stop in at the local convention and visitors bureau for further information.

NEW FRIENDS BY ASSOCIATION

Do you belong to a social club, alumni association, or professional society? If so, give them a call and see if there are any chapters of your association in the destination where you are going. Or, maybe they have reciprocal agreements with clubs elsewhere. For instance, we belong to the Overseas Press Club in New York City, which has reciprocal relationships with press clubs in cities throughout the world.

Similarly, if you belong to the Kiwanis, the Lions, or other lodges, you might want to call the president, chairman, or other members in the place you plan to visit to say hello and find out when the next meeting is. Or, you might wish to meet some people in your destination who are involved in the same business or profession, whose names and phone numbers you could probably get from professional associations to which you belong. Think of any possible connection to new friends where you are going that your hometown activities may supply—church, synagogue, mosque, or temple fellowships, photography clubs, etc. Call or write people before you leave, and call them when you arrive.

The point is that meeting new people is the best part of Green Travel. Not only does it enrich your trip with personal interactions, but it may also provide you with inside information that only locals can tell you about the best places to go and the most interesting things to see. For instance, during a visit to New Zealand, one of our new-found friends took off from work one day to show us his favorite spots in the back country. We ended up on a breathtaking old mule trail thousands of feet above sea level, closer to the sky and nature than to any other human being. We wouldn't have found it on our own in a hundred years.

Talk to the Experts

To our way of thinking, experts are people who have been where you are going and have special interests similar to yours. Not only would talking with them help you prepare for your trip, you might even make some interesting new friends with whom you would enjoy comparing notes after you return home.

Ask your travel agent if anybody they booked to your destination would be willing to talk to you. Having been there recently, these other travelers can tell you about their personal discoveries, adventures, and insights, as well as those things they were sorry to have missed out on. One woman who visited Bali last year told us that the best part of her trip was attending a funeral, which is an exotic celebration of incredible colors, music, and animation. You won't find that odd tidbit in most of the guidebooks.

If you live in or near a large enough city, go to dinner in a restaurant that specializes in the native food of the country or region where you are going. In addition to enjoying a taste of the culture (literally!), you'll meet people who might give you some insiders' advice. (Who in your hometown would know more about Greece than the Athenian maitre d' of a local Greek restaurant?) Tell them that you will be visiting their home country, ask about their favorite places and things to see, and you'll probably be besieged all evening with stories about their childhood, village life, and why they left. In fact, they may give you the name and phone number of their brother or cousin to call to say hello for them. And that could lead to yet another memorable encounter.

One warning: As friendly as you may become with any individuals, do *not* carry gifts between friends unless the package is unsealed and the contents can be visually inspected. This is for your security, as well as to avoid any problems with customs. (In this day of terrorism and drug couriers, you must be thoroughly sure that you know exactly what you carry.)

Of course, the quintessential expert is the person who devotes his or her career to studying the culture, society, history, wildlife, or other aspects of your destination. Usually, they have more to tell about the subject than people who will listen and therefore welcome a willing and enthusiastic ear. Call a nearby museum, university, or college (or your alma mater), and ask to talk to researchers, professors, curators, naturalists, etc. Once you've made contact and piqued their attention, ask them to tell you what are the three or four things or places most worth visiting.

Let's say you were headed for Australia, and you wanted to be sure to see wild kangaroos. It would be a good idea to call the local zoo and talk to the marsupial specialist to find out where he or she would go. But don't stop there: You might ask what clothing should you wear, whether some colors frighten off the animals, if kangaroos dislike certain smells, how closely can you approach without spooking them, and if they have any suggestions on what to do or how to act.

Or, if you know you want to go somewhere out West to learn more about Native American culture, you might call a local museum that has a collection of ancient Indian artifacts and talk to the curator that was in charge of putting that exhibit together. (Go to see the exhibit first, so you can have genuine enthusiasm for his or her work and have intelligent questions ready.)

All of these people are quite busy and may not have time to talk with you right away. But you can try to make an appointment to meet, or they may refer you to a knowledgeable assistant. More often than not, we have discovered that even busy, important curators and professors really enjoy being asked unusual questions for which they have had the answers waiting for years. The only problem with asking a true expert a question is the answer may seem interminable.

PACKING
▼ ▼ ▼

Most travelers know to pack clothing appropriate to the climate and context. It would be wise to check with the airline beforehand to determine the restrictions on weight, size and number of suitcases. On most international flights, economy class passengers are limited to two bags with a total weight not exceeding 20 kilos (44 pounds) and one carry-on bag small enough to fit under the seat or in the overhead luggage rack. The problems will come in the small bush or domestic flights in other countries that may have even more restrictive luggage limits. Charges for excess baggage can be substantial. Another rule of thumb we've learned from many years' experience is never to bring more baggage than you can comfortably carry yourself. While traditional tourists can usually rely on porters, skycaps, or bellmen to schlep their suitcases, Green Travelers are sometimes responsible for looking after their own luggage. Green Travelers going to remote or wilderness areas would be well advised to try to bring everything in a single, comfortable backpack. For others, soft suitcases with shoulder straps are preferable to heavy, rigid cases, even those with wheels.

Most Green Travel programs and tours are informal, and casual clothing is usually appropriate. On many volunteer programs, you will probably need work clothes. Ecotours and adventure travel may mean packing walking boots, rain pants, and other weather or terrain gear. However, regardless of the program, you might wish to bring along one good outfit, like a sports coat and tie or a dress or pants suit for an evening out on the town or other special occasion.

There may be a lot of "down" time, so pack some paperbacks or magazines (preferably ones you can leave behind with new friends), perhaps a portable chess or Scrabble board, and maybe even a musical instrument like a wooden recorder or a harmonica.

By the way, you could minimize your packing, as well as help out the local economy, by purchasing some of your clothing at your destination. Over the years, we've acquired a wonderful collection of hats, sweaters, books, jackets, gloves, briefcases, and coats from around the world.

If you're expecting to observe animals in the wild, a pair of binoculars is essential. A more often overlooked item is a miniature tape recorder for capturing and preserving lectures, animal sounds, or group discussions. Also, many photographers, both amateurs and professionals, use tape recorders for making notes and caption identifications that correspond with what they capture on film. Having been in the rugged New Zealand countryside during much of the Gulf War, we've come to appreciate the need for a miniature shortwave radio for staying in touch with the rest of the world, although for most trips this would be a superfluous item. One electronic artifact that we always include in our kit is a small pair of Radio Shack FM walkie-talkies. These inexpensive devices have a range of about one-quarter mile and are perfect for staying in constant touch when one of us goes off the trail or out of sight to take a photograph. They're especially helpful when Sally has literally gotten herself up a tree in pursuit of that one memorable photo and can't get down again.

Last but not least, always pack an empty folding suitcase or duffel bag. Chances are you'll accumulate so many mementos, papers, clothing, or artifacts of one sort or another that they won't all fit in your regular luggage. That's when you'll congratulate yourself for having the foresight to bring an extra bag.

FINANCIAL ARRANGEMENTS
▼ ▼ ▼

The cost for Green Travel varies as widely as the programs. You may pay nothing or many thousands of dollars; some volunteer programs even offer a stipend to certain qualified individuals. The prices that we list in the individual organization profiles (Section Two) are ranges based upon costs at the time that this book went to press, which means that many may be out of date by the time you read this. The purpose of providing them is to give you an *approximation* of how much you will have to pay for specific types of programs.

Not included in the published prices are the typical additions, such as taxes, many admission or user fees, soft drinks and alcoholic beverages, personal items, side tours, etc. Also, most tours listed do not include air transportation, since participants come from all over the world. You'll probably have to pay out of your own pocket to get to the assembly point (many tour operators offer discount tickets from certain gateway cities), but after that, other transportation costs are usually included in the basic ticket price. You will almost invariably pay more (125 percent to 200 percent more) if you are a single person not willing to share a room with a stranger. (Most organizations and tour operators will pair singles of the same sex in order to help you avoid such surcharges.)

An additional expense worth considering is trip insurance. It will reimburse you for missed connections, last-minute cancellations (but you have to give them a good reason, such as illness, or else they won't reimburse you), lost or stolen luggage, misdirected reservations, and other definable mistakes, problems, or losses. But it won't cover you if you simply change your mind about your plans. On the other hand, it's fairly expensive relative to the cost of the trip and can add up dramatically if more than one family member is going. We've done without it well enough for years, but given the complexities of contemporary air travel, we might be on borrowed time. If you can afford it, get it, but if not, just hope for the best and pay more attention to what's going on around you.

In the travel industry, and no less in Green Travel, discounting is rampant. If a certain trip hasn't been booked up completely, if the company is looking for a better cash flow, if the moon is in retrograde—whatever the reasons—travel organizers will often discount their prices. Note, however, that they rarely publicize these discounts—you have to ask for them. On a recent adventure tour, a fellow participant tallied up what everyone said they had paid. He asked a dozen people and got a dozen different figures.

If you are a senior citizen, student, or traveling with a child, automatically ask if you might qualify for another price structure. But these aren't the only discounts available. In some cases, it seems the price you pay depends on the mood of the person taking your reservations and how well you can negotiate. Start out by asking how much less you would pay for making a reservation and putting down a deposit well before the trip. Or, conversely, ask what discount you might expect if you are willing to wait until almost the last minute and see if the tour hasn't been sold out. (Rather than let the trip leave with an empty space, the organizer may be willing to give you a bargain. But if your heart is set on a certain program, you may not want to gamble on not getting in; certain popular Green Travel tours often fill up quickly.) Inquire if members of any specific organizations receive discounts. It may be worth your while to join those organizations.

Lastly, ask quite directly but respectfully if there are any discounts possible. (See below for a discussion on discounts available to certain professionals who are willing to work on vacation.) In the end, if you don't get a discount, don't feel cheated, especially if you are signing up for a very popular tour. While some organizations and tour operators can and do discount, others, especially nonprofits and small outfits working on limited profit margins, cannot afford to reduce the price for anyone.

You should also be aware that scholarships, grants, and loans may be available, not just on tours or volunteer programs offered by nonprofit organizations, but also on some of the programs offered by for-profit companies. This is usually, but not always, noted in the brochures. It doesn't hurt to ask directly.

Like all conventional travel arrangements, most Green Travel fees, expenses, or payments due airlines, tour operators, sponsoring organizations, hotels, etc., must be paid in full in advance of the departure date. Usually, you put down a deposit when you sign up for a tour or program and pay the balance in increments some time before you leave on your vacation. (There are a very few Green organizations that will allow you to string out your payments so that the balance isn't paid until sometime after you return from your trip, but they are rare.)

We heartily recommend that you pay by credit card whenever possible, because the credit card company has quite a bit of clout if there are any problems. The one exception to this rule is if the tour organizer is a very small company or a nonprofit organization that can't really afford to pay the 2 percent to 5 percent commission that credit card companies charge. Then, you might wish to temper your need for security against your compassion for the tour organizer.

PLAYING THE PROFESSIONAL CARD
▼ ▼ ▼

Certain programs are willing to give discounts to those professionals who have skills that would be useful to the group.

If you happen to be a medical doctor or a registered nurse, you may qualify for an extra discount on certain programs and tours. A number of organizations have a policy of granting 25 percent or 50 percent reductions for medical personnel on the understanding that they will administer first aid or medical assistance to fellow Green Travelers and staff in the field. Since you'll be going anyway, and your Hippocratic Oath obliges you to render aid in case of need, you may as well be compensated by taking the discount. To find out if you are eligible, check with the organization at the time you sign up.

Other programs (especially research or other volunteer projects) may need a professional photographer, journal writer, chemist, geologist, heavy equipment operator, etc. Check to see if any of your proven skills will entitle you to a discount.

DEALING WITH A TRAVEL AGENT
▼ ▼ ▼

If all things were equal, it would almost always be to your benefit to use a travel agent rather than dealing directly with a tour operator or organization. A good agent can provide essential information, make all bookings, arrange transportation, handle payment submissions, and take care of any snags or difficulties. In addition, if you encounter any problems on your trip, you will have someone to turn to for help who has the added incentive of wanting to keep your business. What's more, it shouldn't cost you a penny more to use his or her services. Agents receive their commissions (10 percent is the industry average) not from you but directly from the tour operator, airline, hotel, etc.

Unfortunately, all things often aren't equal in using a travel agent for Green Travel programs and tours because it is difficult to nearly impossible to find a good travel agent who is well informed about what programs and alternatives are available.

Sadly, most of this country's more than 33,000 travel agencies are ill-equipped to deal properly with Green Travel. The main reason is that travel agents make their money booking as many clients as possible into trips and vacations that don't require an inordinate amount of work and pay prompt commissions. On the other hand, handling a Green Travel booking may involve five or even ten times more effort than normal travel, because many Green Travel tour operators are international concerns and don't have an American office; they work so close to margin that they can't afford to pay travel agent commissions or they take months to pay; they are nonprofit organizations that don't pay commissions as a matter of policy; or they use small, local hotels and facilities that are hard to reach, let alone deal with.

Most travel agents would rather pick up 10 percent on a sure-fire $4,000 family booking to Disney World that will take an easy half-hour's work and promptly pay a guaranteed $400 commission (usually with a bonus or override) than handle a $7,500 camera safari that may consume many hours of paperwork, involve unreimbursed faxes and transatlantic telephone calls, threatens a fair degree of uncertainty and an elevated risk of cancellations, and may take months to pay the $750 commission (minus currency exchange or bank charges).

Besides, except for the larger commercial enterprises, most travel agents have little knowledge of who the Green Travel tour operators are or how to get in touch with them. Travel agents use a variety of trade sources—computer searches, hotel and resort directories, airline guides, etc.—to ferret out the names and phone numbers of all the companies that the traveler will be using or staying at. Often, all they know about a tour operator or program is what they read in the same brochure you might have. Travel agents are limited to a slim publication called the Specialty Travel Index, about the only readily available professional sourcebook that touches on Green Travel. Only a handful of Green Travel operations are listed in it.

That's not to say that you shouldn't talk to your travel agent. According to Laurie Lubeck, director of the Wildlife Tourism Impact Project, the more people who ask for Green Travel programs and tours from their travel agent, the more the industry will perceive a growing demand. And that in turn may help make Green Travel enterprises and operations more popular and accessible to the public.

Even when dealing with a travel agent, be sure that you do your own research and are booked according to what you want to do, where you want to go, and how you want to go about it. Remember, although few travel agents, if any, will book you with nonprofit organizations or volunteer programs, they are still useful for helping you get to the assembly point.

We strongly suggest using a travel agent when you are planning to travel independently. Although a travel agent may not be particularly helpful in arranging most of your trip, especially if you want to keep it unstructured, an agent is useful for arranging such things as airline tickets, car rentals, first and last night motel rooms near the airport and other traditional travel matters.

Listed below are a handful of the travel agencies that specialize in Green Travel tours and programs. We expect more to pop up after this book is published.

TRAVEL-LINKS, Co-op America, 2100 M Street, NW, Suite 310, Washington, DC 20063, tel. (800) 992-1903 or (202) 872-5307. Co-op America is one of the largest and best-known environmentally and socially responsible organizations in the country, and as a service to its members, it offers specially selected socially responsible tours "for the ethical traveler," both for groups and individuals. In addition, a part of the commissions on every booking are donated to Co-op America's Economic Development Fund "to directly help progressive organizations that are working for economic justice." You don't have to be a member to use any of its travel services, but you can find out about joining by calling (800) 424-2667.

BREAKAWAY ADVENTURE TRAVEL, 93 Cherry Street, New Canaan, CT 06840, tel. (800) 955-5635 or (203) 972-6559. As its name indicates, Breakaway Adventure specializes in rugged and soft adventure treks around the world. "The companies we represent are all committed to socially and environmentally responsible travel."

HOLBROOK TRAVEL, 3540 N.W. 13th Street, Gainesville, FL 32609, tel. (904) 377-7111. Fax (904) 371-3710. We don't know much about this agency, except that it is active in ecotourism circles and comes recommended by people who care about the environment.

SAFARICENTRE INTERNATIONAL, 3201 N. Sepulveda Blvd., Manhattan Beach, CA 90266, tel. (800) 223-6046 or (800) 624-5342 (within California). Safaricentre claims to offer "the widest range of unique and imaginative wildlife, nature, and ecology safaris in Africa, Latin America, Asia, and Oceania to suit the budget requirements of the most intrepid adventure travelers as well as the most comfort-conscious environmentalist." The company provides full descriptions of all trips in brochures printed on recycled paper.

STA TRAVEL, tel. (800) 777-0112. STA Travel is an international agency with 120 offices around the world, including branches in Massachusetts, California, and New York. The company specializes in cheap travel abroad for youths and students, including charter flights and Eurail passes.

YOUR TRAVEL WALLET
▼ ▼ ▼

When you travel, although you should try not to carry an excess of cash that would burn in your pocket until you spend it, you will need to bring some extra cash. Many local merchants can't really afford the 2 percent to 5 percent commission that credit card companies charge, but they also can't afford to turn away business even if it means accepting credit cards.

Traveler's checks are valuable because they're so safe and secure—but only *if* you remember to put their numbers in a safe place other than with the checks and then record which ones you use as you spend them.

Be wary of playing the currency black market in Third World countries. It's illegal, it can be dangerous, you can be defrauded, and it does sometimes hurt the local economy. Conversely, some national economies actually depend on the currency black market to keep the country liquid. Let your tour guide advise you; he or she knows the local conditions. However, let your common sense be the final guide. As a *caveat*, be wary of tour guides who themselves dabble in money changing. You'll be much better prepared if you know not only what the official exchange rate is but how much the banks charge for the local currency before entering any transaction.

PHOTOGRAPHY

Photography is perhaps the most pleasurable and pervasive activity people do on vacations, and Green Travelers are even more apt to snap or tape, exposed as they are to strange and exotic lands, rare wildlife, unusual festivals, and other out-of-the-ordinary images. In fact, a disproportionate number of Green Travelers are serious amateurs who spend thousands of dollars on fine photographic equipment. But you needn't be an expert photographer with expensive equipment to be able to capture your memories on film. You'll discover, to your delight, that most Green Travel photographers are willing to help others with questions or problems.

As professional photographers, we'd like to make a few suggestions that may improve both your pleasure and your photographs.

▶ Take more film than you think you could possibly need. Photo stores are few and far between once you get outside big cities, and even if you are lucky enough to locate a source of your brand of film, it will probably be much more expensive than you would pay at home.

▶ If you have them—or can borrow them—bring at least two cameras or camera bodies with you. The worst possible thing that could happen on your vacation, especially if it is a once-in-a-lifetime adventure, is to suddenly be without a camera because it breaks down or is somehow lost. It eventually happens to everyone, amateur and professional, and the best prevention is to have another camera at the ready.

▶ Take along a complement of interchangeable lenses, each with an ultraviolet filter in front. The filters will cut down the excess blue light found at the seashore or in the mountains, and they protect your lenses. If you are on a wildlife trip, be sure that one of your lenses is a telephoto, so you can make the image of the animals fill the frame of the picture. Otherwise, you'll have lots of little, undistinguishable dots in the middle of big landscapes where the wild animal was.

▶ Pack all your film, fresh and exposed, in a clear plastic bag. That way you can send your camera bag through an airport X-ray machine while handing over the bag for a visual hand check. Yes, X rays are generally safe, but they're also accumulative; if your film goes through three or four checks on a trip, it may begin to fog.

▶ Before you attempt to photograph the wildlife, ask your guide or staff member if there are any special instructions or prohibitions. How close can you get? Should you approach downwind? Will a sudden movement scare off the animal? Although the best approach mostly relates to getting better photos while not stressing the animals, it can also involve life-and-death situations. For instance, in April 1991, a 25-year-old tourist was trampled to death in Thailand when she attempted to photograph an elephant and her flashgun startled the beast.

▶ If you photograph people, be sensitive to their feelings; don't simply point and shoot without making eye contact and asking permission. In some cultures, people fear that their souls may be carried away by a camera. Try asking first; often as not, most people will allow you to take their picture, and you may even make friends that way. Some photographers use their long telephoto lenses to take candid photos from a distance without first asking permission, but before doing this, ask yourself: Is this particular picture worth the potential invasion of another human being's sensitivities?

▶ Insure your expensive photo or video equipment. Most homeowners' or renters' policies can be extended at a nominal rate to include cameras, binoculars, portable computers, and other equipment you may take with you on vacation.

▶ Burn film. It's relatively cheap, you may never get back to that place again, and as every pro knows, the more images you shoot, the higher the probability that you'll capture a few memorable, even brilliant photographs.

Chapter Six

COLLATERAL ISSUES

▼ ▼ ▼

YOUR VACATION MAY BE TAX DEDUCTIBLE
▼ ▼ ▼

Sometimes in this world there *is* justice: The parking meter was broken and you got an extra three hours' time, you go off your diet for the weekend but lose weight anyway, all the multiple-choice questions you guessed at in the exam turned out to be correct. And sometimes, when you do a good deed by volunteering for a Green Travel program, or even go on a trip with a Green Travel tour operator, you might end up with certain serendipitous rewards, above and beyond the good experience.

A large percentage of Green Travel nonprofit organizations and even commercial for-profit tour operators are structured in such a way that part or even all of the money you paid for your vacation may be deducted from your income tax. IRS rules permit taxpayers who itemize in the 1040A long form to deduct for certain charitable activities and contributions, if particular criteria are met.

First, the contribution must be to a legitimate, qualified, nonpolitical cause or organization, registered under Section 501(c)(3) of the IRS Code. This includes such foundations as the World Wildlife Fund, as well as most colleges and universities. Also, you must be a member of the organization. Not all charities or nonprofit organizations qualify for IRS approval. For example, the Sierra Club lobbies for environmental legislation in Washington and therefore its trips are not usually tax deductible.

The most important thing to keep in mind is that you can't deduct what you paid for a Green Travel vacation, even if it is taken with a qualifying nonprofit organization, if you didn't do anything other than have a good time. You must spend most or all of your time as a legitimate volunteer, or as part of a delegation, in order to qualify. For example, if you are on a two-week trek through the Amazon, helping to count the parrot population for a university, the trip is probably tax deductible. However, if you spend only ten days doing field work and the rest sightseeing, the new IRS rules will probably disallow any expenses associated with the time you were sightseeing. But if your sole purpose is research or assistance, then you may be able to deduct meals, lodging, all incidentals and even the mileage it took you to drive to the airport.

In order to prove that you are entitled to a complete or partial deduction, keep some sort of daily log of your activities. Also, keep a record of any extra contributions you might make, whether it is in cash, equipment, securities, etc.

Many Green Travel organizations and tour operators donate a specific portion of the revenue they receive from every participant to local causes or charities. It's their way of giving back to the local culture or ecology. Typical amounts range from $20 to $300, which is usually stated somewhere in the brochure or on your ticket. You may be allowed to deduct that amount as a charitable contribution.

Most Green Travel organizations and tour operators are very forthright on whether or not you may claim a charitable contribution, and if so, how much. We have attempted as best as we can to confirm which of the programs listed in this book may be entirely or partially tax deductible. However, because some companies are foreign based, and the charities are local and may not be acceptable to the IRS, we urge you to check with your accountant or tax advisor before putting them down on your return.

COLLEGE CREDITS

Some of the programs listed in this book carry an added bonus: Upon completion, you may be able to claim college credits. Usually, these learning programs have been developed in conjunction with a particular college or university and are taught or conducted by staff or visiting professors. Such programs typically award one or two credits for two or three weeks' work.

Depending upon the particular program, you may have to undertake some field work, submit a paper, or take an exam. Also, in order to have them transferred to your own college or university, you may be required to pay an additional fee per credit. However, it's a relatively painless and rewarding way to continue your education or advance your professional standing while enjoying a Green Travel vacation. (If you are participating in what is normally a tax-deductible program, but you also happen to be receiving college credits, you may not be eligible to take the deduction, unless you are a teacher seeking to advance your accreditation.)

Don't be discouraged if the program or trip you are interested in doesn't specifically offer college credits. Nowadays, many colleges grant credits for what are known as life experiences—things you learn on the job, pick up during leisure time, or experience on your vacations. If you are serious about accumulating college credits, look for programs that offer you an opportunity to both learn and contribute, such as helping conduct nutrition surveys in Zimbabwe, study orangutan behavior in Borneo, or assist in compiling weather statistics in Arctic Norway. One of the best sources for finding volunteer programs likely to translate into college credit is Earthwatch (see page 181), a nonprofit clearing house that matches scientific and academic programs around the globe with potential volunteers willing to pay to work for the pleasure of the experience.

COMING HOME
▼ ▼ ▼

You may not know it yet, but Green Travel, especially after your first trip, is likely to change your life, and in ways you can scarcely imagine. Picture, if you will, how you might feel about suburban coffee klatches, Saturday morning Little League, or office politics immediately after you've just returned from three weeks on a wildlife watch in the Alaskan Arctic, a study tour of war-torn Central America, or a stint at a clinic inoculating infants against cholera in Bengal.

The intensity of experience, adventure, and discovery that is the hallmark of Green Travel and the very reason that you might choose a Green trip can alter your sense of perspective. While you are on the trip, you are infused with a sense of purpose or excitement. Then, when you come home, unpack your bags, and put away your souvenirs and log books, it is difficult to accept the fact that everything is just the way you left it, even though *you* might not be.

What you are going through is an esoteric form of vacation letdown, a very common symptom that is not limited just to returning Green Travelers. While it tends to be more severe with Green Travel, it has rather enjoyable solutions that don't apply to the letdown associated with traditional travel.

The solution is to continue doing whatever it was that you enjoyed so much during your Green trip. That's what's so rewarding about Green Travel. Everything can be translated to something back home.

Did you feel young again, learning about nature through field trips and wildlife encounters? You could become a member of a group like Sierra Club that has local weekend outings through nearby parklands. Or consider joining a nature photography club that works to learn more about the local wildlife and how to see and capture it on film.

Did you enjoy the lectures and learning about, say, art history? You could join the local museum and take some of their classes. Become a member of the local historical society to help identify and preserve historical sites. Or volunteer to help conduct tours in museums during your free time.

Do you feel depressed from no longer having the elation and self-enrichment of volunteering to help out in field research or in humanitarian projects?

Certainly, there are programs that could use your help part time. If there aren't, maybe you could get together with other Green Travelers to start something.

Is it the camaraderie of Green Travel that you miss? Join a study group, or start one. Before we moved out of the city, we held a very informal, once-a-month open house get-together in which we invited friends, associates, acquaintances, and strangers. We talked about whatever was important to us at the time, which generally covered the arts, philosophy, politics, and the news. The only rule was that every two or three times, our visitors were expected to bring someone new to the group. Sometimes it was boring and lifeless, other times exciting and exhilarating.

We aren't suggesting that you change your entire life style, quit your job, or open up your house to strangers. It's just that if you miss something that you found in Green Travel, you can probably find something similar at home.

In other words, don't just travel Green, but begin to *live* Green. That doesn't mean only being good to the world by recycling and standing up for what's right. It also means being good to yourself by seeking out those things in your hometown that will help you keep your mind sharp and your eyes on the horizon.

STAYING IN TOUCH
▼ ▼ ▼

Another important step to healthy decompression from a Green trip is to stay in touch, not only with the people you met but also with what is happening to the societies and wildernesses about which you now care.

If you traveled with a nonprofit organization, you will almost certainly continue to receive newsletters and/or magazines from them. Many for-profit tour operators include appropriate memberships in conservation or humanitarian organizations, too. Of course, you don't need any tour operator to help you seek out those organizations that are working toward the future you would like to see become a reality. As a starter, you may wish to refer to some of the organizations that are listed in the Points of Reference section of this book.

In addition to the regular membership privileges and publications, ask them if they have some kind of task force or committee that focuses on the area or culture you visited. If so, you could ask to be on its mailing list. Keeping informed is the first and most important step to helping to make a difference. The next step is to volunteer to help in some small way.

Such organizations often have regional or local chapters, too. Thus, membership becomes another entré into the Green network, with the bonus of meeting people in your hometown who think as you do and seek the same kind of leisure distractions.

HELPING YOUR FAMILY UNDERSTAND
▼ ▼ ▼

A friend of ours, the CEO of a major bank, started going to Haiti during his vacations two years ago to help out in a clinic. (It had been arranged on a private volunteer program sponsored by his sister-in-law's church.) He would return, simultaneously depressed and exhilarated, filled with a sense of purpose and the need to give to others. (His associates also made sure he didn't have to approve any hardship loan applications for a few months after each trip.) Unfortunately, his wife of many years did not feel the same emotional commitment to the area and did not go with him to Haiti. Thus, he was affected profoundly by an experience that she did not share, and while she remained as always, loving, intelligent, and interesting, she was not quite on the same wavelength as her husband.

This can be a very real problem. Try to help the people you love to understand what it is you are seeking in your Green Travel experiences. If you are involved in a relationship that is important to you, try to take that significant other with you on at least a short version of a Green trip. Let them change with you, and be patient with them if it scares them. You would do no less in meeting up with a stranger in an exotic land whom you have difficulty understanding. If you undergo a metamorphosis due to your Green Travel experiences, please be patient with your friends and family.

To us, that fits in the human element of our Green Travel guidelines, which, as we stated earlier, are:

▶ Be sensitive to local cultures and attitudes.

▶ Take the time to learn about and understand their expectations, taboos, and a few words in their language.

▶ Respect other people (your fellow travelers as well as the locals) as you would have them respect you.

▶ Honor everyone's inherent right to human dignity. Would you do more for strangers than for the people who love you?

THE RETURN TRIP

Green Travel is rather addictive. Once you have escaped the ordinary and experienced a rarefied vacation, it is difficult to go back to anonymous beaches, plastic resorts, and superficial sightseeing. It would be like trading in your color television set for an old black and white. Nothing less than the vivid colors and intriguing encounters of Green Travel will satisfy your new sense of adventure.

Beyond the choice of where to go and what to experience next is the question of whether or not your next Green trip should be with the same organization as the last.

There are advantages to going with the same tour organizer. As a repeater, you will be offered substantial discounts, enjoy a sense of familiarity of people and styles, and may be offered small gifts or other incentives. In addition, certain organizations, such as Sierra Club, recruit future leaders from former participants after they have demonstrated their abilities over a series of trips.

On the other hand, the great diversity of Green Travel options is a veritable smorgasbord of possibilities. If Green is the color of opening up your world as wide as your mind can take it, then the most vivid shades of Green will come from years of expanding your experiences to new places, new adventures, and new tour organizers, constantly widening the network of people of which you are a member.

PART TWO

GREEN TRAVEL
PROGRAMS

▼ ▼ ▼

OVERVIEW
▼ ▼ ▼

Now that you've determined that you want to travel Green on your next vacation, you have some decisions to make. To help you we have chosen over 80 different Green Travel options to profile in this section.

Please remember that between the time this book went to press and the time you picked it up, there may have been a few changes in prices, destinations, types of programs offered, etc. Our purpose in being as specific as possible on details that can change so quickly is to give you a baseline by which you can judge and compare different options.

PRICES
▼ ▼ ▼

Prices are given in two forms: the range of total cost and the range of per diem costs (i.e., the price per day). But when you compare various programs, please be certain to note what each includes. For instance, on first glance the price of a trip may seem very reasonable. But if you have to pay for your own air transportation, most of your meals, and some of your lodging, then you might be better off financially choosing another trip whose higher basic price is all-inclusive.

Of course, almost no tour organizer will pay for purchases of a personal nature, such as laundry, bar bills, souvenirs, independent excursions, or insurance. (Some do include wine, beer, or soft drinks with dinner.) Other expenses you may have to pay for out of your own pocket include passport and visa charges; transfers between the airport and your hotel or assembly point; airport or departure taxes; admission charges or park fees (on an African safari this can run as high as $500); individual excursions; airline charges for excess baggage; and gratuities. Be sure to factor such expenses into your travel budget.

All prices quoted in those programs that offer private rooms are based on double-occupancy (unless otherwise noted). If you are traveling single, most tour operators will help by trying to pair you up with another single of the same sex. Otherwise, you usually have to pay a surcharge for taking up a double room by yourself. On the other side of the spectrum, most tour operators offer group discounts. Because their definition of a group varies, it doesn't hurt to ask if you are traveling with your family or another couple if you qualify for a group discount. Or, if they know of an affinity group that needs a few extra people in order to meet the minimum qualification numbers, they may refer you to that organization so you can either officially join or just informally sign up under its auspices.

All tour operators base their prices on a certain number of people signing up for the trip. If they don't get enough paying guests, they have two options: cancel the trip or raise the price. They reserve the right to do either, but you can usually ask about their track record and your options at the time you make your reservation.

AIR TRANSPORTATION

There are variations in the kind of air transportation that a tour organizer may provide. The most basic requires that somehow, on your own steam and at your own cost, you will have to meet the group wherever they are—at the "assembly point." Usually, that means having to get and pay for round-trip airplane tickets plus ground transfers to wherever the tour will be: Nepal, Belize, or the Grand Canyon. Another variation is when your cost includes "air transportation from a U.S. gateway airport." That means the group will assemble at some major airport, such as New York, Miami, or Los Angeles, and you will have to find and pay for your own "domestic" transportation to get to that gateway airport. Sometimes, but rarely, all transportation from your home state's (or province's) main airport is included in the price.

Even when air transportation is an additional cost, many tour organizers offer group discount tickets. Usually, they are a good buy, but be sure to comparison shop to make sure. Other than price, the advantages to flying on the tour organizer's flights are that transfers and baggage handling are also usually included. Also, if there's a problem or delay, alternative arrangements for the entire group are usually made on the spot. What's more, it gives you an opportunity to meet your fellow travelers. But if you want to go off on your own before or after the tour, to explore the countryside or stay in a nearby city, buying the group air package may (or may not) limit you. Ask if you can change your flights or take a different one from the group before you buy the tour organizer's air package.

Another phrase you may encounter is "in-country transportation" which covers that transportation that you must use to move from place to place during your tour. Just about all tour organizers include this in the tour package.

GRATUITIES
▼ ▼ ▼

Whom do I tip? Who would be insulted by being offered a tip? How much is too much? Too little? Do I tip in dollars or the local currency? When is it more appropriate to give a gift than money?

Tipping practices vary depending upon the local economy and culture, the type of trip you are on, the quality of service you receive, and your tour organizer.

If you are on a volunteer project, reality tour, or a people-to-people program, it is generally inappropriate to tip anyone except waiters, taxi drivers, and other similar service personnel you may encounter on your own. In these cases, tips should range between 10 percent to 20 percent, just as it does at home. However, gifts may be a welcomed gesture. (See page 43.) Similarly, the lecturers and naturalists that are the hallmark of many Green tours are considered highly respected professionals; it is almost insulting to tip them. When you dine out with the group or stay in a hotel with them, the tour organizer usually takes care of your waiters and bellhops.

If you appreciate the work and service they have given you, then do tip local guides (but not guide managers), your driver (if he is with you for a few days), a boat's crew (if you are on the boat overnight), or your safari camp helpers. In a survey of all the tour organizers in this book, we have determined that a budget of $2 to $7 per traveler per day is realistic. (If you are on a safari in which the camp crew works hard in setting up the camp, cooking your food, bringing drinks, and trying to keep your impact on the camp area to a minimum, then you may wish to tip them as much as $10 a day.) In a seemingly unjust tradition, in the poorer nations the going rate for a proper tip is lower than in the richer nations, where the employees don't need it as much. But we suppose that also reflects the buying power of the dollar in each country. Another ironic aspect of international tipping etiquette is that it's quite indelicate to overtip in poor countries, which would demonstrate to the recipient how rich you are and how poor he must seem to you.

On the other hand, on some commercial tours and cruises, where tipping is a normal, integral part of the service, you may be expected to tip up to 10 percent of the basic trip price. If so, you will be advised by a staff member before the last day what the recommended amounts are, who gets what, and how it is handed over.

By the way, don't feel pressured or obliged to tip. A gratuity is a personal gesture of thanks for service, courtesy, and a job well done, not blackmail.

We note information about gratuities (and gifts) in the trip profiles only when the above rules of thumb don't apply.

Chapter Seven

ALL THINGS WILD AND BEAUTIFUL

Experiencing the Wonders of Nature

▼ ▼ ▼

A FEW WORDS

▼ ▼ ▼

For Yuri Gagarin and Alan Shepard, as well as for all the cosmonauts and astronauts that have followed them into space, the single most exquisite sight in the entire universe has been our sparkling blue-green world suspended in the void. The wonder of our earth and the unique diversity of life it supports can only be appreciated when seen from far away—or, in a delightful contradiction of refocused perspective, when you experience the very small, almost pointillist details of beauty on a truly personal level.

The flight of an iridescent blue butterfly among giant ferns in a dank green jungle. A seal nudging her newborn pup to her nipple. A tiny, almost impossibly colorful wildflower in the middle of a high desert. Life on earth in its resplendent natural state is an irresistible symphony of joy and wonder. And all we have to do to enjoy it is take the time to look closely at it, stop and smell the roses, so to speak, and allow ourselves to become part of it all, as we originally were.

Fortunately, for those of us who live far away from nature in the wild, or are caught up in our everyday hectic schedules, there are numerous Green Travel organizations that offer wildlife and wilderness tours designed to reintroduce us to our wondrous world. One can choose from naturalist-led trips to a nearby or national park, African photo safaris, whale-watching cruises, rain forest seminars, birdwatching trips, study tours of unique ecosystems. . . . In fact, there are almost as many different types of nature tours as there are kinds of animals.

Timing is everything when you are planning a trip with the hope of encountering certain wildlife. If you want to see penguin chicks in the nest, January to early February is the best time to visit Antarctic penguin rookeries. Arrive later, and you might see more corpses of the ones that didn't make it than live chicks; most of the survivors will have already followed their parents out to sea.

Any particular animal behavior you wish to witness will probably follow a certain seasonal pattern. For instance, mating rituals usually occur only during the mating season. What is the mating season for bear or beaver may not be for albatross or aardvarks.

Similarly, if you are headed for Tanzania to see the wildebeest migration, keep in mind that although June through August are the most comfortable months of the year to be there, the migrations actually take place in mid-December to mid-March. (In fact, February is the best time to see the wildebeest, because that's also when they calve.) On the other hand, the wildebeest migration in Kenya is mid-July to mid-September. That doesn't mean there aren't wildlife tours of Africa any other time. Some game can be seen all year. For instance, the mountain gorillas are always in their small, ever-diminishing preserves in Rwanda, and you'll see them every month of the year if you have a good tracker.

Travel to Africa, like many other destinations, is significantly affected by the weather. Many experts feel that the best time to go to east Africa (Kenya, Zaire, and Tanzania) is the autumn, which offers an excellent blend of dry, relatively cool weather and the most accessible game. If you went in April or May, you'd find it difficult to move about in the rains. On the other hand, the optimum time to travel to southern Africa (Botswana, Zambia, and Zimbabwe) is mid-May to late September. The rains there are in January through late April, and the rest of the year is quite hot.

In other words, if you have your heart set on seeing certain wildlife or specific behavior, be sure to schedule your holiday to fit with the animal's natural timetable. And also be aware when the rainy, icy, or hot seasons are, because the best animal sightings and experiences can be ruined if you are intensely uncomfortable because of the weather, or because the animals have migrated elsewhere.

But regardless of how carefully you plan your trip, even if you survey all the experts and study the charts of sightings of the past 10 years, there is nothing anyone can do to guarantee that you'll see all the wildlife you wish or witness certain behaviors. Wild animals are, by their very nature, unpredictable and erratic. And conditions in the wilderness can change, forcing you to alter your itinerary. For example, an unseasonably heavy rain can wash out the dirt road to the next scheduled preserve. What's more, if the trip is to a comparatively undeveloped country, our western-style expectations of time schedules, rational responsiveness, or reliable vehicles just aren't appropriate or possible in many local societies.

A certain degree of flexibility (seasoned with a healthy sense of humor) is required if you are to enjoy yourself. Don't get bogged down in frustration of what you won't see, but enjoy the adventure of never really knowing what will happen when dealing with wild things (or exotic cultures).

When considering various itineraries, it is valuable to realize that the more miles you will cover, the less you will probably see. In the tourism industry, this is known as the If-It's-Tuesday-It-Must-Be-Belgium syndrome. Programs that take their time to see an area in more detail usually provide a greater opportunity for wildlife sightings and allow you to learn more about their environs. For instance, many tours go to Denali National Park in Alaska for one night only, so you may catch only fleeting, faraway glimpses of the backsides of bear, caribou, and moose. Stay three days, however, and there's a far greater opportunity to come across wild animals up close, as well as to more fully experience that spectacular and enormous reserve. Of course, that may mean that you will spend less time elsewhere during your Alaskan vacation, but since you'll never be able to see it all in a couple of weeks, you might as well make quality choices.

Green Travel nature tours are very popular and highly accessible programs, with a wide range of prices, accommodations, and transportation. The groups, too, are very diverse. It is not uncommon for a tour to consist of singles, couples, teenagers, and an octogenarian or two. As a rule, the smaller the group on a nature tour, the more wildlife sightings you'll share and the less impact you'll make on the wilderness.

THE FLYING DOCTORS
▼ ▼ ▼

A brief word about African safaris and The Flying Doctors Society. The Flying Doctors Society provides emergency medical care, not only for tourists on safari but also for the local people who live in isolated areas. So, when some tour organizers arrange for you to have temporary membership in the society, they are not only protecting you but also supporting and subsidizing an important local organization.

NATIONAL AND STATE PARKS
▼ ▼ ▼

Although it seems statistically improbable and realistically incredible, approximately 90 percent of the total land mass of North America is in essentially the same condition as it was before Christopher Columbus bumped into the West Indies. Once you subtract the cities and suburbs, farms and small towns, you are left with a vast expanse of prairies and plains, mountains and deserts, forests and tundra. What's more, North America is fabulously rich in wildlife. It could very well be the most diverse and majestic ecosystem in the world.

Much of this vast, empty wilderness belongs to you. How so? Because it is federal, state, and provincial land, set aside for the enjoyment of everyone. So you don't have to travel to some exotic and far-off country to participate in a memorable nature tour.

The park systems present a wealth of opportunities. Park Rangers lead free walking tours and hikes and are generally available to answer any questions you may have. This can involve a lengthy discussion on the behavior of a local critter, advice on where to walk for the best views, or information about the history of the region. Today, when the age of heroes seems only a distant memory or a myth, we nominate park rangers as the unsung heroes of conservation. No matter where we have traveled in the various park systems on this continent, every park ranger we have met has been generous with time and information and more than happy to share his or her unique brand of knowledge.

Facilities in or near the parks can include lodges, hotels, and campgrounds. At the entrance, there is usually a display (sometimes quite large) about the natural history, geology, flora, and fauna of the region. There may also be ongoing free documentary films. In addition, seminars, workshops, and other events may be available from time to time.

How much will all this cost you? Frequently, nothing except the expense of driving or taking a bus to the park, lodging, and meals. Some places, especially the larger national parks, charge a nominal admission fee, and if you bring your own tent and sleeping bag, there might be a small cost for using the campsite amenities. Many of the programs and guided tours are also free, but if not, the charge will usually be less than you would spend to go to a movie.

Parks are more popular than ever. The Cassandra-like reports on television might lead you to believe that they're hopelessly overrun with tourists, especially during holidays. However, according to a recent CNN report, 95 percent of all park visitors stay within a short walk of the paved roads. All you have to do is wander five minutes or so off the path and you'll be almost alone in the wilderness. But if the prospect of bumper-to-bumper traffic at ever-popular places like Yellowstone or the Grand Canyon really puts you off, consider going to some of the less famous parks.

For information about various state, provincial, or regional parks, contact the park service in the capital of the state or province. For information about national parks, contact: *U.S. National Forest Service*, 201 14th St. NW, Washington, DC 20250, tel. (202) 447-3760; *U.S. National Park Service*, 18th & C Sts. NW, Room 3424, Washington, DC 20240-0001, tel. (202) 343-7394; *Bureau of Land Management*, 1849 C St. NW, Washington, DC 20240, tel. (202) 343-5717; *Environment Canada Information Center*, 351 St. Joseph Blvd., Hull, Quebec, K1A OH3, tel. (819) 997-2800; or various regional offices.

ABERCROMBIE & KENT
▼ ▼ ▼

Back in the early 1960s, A & K started out as an African wildlife safari company. It has since spread its operations throughout the world, becoming one of the trendsetters and standard bearers in adventure, natural history, and exotic culture travel. Over the years, A & K has earned a reputation for providing the best of whatever is available in any destination for its elite clients. Of course, such quality has its price, with some of A & K's more extravagant or extraordinary tours costing something up in the stratosphere. But many feel it's worth the price to travel with the best. (On the other hand, some of their tours are no more expensive than those offered by competitors.)

Every little detail is handled with meticulous planning and style. For many A & K tours throughout the world, your meals are included in the price, but you can dine just about anywhere you wish and whenever you wish as part of their a la carte plan. As Jan Wolf of A & K said, "Our policy is not to nickel and dime our guests, but to include everything that is within our control to include."

A & K's destinations are mostly on the edges of civilization, where life is unpredictable and politics occasionally precarious. That, too, is part and parcel of the adventure: to go where your friends and neighbors have never gone before. But that also means that you should strongly consider purchasing trip and emergency medical insurance. Then relax and roll with whatever happens. Chances are that not everything will go as planned (which is to be expected on any wildlife tour), but that doesn't mean the surprises will be unpleasant. In fact, A & K plans carefully to provide whatever emergency assistance may be necessary, such as providing membership for all their clients to Africa in the East African Flying Doctor's Society. (A & K does have a few tame destinations, such as manor houses of the English gentry.)

Most of A & K's clients are quite used to both comfort and adventure. Sophisticated and with enough time and money to see the world at a leisurely pace, they often take advantage of the many unusual optional extensions to the tours. A & K's independent traveler programs (including private air excursions into the wild) are quite noteworthy for their creativity.

(See pages 221–224 for a description of A & K's adventure cruises; other nonadventure river cruises are available.)

DESTINATIONS: Kenya, Tanzania, Rwanda, Zaire, Egypt, Botswana, Zimbabwe, Zambia, the Seychelles, New Zealand, Australia, Papua New Guinea, Fiji, Polynesia, Great Britain, France, Ireland, Scotland, Germany, Austria, Hungary, Yugoslavia, Romania, Danube River, Turkey, Black Sea, U.S.S.R., Spain, Switzerland, Italy, India, Nepal, Pakistan, Thailand, Hong Kong, China, Japan, Indonesia, Malaysia, Singapore, Laos, Borneo, Tibet

Season: All year

Length of Programs: 5 to 31 days

Enrollment: Varies, depending upon the program, but A & K tends to keep the numbers down to maintain their status as an elite tour operator.

Total Cost: $1,585 to $17,000

Cost Per Diem: $157 to $851

Tax Deductible?: No

Cost Inclusive Of: Lodging, all meals during tours, transportation during tour, pretrip information packet, flight bag, passport wallet, welcome cocktail party and farewell dinner, transfers for those on group flights, sightseeing and entrance fees during tour, most gratuities

Cost Exclusive Of: Air transportation to the tour's assembly point, airport taxes (most tours), transfers for independent passengers, gratuities to some local guides and drivers

Amenities, Facilities, and Realities: A & K endeavors to provide the best available in any destination. Their chefs are inventive, cold drinks are served in the hottest and least-likely locales, comfort is a bylaw of the company, luxury expected even in the bush. Some of their tents have private bathrooms with showers and toilets. A & K clients take for granted that everything will be taken care of graciously and stylishly; it usually is.

Other Comments: A & K donates $10 per African traveler to Friends of Conservation, "an organization dedicated to the preservation of African wildlife and habitats," with which Jorie Kent, cofounder of Abercrombie & Kent, is very active. As a matter of policy, there is no smoking in A & K sightseeing vehicles.

Contact: Abercrombie & Kent, 1520 Kensington Rd., Oak Brook, IL 60521-2106, tel. (800) 323-7308 or (708) 954-2944.

Alaskan Wildland Adventures
▼ ▼ ▼

Sometimes, we stumble across a small operation that does something unusual and does it well. After we gave our papers at the 1990 Ecotourism Symposium in Miami, a soft-spoken, bearded young man approached us to tell us about his company—Alaskan Wildland Adventures. What he had to say about showing travelers an Alaska that outsiders seldom see, plus the sincerity with which he spoke, caught our attention. So, we decided to look into the company further.

Established in 1977, AWA is run by Alaskans who love their state and take pride in showing visitors the best that it has to offer. Their programs take only small groups into the interior to see wildlife up close and include tent or cabin wildlife safaris, senior citizens' safaris, family tours designed to intrigue children and their parents, sport fishing, whitewater rafting, yacht trips through Prince William Sound, and other unusual expeditions. The most rugged of their tours—the Alaska Wildland Expeditions—can involve being a member of a very small group dropped off in the wilderness "by small plane, hundreds of miles away from roads." Among their land tours, you can choose between roughing it or staying in a heated lodge or hotel with all the comforts of home. But whatever tour you do take, you will agree with AWA that "the real experience begins where the crowds don't go."

AWA's reputation is well established, and they have been affiliated with numerous prestigious tour organizers as Alaska land packagers. Some of these organizations include: International Expeditions, Sobek, the Audubon Society of Massachusetts, the Delaware Nature Center, and others. By the way, AWA offers to provide a list of past clients who would be willing to talk about their personal experiences with this tour operator. We recommend taking them up on the offer.

DESTINATIONS: Alaska

SEASON: Mostly June to early September, with some off-season (and generally less expensive) programs in March to May and September to mid-October

LENGTH OF PROGRAMS: 2 to 12 days

ENROLLMENT: 12 to 18 participants

TOTAL COST: $1,195 to $3,405

COST PER DIEM: $199 to $417

TAX DEDUCTIBLE?: No

COST INCLUSIVE OF: Lodging, all meals, all gear and equipment (as needed), guide, tax

COST EXCLUSIVE OF: Transportation to pickup point in Alaska, gratuities to guide, drinks, sleeping bag, and water bottle (if needed)

AMENITIES, FACILITIES, AND REALITIES: When making a reservation with AWA, be honest with them about your level of physical fitness, as well as just how much comfort you need or want on a trip. They probably can accommodate you, whatever your preferences and needs. But if they feel you would be happier with another tour operator, they will make suggestions to you about others you should consider calling. Some of their lodge and hotel-based tours include private bathrooms and all the comforts you would expect on a traditional tour. Others, such as some of their fishing lodges, involve showers and toilets that are in outbuildings. A few programs offer some nights with private facilities and other nights not. As Kirk Hoessel, the director of AWA, said, "For the richness of experience that you can have in Alaska, you sometimes compromise your desire for a bathroom in your room." On most camping trips, AWA guides take care of most of the work involved, such as setting up camp, cooking, and cleaning. But on the Alaska Wildland Expeditions, participants will be expected to assist in those duties. AWA's brochure is very clearly written, so that you can determine just which program offers what kind of amenities and requires what level of fitness. But, if you are uncertain, it is best to talk with them directly. They are a very unassuming, helpful, and well-informed group of people.

CONTACT: Alaska Wildland Adventures, P.O. Box 389, Girdwood, AK 99587, tel. (800) 334-8730 or (907) 783-2928. Fax (907) 783-2130.

AUDUBON SOCIETY
▼ ▼ ▼

For more than half a century, the National Audubon Society's summer camps have attracted adults and kids alike to learn about nature from firsthand experience and encounters with nature under the guidance of the experts. They study such things as geology, ecology, photography, field ornithology, marine biology, and Native American culture in some of the most beautiful settings in the world, which are, fortunately, very close to home. In addition to field studies and lectures, there is usually time for hiking, rock climbing, and, when near water, swimming. What makes this exceptional experience even better is that the prices are quite reasonable, even bargains. Some of the adult camp programs include: "Maine Coast Field Ecology" and "Field Ornithology."

In addition, Audubon conducts ecology workshops in wilderness areas in the United States and the American tropics (such as Costa Rica, Trinidad, and Venezuela). The purpose is to learn to understand and cherish what must be preserved while still having a wonderful adventure. For an additional charge, you may earn college credit on some programs.

DESTINATIONS: Wyoming, Yellowstone National Park, Grand Teton National Park, Maine, Connecticut, Hawaii, Texas, Arizona, Washington State,

Grand Canyon, Zion National Park, Bryce National Park, Costa Rica, Trinidad and Tobago, Venezuela, Belize, Amazon River, Brazil

SEASON: Mostly summer, though there are programs at other times of the year.

LENGTH OF PROGRAMS: 6 to 12 days

ENROLLMENT: 28 to 55 participants domestic; 15 to 30 international. A limit of 48 campers in the camp for kids (10 through 14 years old).

TOTAL COST: Domestic: $495 to $975; Hawaii and international: $1,695 to $1,895

COST PER DIEM: Summer youth camp: $60; Domestic: $70 to $139; Hawaii and international: $154 to $211

TAX DEDUCTIBLE?: No

COST INCLUSIVE OF: Lodging, meals (in Maine, Connecticut, Wyoming, and international programs, others cover only some meals), instruction, transportation during the program

COST EXCLUSIVE OF: Transportation to assembly point, some meals on some tours

AMENITIES, FACILITIES, AND REALITIES: Generally speaking, accommodations are rustic, reminiscent of the camp days of your childhood. Rooms are usually double occupancy, sometimes with private bathrooms. (In Connecticut the bathrooms are private; in Maine and Wyoming, they are shared. Elsewhere, it depends upon what facilities they use.) If they know in advance of any disabilities, Audubon staffers try to help physically limited participants to fully enjoy the programs. Some ramps are available, but the trails are not paved and are very hilly. No special diets are possible. Gratuities are generally not appropriate on these tours except on international programs where the tipping customs vary.

OTHER COMMENTS: The youth camp fills up so quickly that if you want your kids to get into it, make your reservations before the brochures come out, which is in the autumn.

CONTACT: Audubon Ecology Camps & Workshops, National Audubon Society, 613 Riversville Road, Dept GT, Greenwich, CT 06831, tel. (203) 869-2017. In addition, international tours and cruises are sponsored by National Audubon Society, 950 Third Avenue, New York, NY 10022, tel. (212) 546-9140. Some local chapters offer various travel programs.

BIG FIVE EXPEDITIONS

Big Five has long been a term used by hunters to describe the five big game animals they sought in Africa—lion, rhinoceros, elephant, buffalo, and leopard. So it should come as no surprise that this tour operator specializes in African safaris. Of course, they are nature and photography tours rather than hunting expeditions.

What sets Big Five apart from its competitors is that it is owned and operated by a Kenyan family. Mahen Sanghrajka, who was born and raised in Nairobi, started the company with his brother and their friend in 1973. With pride, Sanghrajka said to us, "Every group that arrives in Nairobi has dinner in my family's home in Nairobi. Also, when we make a promise, we know we can deliver it, because we have all the personal connections for whatever has to be done." They don't depend on subcontractors to provide necessary services. What's more their African guide/drivers are all shareholders in the company.

Recently, Big Five has branched out to other areas in the world where adventure and nature are still wild and romantic to offer special-interest and soft-adventure tours. For instance, Big Five travels to Manitoba to see polar bears, to Baja California for the whales, to the Amazon and Costa Rica for the rain forests, etc. They also head out to England and Wales for much tamer programs. Big Five also designs custom programs for individuals and organizations. But it is in Africa where they are the specialists, because it's their home.

DESTINATIONS: Botswana, Kenya, Tanzania, Egypt, India, Nepal, England, Wales, Galapagos, Ecuador, the Amazon, Peru, Costa Rica, Alaska, Baja California, Canadian Rockies, Canadian Arctic, Australia, Indonesia, New Zealand, Yellowstone National Park

SEASON: All year

LENGTH OF PROGRAMS: 3 to 20 days

ENROLLMENT: Never more than 18, a maximum of 6 people per minibus. Camping safaris are limited to no more than 12 participants.

TOTAL COST: $579 to $3,825

COST PER DIEM: $80 to $279

TAX DEDUCTIBLE?: No

COST INCLUSIVE OF: Lodging, some meals, transfers, porters, sightseeing, most park and entrance fees, membership in Flying Doctors Society (for those on the east Africa trips)

COST EXCLUSIVE OF: Air transportation to the assembly point, some meals, gratuities, airport taxes

AMENITIES, FACILITIES, AND REALITIES: The African tours are usually tent-based. Each tent is 20' × 12' and has private shower and toilet *ensuite*. In addition, Big Five's African equipment includes a fleet of 8 4-wheel drive vehicles and 40 6-passenger minibuses, each outfitted with seat belts, a few reference books, several binoculars, an ice chest filled with cold soft drinks, dust masks (for passengers), plastic bags to protect camera equipment, and the usual pop-up roofs for better photographic views. Their facilities elsewhere in the world vary, depending upon the destination. As a rule, Big Five attempts to book accommodations that have private bathrooms, when they are available.

CONTACT: Big Five Tours, 110 Route 110, South Huntington, NY 11746, tel. (800) 445-7002 or (516) 424-2036. Fax (516) 424-2154.

BORROBOL BIRDING
▼ ▼ ▼

Tucked far up in the northern tip of Scotland, in the Highlands, in the midst of a dramatic isolated landscape, Borrobol is an Edwardian sporting lodge in a 23,000-acre estate. Beyond its own beauty and charm, what makes Borrobol noteworthy is that it is smack in the middle of the migration path of over 100 species of birds, some that are just passing through but many that come to lay their eggs. Golden eagles, Scottish crossbills, peregrine falcons, hen harriers, merlins, sparrowhawks, kestrels, buzzards, goshawks, owls, geese, ducks, plovers, red grouse, black grouse, greenshanks, dunlins, curlews, oystercatchers, ptarmigans, waders, crows, herons, and many more may be sighted here. On nearby sea cliffs, you'll see swarms of nesting sea birds. It's a birdwatching smorgasbord and birding tours are led by a field ornithologist from the Royal Society for the Protection of Birds.

When you tire of squinting through binoculars at the profusion of birds, there are also archeological and historic sites, such as castles, Iron Age forts, standing stones, and neolithic defense towers. Or you can take a few swings at the challenging Dornoch golf course. Other wildlife you may see include: red deer, roe deer, wild goat, fox, mountain hare, badger, otter, and Scottish wild cat.

DESTINATIONS: Scotland

SEASON: Late April to mid-July

LENGTH OF PROGRAMS: One week, beginning on Saturday

ENROLLMENT: Up to 6 guests

TOTAL COST: $1,395

COST PER DIEM: $199

TAX DEDUCTIBLE?: No

COST INCLUSIVE OF: Meals, wine and spirits, accommodations, daily birding and sightseeing excursions, transportation and admission to local historical and cultural attractions, gratuities

COST EXCLUSIVE OF: Transportation to Borrobol

AMENITIES, FACILITIES, AND REALITIES: The lodge has four charming guest bedrooms (two with double beds) and three bathrooms, plus two drawing rooms, a large dining room, and a library filled with bird books, stuffed birds, and paintings of birds. Michael Wigan, the owner, is very available and ever-present. This is a most gracious way to go birding.

CONTACT: Michael Wigan, Borrobol, Kinbrace, Sutherland, Scotland KW11 6UB, United Kingdom, or Selected British Hotels, 519 Park Drive, Kenilworth, IL 60043, tel. (800) 323-5463 or (312) 251-4110.

EXPLORAMA TOURS (EXPLORACIONES AMAZONICAS S.A.)

▼ ▼ ▼

The Amazon Jungle, the granddaddy of all the rain forests in the world, simply can't be fully experienced from some aloof tour bus or on a two- or three-hour shore excursion from a cruise ship. It's too immense, too diverse, with so many little details of life. It takes hours just to refocus the way you look at things. The only way to really see the Amazon is to become a part of it, if only for a few days.

Explorama Tours was established in 1964 by Peter Jenson, an American anthropologist who wanted others to have the same opportunity he had to really delve into the mysteries and beauty of the Amazon Jungle. Today, Explorama has three very different properties, right in the middle of the forest: the Explorama Inn with private palm-thatched cottages; the Explorama Lodge, with its lodges of sleeping rooms; and the Explornapo Camp, with Indian-like dormitory accommodations.

According to Peter Jenson, who is now the president and general manager, they guarantee that the majority of the money you pay Explorama will stay in country with the locals. Also, he added, "Out of 90 employees, Explorama has only 2 employees who were not born in the Amazon Rain Forest and who have not lived in the Rain Forest their entire life: Pam, our lodge hostess, who is married to one of our guides, and myself." In addition, not only are all the Explorama investors Peruvian (other than Jenson), but Jenson has signed a contract with the government that he will not remove any of his own investment earnings from Peru. This is quite an unusual arrangement that exhibits a real commitment to what is best in the Green movement.

Their reputation is such that numerous well-known tour operators use Explorama as their Amazon subcontractor, most notably International Expeditions, with which Explorama has a very close relationship based on heartily expressed mutual respect. Also, International Expeditions has joined with Explorama to create what will probably be the most exciting and innovative site for rain forest research and education—the new Amazon Center for Environmental Education and Research. (See page 94.)

Explorama offers such an intimate experience of the Amazon that Earthwatch bases their katydid project there, and other scientists have used the facilities for research programs. In fact, Explorama neither charges many scientists who need to use their facilities (including lodging and food) nor bothers them with requests to guide visitors. As Jenson explained to us, the use of resident scientists to show visitors around would effectively restrict the hiring of locals for the most prestigious jobs—that of guides.

DESTINATIONS: The Peruvian Amazon

SEASON: All year. The high-water time is usually November to mid-July when you can paddle almost wherever you want or trek on high ground. The low-water time is usually mid-July to October, when many of the small streams become trickles and unnavigable, but there are more dry areas in which you can walk. Different "experts" prefer the different times of year based upon whether they prefer going by water or by foot.

LENGTH OF PROGRAMS: 3 to 7 days

ENROLLMENT: Explorama Inn has 26 private cottages available for single, double, or triple occupancy; Explorama Lodge has 72 rooms, most of which are doubles; Explornapo Camp holds up to 40 participants.

TOTAL COST: $96 to $1,000, depending upon which property you choose, how many people are traveling with you, and the number of nights you stay. There are also combination packages that allow you to stay a couple of nights in each of the three properties.

COST PER DIEM: $48 to $200

TAX DEDUCTIBLE?: No

COST INCLUSIVE OF: Airport reception in Iquitos, transfers, land and river transportation, accommodations, meals, guided excursions, taxes

COST EXCLUSIVE OF: Air transportation to Iquitos

AMENITIES, FACILITIES, AND REALITIES: The three properties are very different from each other, which is why you may wish to try more than one by purchasing a combination package. The Explornapo Camp is the most basic, even primitive, of the properties. You stay in open-air dormitories, under mosquito-proof tents. Showers and latrines are communal. The much newer and more comfort-oriented Explorama Inn has private cottages, each with *ensuite* bathrooms, electric lights, screens, and a private porch that overlooks the Amazon. The Explorama Lodge is a compromise property that has private sleeping rooms in large thatched buildings, but the toilets and showers are in outbuildings. All are surrounded by nature preserves. Of course, you must keep in mind that the Amazon is about as far off the beaten track as you can get. Explorama denies any health or accident responsibilities outside the urban area of Iquitos. And there are few, if any, facilities nearby in case of emergencies. By the way, your shoes are sure to get wet at one time or another, so pack an extra pair of sneakers. As Peter Jenson says, "Our part of the Amazon is what is called an 'Everwet' or 'Humid Rain Forest.' " Expect it to rain at some time during almost every day you are there. (The area has rain about 250 days a year.) But that is one of the important factors that makes this region the most diverse in the world. According to botanist Dr. Alwin Gentry, you can find more tree species here than anywhere in the world. Besides, the rain is usually in short spurts, not all day long.

OTHER COMMENTS: When in the Amazon, you will have the opportunity to trade goods with Indians living in the jungle. Generally, they don't want money. While some tourists bring cigarettes, cosmetics, and tee shirts, we discovered the high value the locals place on such useful items as inexpensive hammers and umbrellas. Metal deteriorates so quickly in the jungle that we had brought one of the most desired commodities. In fact, while our fellow travelers bartered with members of the tribe for souvenir-sized replicas, the headman would not have insulted us with anything less than authentic blowguns, headdress, and a pictographic bark skirt. When packing for barter, think of what might be practical, needed, and rare in the region to which you are going. These items may actually be clothes, tools, or hardware that are in good condition and are just taking up space in your closet.

CONTACT: Exploraciones Amazonicas (Explorama Tours), Box 446, Iquitos, Peru, tel. 011-51-94-23-5471. Fax 011-51-94-23-4968. Or contact their U.S. representatives: Selective Hotel Reservations, 9 Boston St., Suite 10, Lynn, MA 01904, (800) 223-6764 or (617) 581-0844.

FOOTHILLS SAFARI CAMP AT FOSSIL RIM
▼ ▼ ▼

You don't have to spend the money and time to go all the way to Africa to participate in a tent safari. Right in Texas, within a comparatively short drive of the Dallas/Fort Worth airport, is a 3,000-acre wildlife conservation park "dedicated to breeding endangered animals with the ultimate goal of returning them to their natural environment." Wildebeest, cheetah, oryx, zebra, giraffes, white rhinos, exotic birds, Mexican Grey Wolf—about 30 species of endangered animals roam the African-like savannah of Fossil Rim.

Foothills is a very small operation that almost seems like your own private wildlife preserve. Some of the activities in which you can participate are visits to see (and perhaps feed) the young in the breeding grounds, birdwatching, nature walks, and jeep tours, discussions on conservation with the experts who are being so successful with their breeding projects, campfire storytelling, stargazing, horseback riding, etc. You can also go fossil hunting in an area that has been rich in finds. Though they cater to individuals, the safari camp can be reserved whole for a group, without breaking the bank.

DESTINATIONS: Texas

SEASON: All year

LENGTH OF PROGRAMS: 3, 4, or 5 days

ENROLLMENT: Limited to 12 participants, at 2 to a tent

TOTAL COST: $398 (3 days); $596 (4 days); $795 (5 days)

COST PER DIEM: $133 to $159; the price per diem per person is less if you are part of a group of 12 that book the entire camp.

TAX DEDUCTIBLE?: No

COST INCLUSIVE OF: Lodging in tents, meals, soft drinks, naturalist-led jeep tours and photo walks, use of a 10-inch Celestron computerized telescope (for star gazing), membership (during your stay) to the Foothills Safari Club

COST EXCLUSIVE OF: Transportation to the camp

AMENITIES, FACILITIES, AND REALITIES: The tents are luxuriously appointed, with central air conditioning and heat, private bathroom, and a view of the watering hole where some animals congregate. Everything is done with a sense of style and comfort, making roughing it a misnomer, even though you are living out in the "wild." The food is made to order for such a small number of people that the chef has the leisure to be creative. If any of your party have physical limitations, talk to Foothills when you make your booking, and they will do whatever they can to make the visit comfortable and the activities accessible. No gratuities are accepted. Any gratuities that you want to give will be turned over in your name to the Fossil Rim conservation foundation, which is responsible for the care, breeding, and preservation of the animals.

OTHER COMMENTS: Once a month there are special family safaris on which children are welcome. Children under 2 are free; 2 to 6 years old cost about $108 per diem; 7 to 18, $133 per diem.

CONTACT: The Foothills Safari Camp at Fossil Rim, P.O. Drawer 329 (Route 1, Box 210), Glen Rose, TX 76043, tel. (817) 897-3147. Fax (817) 897-3785.

INTERNATIONAL EXPEDITIONS
▼ ▼ ▼

International Expeditions is a private tour operator whose travel programs to some of the more remote areas of the world focus on enjoying the diversity of nature, especially wildlife, with a close eye on conservation and protection. All their tours include field trips led by expert naturalists. What's more, International Expeditions spends a considerable amount of effort on trying to minimize their negative impact on local cultures and natural habitats, while attempting to seek ways to make their presence a positive influence. This appears to be much more a commitment to a travel ethic than just a marketing stance. They've certainly been at it since well before the current "ecotourism" bandwagon started gathering momentum.

In March 1991, International Expeditions co-sponsored (with Explorama Tours, The Nature Conservancy, and the Peruvian Foundation for the Conservation of Nature) the first International Rain Forest Workshop. The location was the Amazon Jungle, and the purpose was to study the problems and possible solutions for saving rain forests around the world. It was such a successful workshop that it is scheduled to be an annual event, open to the public, that may be booked through International Expeditions. The next workshop will be March 21 to 28, 1992. (See Other Comments below about the new Amazon Center for Environmental Education and Research, which will be the site of future workshops.)

International Expeditions' other programs include journeys to Churchill in Manitoba, Canada, to see the polar bears, visits to the Magdalen Islands when the harp seals pup, treks up into Rwanda to see Dian Fosse's mountain gorillas, and many other exotic wilderness areas where wildlife sightings are the main attraction. Some of the special interest groups that travel with International Expeditions include: American Museum of Natural History, Friends of the National Zoo, North Carolina Zoological Society, Scranton University, Georgia State University, Baltimore Zoological Gardens, and others.

DESTINATIONS: Kenya, Tanzania, Rwanda, Zambia, Zimbabwe, Botswana, Madagascar, India, Nepal, Thailand, Malaysia, China, Australia, New Zealand, Papua New Guinea, Hawaii, Alaska, Manitoba, Quebec's Magdalen Islands, Iceland, Belize, Costa Rica, Venezuela, Ecuador, Galapagos, Peru, Brazil, Antarctica

SEASON: All year, the season depending on the destination

LENGTH OF PROGRAMS: 8 to 22 days

ENROLLMENT: 12 to 15 participants

TOTAL COST: $699 to $5,398

COST PER DIEM: $142 to $320

TAX DEDUCTIBLE?: No

COST INCLUSIVE OF: Air transportation from a U.S. gateway airport, meals, transportation during the tour, accommodations, information booklets

COST EXCLUSIVE OF: Domestic transportation to the gateway airport, gratuities

AMENITIES, FACILITIES, AND REALITIES: Accommodations vary depending upon the destination. In the wilds, sometimes there are shared toilets or showers, or even just outdoor latrines. But on other programs, the facilities may include private bathrooms on every evening. According to Tom Grasse of IE, "We cater to a slightly older clientele. We are not an adventure company, so there is no trekking, but there are sometimes extensive walks through the forest." However, none of the activities are strenuous. Of course, he added, no one pressures anyone to participate in every activity, especially if they don't feel up to it. "They can just lie back in a hammock and drink a beer."

OTHER COMMENTS: The first International Rain Forest Workshop in March 1991 was a launching pad for a rather unusual and exciting project. International Expeditions and Explorama Tours (see pages 88–91) have purchased 44,000 acres of the rain forest to be set aside as a permanent preserve, called the Amazon Biosphere Reserve. On the Reserve, which is in the middle of the most diverse ecosystem in the world, they are building the Amazon Center for Environmental Education and Research (ACEER). Among ACEER's more exciting features will be a canopy walkway, suspended high in the trees, to allow visitors to observe life among the treetops, which is so very different from that on the forest floor. ACEER will provide free transportation, meals, lodging, and a complete laboratory to scientists. All they will be asked is to disclose their findings and to explain their work to visitors. Lodging will also be available to paying visitors. And it is hoped that the Orejones Indians who live nearby will become involved as park rangers, thereby providing them with a decent livelihood while maintaining their traditional culture and protecting the rain forest. Explorama and International are hoping that the proceeds from next year's International Rain Forest Workshop will be enough to allow them to purchase another 50,000 acres to add to the new protected area and provide the momentum for more annual workshops followed by additional annual purchases of land. If they accomplish only a portion of what they plan, Explorama and International will have set new precedents for corporate sponsorship of the alliance of conservation, responsible tourism, and respect for local people. In other words, Green Travel. ACEER is scheduled to open in early 1992.

CONTACT: International Expeditions, One Environs Park, Helena, AL 35080, tel. (800) 633-4734 or (205) 428-1700. Fax (205) 428-1714.

NATURAL HABITAT WILDLIFE ADVENTURES
▼ ▼ ▼

Natural Habitat is more than a tour operator. They endeavor to offer local populations an economic alternative to hunting—tourism. For instance, on Canada's Madelaine Islands (in the Gulf of St. Lawrence), local people are still permitted by law to kill seals on a small scale (commercial hunting is outlawed). But Natural Habitat brings tourists up to visit the ice floes and even cuddle baby seals. Not only does the presence of the tourists inhibit hunting, but tourism creates jobs and brings in needed money to a community that is otherwise dependent on the hunting.

Their various programs center around wildlife and are called "Polar Bear Watch," "Seal Watch," "Whale Watch," "Primate Watch," and "Galapagos

Wildlife Watch." The polar bear program sets out from Churchill, Manitoba (Canada), which is so close to the migratory path of the creatures that it is called the "Polar Bear Capital of the World." Like so many other whale programs, Natural Habitat takes advantage of the warm, friendly waters of Baja California. And the Primate Watch includes visits to the Mountain Gorillas of Rwanda (made famous by Dian Fosse and the film *Gorillas in the Mist*).

Groups are kept small, and guides are very experienced photographers who will give advice and assistance to help you get memorable pictures of the animals—some quite close. (By the way, the head of Natural Habitat is also the founder of the International Fund for Animal Welfare.)

DESTINATIONS: Alaska, Manitoba, Baja California, Rwanda, Zaire, Galapagos

SEASON: Various times through the year, following the seasons of the animals

LENGTH OF PROGRAMS: 6 to 12 days

ENROLLMENT: 17 to 150 participants, depending upon the program

TOTAL COST: $1,295 to $4,995, depending upon the area of the world visited

COST PER DIEM: $185 to $416

TAX DEDUCTIBLE?: No

COST INCLUSIVE OF: Transportation during the tour (which includes some international flights for the Africa and Galapagos programs), lodging, meals, photography instruction, transfers, airport taxes, entrance and park fees, the use of arctic suits (during Seal Watch program)

COST EXCLUSIVE OF: Transportation to assembly point (which may include some international flights for some of the tours), gratuities for local guides

AMENITIES, FACILITIES, AND REALITIES: The Seal Watch program is sold based upon the number of helicopter trips you want to make to the ice to see the seals—one, two, or three. The rest of the time is spent in photography workshops, nature walking tours of the Madelaine Islands, lectures, birdwatching, cross-country skiing, snowshoeing, and moonlit hikes. The Polar Bear Watch involves spending up to seven or eight hours a day for three days in specially designed, heated vehicles (called Tundra Buggies) to view the bears through large windows. The Baja and Galapagos programs are both boat-based and do not offer private bathrooms. On the Alaska trips, the lodge that they use in Katmai National Park requires that the group split up by gender (including couples), with four people per room. It's only for a couple of nights, and the locale is certainly rich in wildlife. If you so wish, vegetarian meals are available on all the trips. The assembly point for most programs is somewhere near the basic tour. For instance, for the Seal Watch, the assembly point is Halifax, Nova Scotia, from where you fly further north with the group. The assembly point for the Africa trip is New York, and for the Galapagos, it's Miami.

OTHER COMMENTS: Natural Habitat attempts to make their trips accessible to as many people as possible, regardless of financial or physical limitations. Ask about their payment plans that don't carry any interest or other finance charges. And for those who are limited physically, their brochures state, "The Natural Habitat staff has the commitment to do whatever is necessary to assure your enjoyment and comfort."

CONTACT: Natural Habitat Wildlife Adventures, One Sussex Station, Sussex, NJ 07461, tel. (800) 543-8917 or (201) 702-1525. Fax (201) 702-1335.

THE NATURE CONSERVANCY
▼ ▼ ▼

According to The Nature Conservancy, "By the year 2000, if present trends continue, the world will be losing one plant or animal species every hour of every day." At present, "Every day, 140,000 acres of tropical forest are axed for timber, burned for cultivations, or clear-cut for cattle grazing. An area of forest the size of Great Britain is destroyed every year."

The Nature Conservancy has taken a very pragmatic stance in preserving threatened species and their habitats. Put simply, working with partner organizations throughout the world, they solicit funds to buy up and maintain wild areas to safeguard them from development. What makes them so successful is their no-nonsense approach to finance that makes it possible (and even profitable) for poor nations and major corporations to cooperate in the conservation efforts. Especially noteworthy is their Debt-for-Nature swap program that arranges for indebted nations to unload some of their debt while protecting some of their wildlands. Other programs include building self-sustaining conservation organizations in other countries and developing conservation data centers to help identify and catalog the diversity of life in the tropics, much of which is as yet unknown. Whether or not you travel with The Nature Conservancy, they are worthy of your support. If you do travel with them, the proceeds from the trip will go to further their important work.

While the national organization offers interesting and informative international trips, many regional chapters have exciting domestic trips that any member from any region can join. Some of their unusual domestic tours include: an Alaskan winter wildlife trip by dog sled or cross-country skis, a study tour of the hummingbirds of Arizona or botanical Oregon, learning how to track mammals in Montana, and tracing the San Andreas fault. Their trips—both domestic and international—are intensive, exciting nature expeditions led by a Conservancy representative and a local expert naturalist. They include field trips into the wilds to study the flora, fauna, geology, and history, plus lectures by local conservationists.

DESTINATIONS: Alaska, Arizona, California, Montana, Oregon, Texas, Wyoming, Belize, Costa Rica, Venezuela, Argentina, Yucatan, Galapagos, the Andes, the Amazon, and other areas

SEASON: All year

LENGTH OF PROGRAMS: 4 to 21 days

ENROLLMENT: 6 to 20 participants

TOTAL COST: $465 to $4,425

COST PER DIEM: $115 to $626

TAX DEDUCTIBLE?: The Nature Conservancy states that "the fair market value of each trip is $300 less than the price listed." That $300 is treated as a charitable donation to the Conservancy.

COST INCLUSIVE OF: Air transportation from a U.S. gateway airport (for international programs), transportation during the program, lodging, meals

COST EXCLUSIVE OF: Domestic transportation to the assembly point or to the U.S. gateway airport

AMENITIES, FACILITIES, AND REALITIES: Because these trips are designed to focus entirely on nature, they stay wherever they can that is closest to the wilderness. In the international trips, they try to find a lodge or similar accommodation that is near a protected area, that offers private bathrooms and hot and cold running water but is definitely a lodge situation rather than a typical hotel. On the other hand, in areas such as the Amazon, it is unlikely that you'll have such amenities. As is to be expected, the Galapagos trips are by boat, where it is doubtful that you will have a private bathroom. According to their brochure, "These trips are designed for those who enjoy the diversity and adventure of natural history travel in the tropics and exposure to a variety of cultures. . . . While these trips are not designed to be physically demanding, we will be visiting remote areas. Trails may be slippery or somewhat rocky; tropical weather ranges from hot to cold; accommodations and transportation modes may be rustic; and the occasional 'travel day' can be tiring. Travelers should enjoy general fitness and good health." The accommodations for the domestic trips vary widely.

OTHER COMMENTS: Among the various informative material that you receive when you become a member is a subscription to their bi-monthly magazine. Every issue lists upcoming programs, including tours, plus the contact names and addresses for the regional chapters.

CONTACT: The Nature Conservancy, 1815 N. Lynn St., Arlington, VA 22209, tel. (703) 841-5300. Fax (703) 841-1283 or (703) 841-4880.

NATURE EXPEDITIONS INTERNATIONAL
▼ ▼ ▼

David Roderick, the president of NEI, brings to the company's tours a dedication to education and to travel as a learning experience. In fact, he started out as a teacher, and when his students started requesting field trips to the places studied, he ended up in the tour business. "Education has always been our first goal, adventure the second. In some of the most fascinating regions of the world we study wildlife, environment, people, and history." NEI's pride in this commitment to learning is obvious in their brochures, which give detailed and informative biographies of their guides and staff—all are curators, professors, and naturalists associated with important universities, research organizations, and museums. NEI programs are therefore well seasoned with lectures and interpretive field trips.

In addition to the tours that they offer the public, NEI arranges expeditions for prestigious organizations, such as the California Academy of Sciences, Pacific Science Center, Stanford Alumni Association, and the New York Zoological Society. They are also willing to arrange private trips for groups as small as five participants.

DESTINATIONS: Kenya, Tanzania, Rwanda, Nepal, Bhutan, Tibet, India, Japan, Australia, New Zealand, Papua New Guinea, Easter Island, Galapagos, Amazon Jungle, Peru, Costa Rica, Mexico's Yucatan Peninsula, Guatemala, Baja California, Trinidad, Martinique, Dominica, Alaska, Hawaii, Utah, Colorado, Arizona, New Mexico

SEASON: All year

LENGTH OF PROGRAMS: 9 to 30 days

ENROLLMENT: 6 to 16 participants

TOTAL COST: $1,490 to $4,990

COST PER DIEM: $118 to $230

Tax Deductible?: No

Cost Inclusive Of: Accommodations, most meals, transportation during the program, sightseeing, porters, guides, lectures

Cost Exclusive Of: Transportation to the assembly point, some meals, airport and departure taxes, gratuities

Amenities, Facilities, and Realities: NEI's brochure identifies the "trip grades" as easy, moderate, comfortable, or challenging to help you determine the level of physical fitness you must have to participate in each. Hotel rooms generally have private bathrooms where possible. The African trips are tent safaris, in which the crew takes care of all work, and the toilets and showers are in separate tents. The Galapagos cruises are in small boats that accommodate up to 20 passengers. NEI requires that every participant fill out a health questionnaire. Anyone over 70 years of age or on a "challenging"-rated trip must provide a signed doctor's certification that they are fit and able to join the trip.

Contact: Nature Expeditions International, P.O. Box 11496, Eugene, OR 97440, tel. (800) 869-0639 or (503) 484-6529.

Trans Niugini Tours
▼ ▼ ▼

Papua New Guinea is like no other place on earth. The second largest island in the Pacific, its exotic diversity of wildlife, landscapes, and native people is dazzling. It has over 750 species of birds (including 13 species of bird of paradise), 2,500 species of orchids, over 200 mammals (including marsupials), a profusion of butterflies and moths, timberland that ranges from tropical rain forest to mist forest to alpine grasslands, snow-capped mountains only a few hundred miles from the equator, and waterways that wind past fishing villages that have remained virtually unchanged since the Western world discovered them not so long ago. And, of course, there are the people, with their flamboyant rituals and dances, vivid body paints and sculpted scars, incredible masks and definitive pottery.

Trans Niugini is a rather successful home-grown tour operation run by Bob and Pam Bates, who have lived in Papua New Guinea since the 1960s. Their involvement with the country is based on a dedication that one can give only to their home. In fact, they are well respected throughout the travel industry, and many major tour operators use Trans Niugini to provide their land (and riverboat) arrangements in Papua New Guinea.

Trans Niugini owns and operates three lodges (Karawari, Ambua, and

Malolo Plantation) and a river boat (Sepik Spirit). Because PNG is so diverse, with a wide variety of ecosystems, terrain, and people, each place offers a different view of this unusual country. Spectacular scuba diving (according to U.S. safety standards) is available at Malolo Plantation Lodge, which is a coconut plantation with a black sand beach, not far from the Madang Barrier Reef. Ambua Lodge is high in the mountains (7,000 feet), where the climate is cooler and the vegetation quite different. Moss forests, high-altitude orchids, waterfalls, and the Huli people are highlights of the Ambua area. At Karawari Lodge, you can take excursions by canoe along the Karawari River to nearby villages or enjoy nature walks through the jungle. The Sepik Spirit is probably the strangest-shaped boat afloat, more a small barge carrying a rectangular lodge. But it is comfortable and offers large window views of one of the most remote areas in the world—the Blackwater and middle Sepik—where few tourists have ever been.

DESTINATIONS: Papua New Guinea

SEASON: All year

LENGTH OF PROGRAMS: 6 to 10 days

ENROLLMENT: 18 passengers on the Sepik Spirit boat; 30 to 80 guests in the land lodges

TOTAL COST: $1,154 to $2,062

COST PER DIEM: $186 to $210

TAX DEDUCTIBLE?: No

COST INCLUSIVE OF: Accommodations, most meals (vegetarian available), tours, transfers

COST EXCLUSIVE OF: Transportation to Papua New Guinea, some meals, some transportation within Papua New Guinea, entry and exit visa, airport taxes

AMENITIES, FACILITIES, AND REALITIES: The rooms in all the lodges and on the boat include private bathrooms with hot water. But it is important to understand how different the facilities are in comparatively undeveloped countries. The electricity may cut off during heavy rains and the quantity of hot water may be limited. However, Trans Niugini does provide some unexpected comforts. For instance, in Ambua Lodge where the Highland evenings can be quite cool, all beds have automatic electric pads.

Down at sea level, the air hangs with humidity, especially during the summer (November to March or April). Other problems of the climate, which Papua New Guinea shares with any tropical area, are: a profusion of voracious insects (take your malaria prophylactics); an intense, searing sun; and tropical rains, which tend to occur during the night or in short, hard spurts during the afternoon. Long sleeves, long pants, insect spray, sunblock, and shading hats are strongly recommended. Your shoes are sure to get wet at one time or another, so pack an extra pair of sneakers. Trans Niugini suggests the following precautions when traveling in PNG: Don't wander about at night (crime is not unknown); time is a relative notion, where "sometime soon" is the most accurate timetable; and baggage limits are strictly enforced.

Bargaining or haggling is considered vulgar in Papua New Guinea, though you may politely ask for a "second price." Credit cards are not commonly accepted. With the introduction of Western communication to Papua New Guinea, there have been some problems, mostly related to the undermining of the tribal traditions by the new availability of currency. There has been a rise in crime, most notably in the urban areas. Curfew has been imposed in some towns. According to Christiane Emonin of UNIREP, "It is Western crime that has been introduced by Western civilization, not tribal crime. In the villages, they are very happy. You might feel that they are poor, because the children wear Western clothes with holes. But they are not poor, because they live on the land. These people live in the Stone Age. The women are still half-naked, with bare breasts; they wear tatoos and shell leis. But when they see white people, our color is such a shock for them, we try not to have a provocative attitude. We don't wear tight tank tops or short shorts."

OTHER COMMENTS: Generally, there is no tipping in New Guinea. Trans Niugini does have a "general staff" fund to which you may wish to contribute. The locals appreciate small, useful gifts (such as cigarettes, pens, pads of paper, etc.), but please don't give sweets or money to the children. In fact, Trans Niugini suggests that all gifts should be given to the Headman of any village, who will then distribute them. This is out of respect for native social traditions.

CONTACT: Trans Niugini Tours, P.O. Box 371, Mt. Hagen, Papua New Guinea, tel. 011-675-52-1438. Fax 011-675-52-2470. Or c/o UNIREP, 850 Colorado Blvd., Suite 105, Los Angeles, CA 90041, tel. (800) 521-7242 or (213) 256-1991. Fax (213) 256-0647.

VOYAGERS INTERNATIONAL

▼ ▼ ▼

The founder and managing director of Voyagers, David Blanton, is a prime example of how the personality behind these organizations determines the kind of experience that you will have on one of their tours. Blanton first traveled to Africa as a volunteer for the Peace Corps for two years, then stayed on for an additional five years as a photographer and writer. "Coming back to the States," he explained to us, "I was sometimes appalled at the lack of awareness that people here have about the rest of the world. So, I decided to use travel as a vehicle for consciousness raising rather than just a leisure activity." But his efforts haven't just been directed toward the North American populace. See below in Other Comments about the program he designed to help Kenyans understand us.

Blanton is personally involved in scouting out Voyagers' destinations. He says he seeks opportunities to give travelers a more in-depth learning experience by avoiding the normal tourist roads, looking for small-scale, locally oriented activities and events.

One of their more noteworthy tours is an African safari that includes walks through Kenya to explore the Maasai culture and discover a rawer, more honest Africa. However, these do not require a greater physical fitness than the ability to walk about 8 or 10 miles a day at a leisurely pace. Evenings are spent in comfortable camps and lodges, where the staff does all the cooking and other chores associated with camping. Nor will you have to carry your own gear other than a small pack with your water, binoculars, and camera.

Voyagers also offers photo workshops in various areas of the world. Instead of formal lectures, the instructors use the natural history and unusual locales of the region as their classroom. In those places where film processing is readily available, it may be possible for the leader to critique your work in progress.

Some of the clients for whom Voyagers has designed travel programs include: Harvard Biological Expeditions, Cornell Laboratory of Ornithology, University of Minnesota, National Association of Biology Teachers, American Birding Association, Academy of Natural Sciences, and various regional Audubon Societies. They also put together customized tours for individuals or small private groups, such as the private tented safari for two.

DESTINATIONS: Alaska, Hawaii, Manitoba, Belize, Costa Rica, Brazil, Galapagos, Ecuador, Amazon, Andes, Ireland, Kenya, Tanzania, Rwanda, Borneo, Indonesia, Australia, India

SEASON: All year

LENGTH OF PROGRAMS: 9 to 21 days

ENROLLMENT: 8 to 18 participants

TOTAL COST: $1,690 to $5,695

COST PER DIEM: $113 to $335

TAX DEDUCTIBLE?: No

COST INCLUSIVE OF: Air transportation from a U.S. gateway airport (for most programs, including the African ones), transportation while with group, accommodations, entrance fees, most meals, membership in the Flying Doctor Society (during east Africa trips), pretrip information packet (including background material, reading lists, maps, etc.), flight bag

COST EXCLUSIVE OF: Domestic transportation to the U.S. gateway airport (on some programs, you may have to add the price of international flights), some meals, optional scuba diving or hot air ballooning (where available), airport and departure taxes, gratuities

AMENITIES, FACILITIES, AND REALITIES: On African safaris, accommodations vary, depending upon where you are and on which itinerary: permanent tented camps, camping out in tents, hotels, and lodges. (Tented camps are permanent fixtures that tend to have more amenities than those available in the tents that are set up for your arrival and then taken down again.) In Africa, a maximum of seven passengers are carried in each nine-passenger minibus, so that everyone has a window seat. In the Galapagos, Voyager books a variety of boats and ships, depending upon your budget and preferences. The more expensive yachts all have private bathrooms in every cabin as well as air conditioning. Some of the economy boats have shared showers, though the cabins usually have private toilets. Or, you can choose a ''cruise ship'' that carries up to 90 passengers with cabins with private facilities. In other areas around the world, they will provide private bathrooms and air conditioning where it is available or appropriate. Please note that many of Voyagers' prices include international air transportation, so when you compare the cost with other programs that may not include air transportation, be sure to factor that into your calculations.

OTHER COMMENTS: When David Blanton was living in Africa, he was asked by Utalii College in Nairobi to help put together a cross-cultural training program for Kenyans studying to work in the tourist industry. (Utalii means tourism in Swahili.) A survey had shown that 70 percent of the students thought that the tourists who came to their country never had to work but that they just toured around the world all year. What's more, the Westerners the students knew in Kenya tended to live quite luxuriously, with servants doing all the work around their very comfortable homes. Blanton made several videotapes for the school. The first series showed people from the U.S., Germany, and Switzerland in their everyday lives, cleaning toilets, working at the office (or wherever they worked), shopping for groceries, and generally going about their lives. The students were quite surprised and now understand to some extent why a visitor is so anxious to not waste time. (To an African, our anxiety over time passing and our desire to deal with people who are usually on time is a bit of a fuss about nothing. Time will come and time passes and life goes on.) Eventually, the students began to partially accept the fact that these visitors had saved all year in order to be able to afford to travel to their country and see it all in just a couple of weeks. Blanton also made a series of videotapes of Kenyan elders explaining what hospitality means in their tradition. The elders discussed how to treat guests properly and make them feel welcome. He also helped the students to understand the prejudices and myths about Africa that visitors may have and how to educate their clients about African culture and give them the kind of experience that would cut through those stereotypes.

Finally, Blanton worked out case studies to help students deal with their discomfort in having to control an entire group of tourists. For instance, how can a gracious, easygoing, soft-spoken guide deal with a smoker on a nonsmoking bus? The program that Blanton developed for the school is still used today to train many of the guides and other service personnel who work for various tour operators throughout the country.

CONTACT: Voyagers International, P.O. Box 915, Ithaca, NY 14851, tel. (800) 633-0299 or (607) 257-3091. Fax (607) 257-3699.

WORLD WILDLIFE FUND
▼ ▼ ▼

A very large, private conservation organization, World Wildlife Fund actively works to not only protect natural habitats but also to make it feasible and even profitable for poor communities to assist in this work. As Prince Philip, the Duke of Edinburgh and international president of WWF, has said, "It has also become apparent that the rural poor, who depend for their survival on the resources of nature, are suffering from the rapid destruction of the natural environment. World Wildlife Fund is therefore working closely with governments, development institutions, and the private sector to persuade those agencies to use their vastly larger resources to explore the potential of development projects that work with, rather than ignore, natural systems." In other words, in their programs to protect natural habitats, World Wildlife Fund keeps in mind the need to protect and improve human habitats. This includes working toward the sustainable use of natural resources, rather than divorcing nature from any human consideration.

World Wildlife Fund offers various trips to experience some of the world's most beautiful natural areas with the purpose of educating individuals about what needs to be preserved and how to go about it. Often included in these tours are visits to ongoing projects, such as the Poco das Antas Reserve in Brazil, which is involved in reintroducing golden lion tamarins into the wild. But the prime focus is on leisurely nature walks through wilderness areas, where wildlife may be observed, some of it quite close. Escorts include professional naturalists and at least one World Wildlife Fund representative.

Some of the programs World Wildlife Fund offers are packaged through Special Expeditions (see pages 243–245) and other tour operators and are available generally to the public. But others, such as the national parks safari in Brazil or the expedition through the rain forest of the beautiful Caribbean island of Dominica are especially packaged for World Wildlife Fund. Members are sent frequent mailings to keep them informed about upcoming travel programs, which is another incentive (other than the desire to support a worthy organization) for joining World Wildlife Fund.

DESTINATIONS: Alaska, Baja California, Dominica, Argentina, Brazil, Galapagos, Botswana, Kenya, Tanzania, Zimbabwe, Madagascar, India, Nepal, Thailand

SEASON: Various times throughout the year

LENGTH OF PROGRAMS: 7 to 22 days

ENROLLMENT: 14 to 70 participants, depending on the program, with most tours being limited to under 25.

TOTAL COST: $1,720 to $5,566

COST PER DIEM: $209 to $427

TAX DEDUCTIBLE?: No

COST INCLUSIVE OF: Transportation during the tour; accommodations; most meals; activities, lectures, and field trips; transfers from and to the airport (if you purchase air transportation with the group); entrance fees; baggage handling; pretrip notes and materials; service charges; airport taxes; gratuities

COST EXCLUSIVE OF: Transportation to the program (though on some trips international airfare from a gateway city such as Miami or New York may be included), transfers if you don't fly with the group, some meals

AMENITIES, FACILITIES, AND REALITIES: Accommodations vary in comfort, depending upon where you go with World Wildlife Fund. On the cruises (except to the Galapagos), everyone will generally have private bathrooms and air conditioning in their cabins. On land tours, World Wildlife Fund attempts to provide basic comforts such as private bathrooms. But that is not always possible in every place they visit. As their Madagascar brochure states, "Please note that basic tourist services are lacking in Madagascar's remote areas, where important parks and reserves are found. Thus, you should expect to forego some creature comforts to enjoy excellent bird watching and close observation of lemurs and other wildlife." They go on to warn that the beds might not be comfortable and running water won't always be available. On most trips, the nature walks tend to be leisurely rather than strenuous, though they may last a few hours.

CONTACT: World Wildlife Fund, 1250 24th St NW, Washington, DC 20037, tel. (202) 293-4800.

FURTHER POSSIBILITIES
▼ ▼ ▼

BIOLOGICAL JOURNEYS, 1696 Ocean Drive, McKinleyville, CA 95521, tel. (800) 548-7555. A small organization, Biological Journeys offers mostly boat-based wildlife expeditions to Alaska, Galapagos, Australia, and Baja California. (See pages 226–228 in the Green Cruise chapter for a full write-up on Biological Journeys.)

THE COUSTEAU SOCIETY, 930 W. 21st. St, Norfolk, VA 23517, (804) 617-1144. Every year, in the summer, the Cousteau Society offers a "Project Ocean Search" in two-week segments. The locale changes each year, but it always involves scuba diving, underwater photography workshops, lectures, and discussions groups. Jean-Michel Cousteau is usually quite active during the program. Enrollment is limited to around 35 participants. Unfortunately, it fills up almost as soon as it is announced where the project will be. The best bet is to keep in touch with the society and, if you are that avid to join the upcoming trip, sign up even before the announcement of where it will be is made.

THE DOLPHIN NETWORK, 524 San Anselmo Avenue, San Anselmo, CA 94969. The Dolphin Network occasionally has trips to areas such as the Florida Keys during which participants swim with and learn about dolphins.

DYNAMIC TOURS, Suite 206, Rakesh Deep, 11, Commercial Complex, Gulmohar Enclave, New Delhi 110 049 INDIA, tel. 011-9111-666-770. Fax 011-9111-686-5212. A small decade-old, family-run business that specializes in natural history and cultural tours of India. They also run a "jungle lodge" in the Kanha National Park, where tigers and other wild creatures may be seen.

ELITE CUSTOM LATIN TRAVEL, 2817 Dumbarton St. NW, Washington, DC 20007, tel. (800) 662-4474 or (202) 626-6500. Fax (202) 625-2650. Specialists in travel to Argentina, Elite offers nature tours to Patagonia and Tierra del Fuego.

EXPEDICIONES MANU, P.O. Box 606, Cusco, Peru, tel. 011-084-22-6671 or 23-9974. Fax 011-084-23-6706. Expediciones Manu offers tours through Peru's incredible Manu National Park, which is a beautiful area of cloud and rain forest (designated a Biosphere Reserve by UNESCO).

GEO EXPEDITIONS, P.O. Box 3656, Sonora, CA 95370, tel. (800) 351-5041 or (209) 532-0152. A private company that offers expeditions to Africa, Australia, Japan, China, Pakistan, Nepal, and Costa Rica, as well as boat tours of the Galapagos.

HORIZONTES NATURE ADVENTURES, P.O. Box 1780-1002, Paseo Estudiantes, San Jose, Costa Rica, tel. 011-506-22-2022. Fax 011-506-55-4513. Costa Rica is one of the Greenest nations on earth, not only because it is beautiful but because its people work to preserve this beauty. Ten percent of its land is dedicated to National Parks, with another 17 percent protected as wildlife sanctuaries and areas of special ecological interest. Horizontes is a Costa Rican company, owned and operated by locals who take pride in showing the best their country has. Their tours are led by naturalists and professional biologists.

KAIKOURA SEAFARIS, 89 S. Bay Parade, Kaikoura, South Island, New Zealand, tel. 011-64-513-5145. Kaikoura Peninsula is more a destination for the independent traveler to New Zealand, because we have not come across any tour organizers who include it. But if you are headed Down Under, it is the one place you should not miss. There's nothing slick or even well marketed here; it's simply the marine mammal-watching capital of the southern Pacific. Numerous small operations offer whale-watching boat tours, scuba diving with dolphins, canoe safaris and other close encounters with marine wildlife. Kaikoura Seafaris is a tiny company, run by Ron and Elizabeth Rae that has a uniquely designed glass-bottom boat. Call ahead to book one of their seal swims. You'll be loaned threadbare wet suits and taken to a cove where the fur seals cover the rocks. Within minutes of jumping in the water, you will be surrounded by many of the seals who slip into the surf to play with you. They are completely wild—in other words they come to you just for the pleasure of it and out of curiosity—and the experience is one of the most exciting we have ever had in the water or on land. Plan to stay at least two or three days in Kaikoura, to take part in some of the other activities in the area. And try to book some of your activities ahead of time. Contact also: Kaikoura Information Centre, P.O. Box 6, Kaikoura, New Zealand, tel. 011-64-319-5641, or New Zealand Tourism Office, 501 Santa Monica Blvd., Suite 300, Santa Monica, CA 90401, tel. (800) 388-5494 for the phone numbers and addresses of other operators in the area.

LIHUÉ EXPEDITIONS, Belgrano 262, of. 104, San Isidro (1642), Provincia de Buenos Aires, Argentina, tel. 011-541-747-7689. Fax 011-541-11-2206. An Argentinian-operated company, Lihué specializes in wildlife, natural history, culture and archeology tours of their own country. Their descriptive sheets are the various regions of Argentina are quite informative, and their corporate emphasis is on ecotourism.

MICATO SAFARIS, 15 W. 26th St., New York, NY 10010, tel. (212) 545-7111 or Moi Ave., Postal Drawer 43374, Nairobi, Kenya, tel. 011-254-2-226-138. A Kenya-based company owned and operated by the Pinto family, Micato operates east African safaris with a personal touch that includes dinner in their family home. They also travel to India, the Seychelles and Egypt.

MOUNTAIN TRAVEL, 6420 Fairmount Avenue, El Cerrito, CA 94530-3606, tel. (800) 227-2384 or (415) 527-8100. Fax (415) 525-7710. One of the largest and best-known adventure tour operators, Mountain Travel also offers programs that visit wilderness areas to observe the wildlife. (See pages 129–131.)

OVERSEAS ADVENTURE TRAVEL, 349 Broadway, Cambridge, MA 02139, tel. (800) 221-0814 or (617) 876-0533. Fax (617) 876-0455. In addition to its physically active tours (see pages 134–136), OAT offers trips that focus on a region's cultural traditions and wildlife.

SIERRA CLUB, Outing Department, 730 Polk St., San Francisco, CA 94109, tel. (415) 776-2211. The Sierra Club offers outings through wilderness areas in the United States and elsewhere in the world. Some of their more than 300-plus outings are appropriate for individuals less interested in roughing it than in being involved with the beauty of wild places. Also, they have special programs just for the physically disabled. The purpose of Sierra Club's outings is not to test your woodsmanship, but to bring as many people, regardless of their physical or financial situation, closer to nature. Reasonably priced compared to more commercial operations, it provides a high-quality experience in small groups. (See pages 136–138 for more information on Sierra Club travel programs.)

SPECIAL EXPEDITIONS, 720 Fifth Avenue, New York, NY 10019, tel. (212) 765-7740. In addition to their numerous adventure cruises, Special Expeditions also has occasional land journeys to unusual places of great beauty, such as their "Walls of Time" tour of the native cultures of northern new Mexico and southwestern Colorado. (See the write-up on Special Expeditions, pages 245–247.)

WILDLIFE TOURISM IMPACT PROJECT, 524 San Anselmo Ave., Suite 103, San Anselmo, CA 94969, tel. (415) 453-4933. Fax (415) 456-9197. Wildlife Tourism Impact has recently published a "Safari Sourcebook," which is meant as a tool for travel agents to help them determine which safari operators in east Africa are contributing to the local community, involving participants with projects, and generally being responsible about the potential of their impact. Because travel agents aren't always responsive to Green Travel needs, you may wish to call Wildlife Tourism Impact directly and buy a copy of the handbook so you can do your own research. You may also ask their advice on your African travel plans, but be prepared to pay a donation for their services.

Chapter Eight

BY YOUR
OWN STEAM

*Travel for
the Physically
Adventurous*

A FEW WORDS

It's one thing to look at the world through the window of a fast-moving vehicle or a high-flying airplane, and quite another to see it at a pace no faster than our ancestors traveled for untold millennia. In our haste toward efficiency, technology, and progress, we've overlooked many fundamental truths, such as the quiet beauty of a mountain sunset, the joy of seeing magnificent animals in the wild, or the satisfaction that comes from meeting and mingling with peoples and cultures so different and alien, and yet so similar and fascinating. We're beginning to rediscover those truths in ourselves, both here at home and halfway around the world.

We are also a nation of thrill-seekers. We patronize amusement park roller coasters and skydive on weekends, catch large breakers on surfboards and ski down steep slopes, play rough contact sports and even bungee off tall bridges. And given the chance, we'd love to raft down a raging river, trek up a rugged mountain path or gallop a horse across the empty plains. Not on some tame and well-manicured river, ranch, or prairie but somewhere authentic, isolated, and unpredictable. It doesn't matter whether it is the buzz or surge of adrenaline that drives us to try daredevil, foolhardy, or even life-threatening challenges—or even the sense of relief and the feeling of being alive that comes from cheating death. What's important for many of us is that excitement and adventure is almost as vital to being human as food, clothing, and shelter.

Then, too, we've become more concerned, even obsessed, with keeping our bodies healthy. We've taken to walking and running, biking and hiking in order to get the pulse rate up to aerobic levels. The last thing we want to do on our vacations is slack off, sit back, and do nothing.

Green Travel often combines these feelings and concerns in adventure-style tours. Such tours give participants the opportunity to experience remote and exotic parts of the world, reached or traversed at a slower pace by foot, animal, or river power, and with the thrill and excitement that ensues from testing ourselves physically. Of course, there are soft-adventure tours that don't demand quite as much from you physically, but you're never really inactive on any of these trips.

In this section, we have listed an eclectic sampling of adventure-style vacations. They range from relatively inexpensive weekenders in national parks to pricey but unforgettable month-long treks through some of the most remote mountains or forests in the world. What they all have in common is the fact that they involve active, physical participation on your part. Instead of sitting in the back of a bus, you'll be walking, trekking, backpacking, bicycling, canoeing, kayaking, skiing, horseback riding, or whitewater rafting. For the most part, adventure vacations avoid cities and populated areas in favor of country roads, infrequently traveled paths, distant rivers, faraway mountains, solitary plains, and other areas where Nature still reigns supreme. Depending upon the program, you may be roughing it in a sleeping bag on the ground or sleeping in an antique four-poster bed in a fourteenth-century chateau, eating campfire-style or having a world-class meal in a private dining room, or maybe something in between. The choice is yours.

There are several important points to consider before selecting an adventure tour. First and foremost, just how physically fit are you? Most adventure travel involves anywhere from modest to extreme degrees of physical exertion. Even on some soft-river-rafting trips, in which most of the hard work is done by a boatman or even a motor, you will probably be required to do some hefty walking or even climbing to get to the launch site and the terminus point or to explore canyons and meadows along the way. (Other more strenuous whitewater rafting requires everyone to paddle and pull his or her own weight.) Or, while the horse does the actual traversing, sitting in the saddle for hours on end and controlling the animal takes a fair degree of strength and stamina. If you're out of shape, overweight, or have a physical problem or disability, participating in a program that's beyond your capability is not only foolish, it can be dangerous.

Similarly, try to accurately assess your skill level. If you're a Sunday nose-to-tail equestrian, then do you honestly feel that you are ready for a ten-day trek through the high country? Perhaps a five-day amble along easier trails might be more realistic, not to mention safe. The same holds true for trekking, skiing, mountaineering, and other skills and experiences.

Most adventure tour operators and organizations rate their trips according to physical difficulty or level of skills required. If you're uncertain about what level fits your ability, talk with them honestly, so they can advise you. Also, be honest with yourself, and don't play macho when you know in your heart that a particular trip is beyond your abilities. You'll have more fun—and may even save your life—if you choose a trip that best fits your physical capability.

Many tour operators and organizations that run adventure trips require a doctor's certificate before accepting applications. Even if your tour operator doesn't, for safety's sake, it's an excellent idea to have your doctor examine you, especially if you are over 40 years of age. Tell him or her in some detail what the trip you intend to take actually entails, and ask point blank if your body is up to it. (It's a good idea to give your doctor a copy of the trip brochure.)

This is not to say that you are permanently disqualified from selecting an adventure trip if you happen to be out of shape. Just choose one that doesn't require a great deal of strength or prowess. Countryside walking tours can be quite delightful and yet tame. And, if they are accompanied by a following van, you can always ride when you want.

Whenever we know we are headed out on a trip that will demand more of us physically than we have been putting in at our desks, we make a concerted effort for several months before we leave to build up our stamina and strength. We start simply by putting on our jogging shoes and walking for a half-hour, three times a week. Gradually, we build it up to an hour every other day. Then speed up the pace, or seek out walks with some hills. We also go to the local YMCA to work out as often as we can and get in shape. Yes, it's tough at first, and downright intimidating to see muscle-bound Apollos and Venuses flex with effortless ease. But we're always surprised (and pleased) how our bodies change significantly within a month or two. Of course, that is one of the reasons we choose such adventure trips, to prod us into going back to regular exercise.

Another thing to keep in mind is that the adventure trip may take you many miles or days away from the nearest doctor or hospital. So, if you have a chronic health problem, such as a tender gallbladder that may suddenly require surgery, take care of it before going off into the bush or veldt.

Adventure travel usually carries a higher degree of risk than almost any other vacation experience. It's not that common, but many tour operators report that once or twice a season, people do suffer from sprained ankles, broken arms, exposure, snakebite, and other accidents or emergencies that require medical assistance. Most minor crises can be taken care of with a first-aid kit, but if it's more serious, you may have to be transported by helicopter or flown in private jet back to the States. That, of course, can cost many thousands of dollars. Frequently, the alternative is to literally put your life in the hands of a local doctor or hospital, which may not be up to Western standards or which your regular medical insurance may not cover.

Because of the elevated risk and potential expense, this is one time we strongly recommend obtaining emergency medical insurance before you go. Also, since the chance of missed connections, canceled flights, broken-down buses, and lost luggage increase directly proportional to how far away you are from the United States, Western Europe, and other developed regions, you might also consider buying trip insurance.

Please don't think we are trying to scare you off of adventure travel. To the contrary, it is one of our very favorite ways to go. Nothing else can capture the glory of being alive on this bountiful and beautiful earth. And the overwhelming majority of people who have been on adventure tours will agree with us wholeheartedly and ask: When do we leave on the next one?

ABOVE THE CLOUDS TREKKING
▼ ▼ ▼

Above the Clouds Trekking, a ten-year-old Massachusetts-based adventure travel company, is about as small as you can get and still maintain a worldwide operation. Although it has only 3 full-time employees, it uses over 100 contract people in more than two dozen countries, the majority of whom are natives. As its name implies, the company specializes in treks in rugged, far-from-civilization regions that, often as not, have had very little exposure to tourists. The treks, which are graded according to difficulty, range from gentle walks to steep climbs that require both experience and a moderate degree of physical fitness. Some tours, such as the unique desert journey through just-opened North Yemen, are done primarily on jeeps, while others, like the 18-day Nepal Bike Odyssey, use "Specialized StumpJumper" mountain bikes. Other programs combine trekking with whitewater rafting. Above the Clouds also offers photo workshops in Peru and Nepal, and a medical seminar in Nepal.

Steve Conlon, director of Above the Clouds Trekking, says that "we are operating adventurous programs to truly remote corners of the world, with our strong suit the Himalayan area. Last year, there were 54,000 trekkers in Nepal alone, and out of them, 50,000 were on two trails. We do very little on those two trails. On an average trek, we encounter maybe 2 or 3 trekkers the entire way around. Thus we can encounter local people who are not in the habit of meeting foreigners and therefore don't have the concept of tourists in their mind set. If they don't treat us like tourists, we don't have to act like one. Thus there's a lot of opportunity for cross-cultural interaction."

DESTINATIONS: Peru, Mexico, Belize, Ecuador, Argentina, Kenya, Madagascar, Zaire, Tanzania, Zimbabwe, Ireland, Yugoslavia, Romania, Spain, Switzerland, Turkey, Nepal, India, Sikkim, Bhutan, India, Japan, North Yemen, New Zealand, U.S.S.R.

SEASON: All year

LENGTH OF PROGRAMS: 10 to 32 days

ENROLLMENT: 1 to 15 participants, but 8 is average

TOTAL COST: $880 to $4,300

COST PER DIEM: $80 to $280

TAX DEDUCTIBLE?: No

COST INCLUSIVE OF: Accommodations, all meals during trekking portion, hotel with breakfasts and private baths in city, all airport transfers and ground transportation, most domestic flights, sightseeing, park entrance fees and trekking permits, bicycles

COST EXCLUSIVE OF: Air transportation, taxes, sleeping bags (may be rented), most meals in cities (about 4 meals total)

AMENITIES, FACILITIES, AND REALITIES: Hotels, all locally owned, are usually more comfortable than most people anticipate. Participants do not have to carry personal or communal gear while on treks, nor are they required to help set up tents, cook, or clean. Above the Clouds boasts that their food is of a quality and prepared with such cleanliness that there is less than a 2 percent incidence of stomach problems on trek, one of the lowest of any trek tour operator.

CONTACT: Above the Clouds Trekking, P.O. Box 398, Worcester, MA 01602-0398, tel. (800) 233-4499 or (508) 799-4499. Fax (508) 797-4779.

AMERICAN WILDERNESS EXPERIENCE

American Wilderness Experience offers a wide range of "soft" outdoor tours and treks. You're not comfortable on horseback, but you want the family to experience the West just like the pioneers? No problem, because you can hitch a ride on American Wilderness Experience's four to six-day covered wagon train journey in Wyoming. Or, you want to go in a covered wagon part of the way and raft the rest of the distance? There's a four-day program in Montana that combines the two. Or would you prefer doing something novel, like hiking with a llama in Wyoming (which you can combine with mountain biking and kayaking), paddling a canoe from country inn to country inn in Vermont, or whitewater rafting in Colorado's Dinosaur National Monument Park?

Then again, would you like to experience one of the dude ranches that American Wilderness Experience markets? Forget the stereotypes and just imagine going on a roundup, trying your hand at roping steers, panning for gold, having an old-fashioned trail barbecue, or jumping into an inviting pool far from everything. With 50 dude ranches in five Western states, you can choose between modern accommodations with all conveniences or semi-authentic but comfortable bunk houses. Depending upon the location, there may be places of historic interest nearby. American Wilderness Experience is a 20-year-old company that provides natural fun rather than serves up an environmental message. While they don't specifically offer Green programs, their tours usually skirt touristy destinations in favor of out-of-the-way, unusual places. Glasnost has made it possible for the company to offer a 22-day trek through the rugged and remote region of Tadjikstan in the U.S.S.R., an area few Westerners have ever seen.

DESTINATIONS: New Mexico, Colorado, Arizona, Montana, Wyoming, Utah, North Carolina, California, Vermont, Idaho, Oregon, Minnesota, New York, Alaska, Florida, Hawaii, Alberta, Canadian Rockies, Baja California, Copper Canyon in Mexico, Peru, New Zealand, U.S.S.R.

SEASON: February to December

LENGTH OF PROGRAMS: 5 to 22 days, with some 3-day trips available; most trips one week or less

ENROLLMENT: 4 to 16 participants

TOTAL COST: $325 to $3,970. A 5 percent discount for repeaters. Special children and senior citizen discounts on some trips.

COST PER DIEM: $98 to $256. AWE can custom tailor a domestic adventure trip for groups at a cost of $95 to $130 per person, depending upon the size of the group.

TAX DEDUCTIBLE?: No, but AWE will plant a tree for every participant in a giant reforestation project undertaken by the American Forestry Association.

COST INCLUSIVE OF: Tent, hotel, or lodge accommodations; all meals; horses, saddles, and tack; camp gear; some in-country transportation

COST EXCLUSIVE OF: Air transportation to assembly point, bushplane/floatplane, bicycle rental, sleeping bag, pretrip lodging, taxes, canoes (in U.S.), some transfers

AMENITIES, FACILITIES, AND REALITIES: Most of the dude ranches come equipped with air conditioning and private bathrooms; some are downright luxurious. While beginners, youngsters, and senior citizens are welcome on most trips, participants must be in relatively good physical condition and able to keep up with the group. The pace is never strenuous, but it can be trying for those not used to the outdoors. Participants are offered guidance and instruction as necessary to help them feel confident in the field.

CONTACT: American Wilderness Experience, P.O. Box 1486, Boulder, CO 80306, tel. (800) 444-0099 or (303) 494-2992. Fax (303) 494-2996.

AMERICAN YOUTH HOSTELS
▼ ▼ ▼

Youth Hosteling has been known for decades as one of the best and least expensive ways for hikers and bikers of all ages to travel through scores of countries. After a long day's rambling about the countryside, it's always a pleasure and a relief to spot the familiar triangular logo on a converted farmhouse, lodge, mansion, or other structure. Then, it's an evening of solid camaraderie and sharing, helping with the cooking and cleanup, a morning of hasty handshakes and goodbyes, and off on the road or path again to the next hostel and a new set of friends.

Of course, you can hostel on your own, or with family or friends. But for those who wish to travel about with a group, AYH offers a wide variety of inexpensive Discovery Tours in the United States, Canada, and Europe. According to David Kalter, manager of American Youth Hostels' programs and education department, "we try to provide a once in a lifetime group experience for people who are looking to be in a participatory trip. It's for the person who wants to get more involved in his or her travel experience, who wants a sense of adventure, and who likes the unexpected. People who come on our trips often come out of them with lifelong friendships."

Depending upon the tour, participants either bike 30 to 50 miles a day or hike 3 to 12 miles a day. (Hikers are transported by minivan some of the distances between hostels.) The idea is to undergo a stimulating physical challenge while still having the opportunity to explore the countryside and do some sightseeing.

DESTINATIONS: British Columbia, New Brunswick, Alberta, Nova Scotia, Quebec, Massachusetts, New England and mid-Atlantic states, New York, Colorado, Washington, Oregon, Nevada, New Mexico, California, Alaska, Appalachia, Washington, DC, England, Scotland, Ireland, France, Germany, Switzerland, Liechtenstein, Austria, Netherlands

SEASON: June to August

LENGTH OF PROGRAMS: 8 to 44 days

ENROLLMENT: 10 participants, including the leader

TOTAL COST: $250 to $2,995

COST PER DIEM: $29 to $98

TAX DEDUCTIBLE?: No

COST INCLUSIVE OF: All overnight accommodations, 3 meals per day, some admissions

COST EXCLUSIVE OF: Transportation to the assembly point, bicycles (if needed), sheet/sleeping sacks, sleeping bags (when camping)

AMENITIES, FACILITIES, AND REALITIES: Despite the fact that you might be staying in a converted castle or chateau, there's nothing elegant or sophisticated about youth hostels. As David Kalter described the accommodations to us, "The hostels range from converted chicken coops to converted castles." Most offer dormitory-style sleeping in bunk beds that are segregated by sex. Most have communal showers. However, some hostels offer family rooms that feature some privacy; they may also be booked by couples upon arrival if available, but never in advance. Everyone sleeping in hostel beds must either buy or rent a sleep sack (which is like a cocooned sheet), or a bring a pair of sheets. Everyone is expected to pitch in with the cooking, buying the groceries, and cleaning. The hiking or bicycling on some tours can be strenuous and not appropriate to out-of-shape travelers, but each tour is rated according to difficulty. Unlike most bike tours, each participant is responsible for transporting luggage, and there's no chase minivan to pick up tired stragglers.

CONTACT: American Youth Hostels, P.O. Box 37613, Washington, DC 20013-7613, tel. (202) 783-6161.

APPALACHIAN MOUNTAIN CLUB
▼ ▼ ▼

Running parallel to the U.S. Northeast corridors, one of the most heavily populated places in the country, is one of the oldest and still unspoiled mountain ranges on the continent: Appalachia. It remains that way in no small part due to societies like the Appalachian Mountain Club, a 40,000-member strong organization dedicated "to protecting the mountains, woods, rivers, and wilderness areas we enjoy.'' The Appalachian Mountain Club is the oldest mountaineering and conservation organization in America, powered mostly by the energy and dedication of its many volunteers and members.

Among the numerous programs and services the Club provides are three to eight-day guided hikes through the White Mountains in Vermont, part of the Appalachian range. Over the years, the Club has constructed a network of ecologically sound huts where campers can spend the night in the company and fellowship of other like-minded people. While the accommodations aren't exactly up to Holiday Inn standards, they're clean, comfortable, warm, and dry. The hikes are led by experienced guides and are graded according to the participants' physical condition and the degree of outdoors experience desired.

DESTINATIONS: New Hampshire

SEASON: June through September

LENGTH OF PROGRAMS: 2 to 8 days

ENROLLMENT: 12 people per hike

TOTAL COST: $175 to $315 for members, $190 to $345 for nonmembers. Reduced rates for children under 12. (Annual membership is $40 for adults, $65 for families, $25 for juniors and seniors.)

COST PER DIEM: $58 to $63 for members, $63 to $69 for nonmembers

TAX DEDUCTIBLE?: No

COST INCLUSIVE OF: Services of two AMC guides, overnight lodging, breakfasts and dinners, transfers to and from trailheads (when necessary), a copy of *High Huts of the White Mountains*

COST EXCLUSIVE OF: Transportation to the assembly point, lunch, hiking clothing and gear, snacks, gratuities

AMENITIES, FACILITIES, AND REALITIES: Pets and children under 8 years old are not permitted on hikes; children under 18 must be accompanied by an adult. There are three levels of hiking: Easier (three to five miles per day, involving no above-the-timberline hiking), Moderate (four to seven miles per day through more rugged territory), and Challenging (five to eight miles per day on steep trails and above the timberline). This is rustic, rugged hiking without a soft edge. Weather conditions can change quickly, so wind-proof parkas, rain gear, and other equipment should be brought. Accommodations are bunk-bed-style in barracks-like huts, although some huts have rooms for four to eight. Pillows and blankets, but no sheets, are provided, with showers available. Meals served cafeteria-style. Hikers must provide their own lunch fixings for the trail.

CONTACT: AMC Guided Hikes, P.O. Box 298, Gorham, NH 03581, tel. (603) 466-2727.

BACKROADS BICYCLE TOURING
▼ ▼ ▼

Backroads Bicycle Touring is one of the largest and best organized bicycle-oriented tour operators, featuring everything from weekend trips to the Wine Country or along the Russian River to 17-day, once-in-a-lifetime treks partially circumnavigating New Zealand's awesomely beautiful and virtually uninhabited South Island. Backroads Bicycle Touring has things down to a science; in fact, the company even designs and manufactures its own 21-speed touring bikes as well as mountain bikes. Another nice touch is the omnipresent chase van, which carries all participants' luggage and roadside purchases, is ready to pick up and transport any weary bikers, and is equipped with refreshments, spare parts, first-aid kit, and all other paraphernalia one could possibly need. If you opt for the camping accommodations, staffers put up and break down your tents, cook wholesome meals, do all the cleanup, etc.

"Gone are the days when bicycle touring meant camping and lugging 50 pounds of gear on your bicycle," said BBT's Bobby Gignilliat. "Today, cyclists discover that bicycling is its own passport, an instant entree into other cultures. This is particularly true in foreign countries, where on a bicycle you never feel like a typical tourist. When you pedal by, the locals murmur approval. They wave to you, ask how far you've come, and wave you over to join them at a sidewalk cafe."

Besides unusual destinations, Backroads Bicycle Touring offers a variety of programs tailored to match participants' interests. For example, there are single tours, family outings, photographic safaris, student adventures, health and fitness tours, art appreciation trips, and even walking tours for those who feel they don't fit in the saddle of a bike. The emphasis is placed less on biking itself than the camaraderie of the group, the physical beauty of the land, and the sense of traveling and touring on your own terms at your own pace.

DESTINATIONS: California, Alaska, Oregon, Washington, Arizona, New Mexico, Colorado, Idaho, Louisiana, Maine, North Carolina, Vermont, Virginia, Hawaii, Canadian Rockies, the Gulf Islands in Canada, Mexico, England, Ireland, France, Italy, Thailand, China, New Zealand, Australia, Bali

SEASON: All year, but mostly during warm weather

LENGTH OF PROGRAMS: 5 to 8 days; 2-day weekend programs in California

ENROLLMENT: 18 to 26 participants

TOTAL COST: $598 to $2,897. Youth and group discounts are available.

COST PER DIEM: $199 to $283 with inn accommodations; $99 to $133 for camping tour

TAX DEDUCTIBLE?: No

COST INCLUSIVE OF: Hotel or tent accommodations, most meals, minivan luggage ferry, helmets, bicycle maintenance, refreshments on the road, some sightseeing

COST EXCLUSIVE OF: Air transportation, transfer between tour assembly point and airport ($20 to $48 van transfer cost on some programs), bike rental ($99 to $169), sleeping bag (which may be rented), some meals, sightseeing side trips

AMENITIES, FACILITIES, AND REALITIES: These tours are not recommended for anyone very out of shape or physically infirm. However, most tours are accessible to beginners, and at the same time challenging to physically fit afficionados. Most daily segments require three to five hours' biking, many with alternative easy and tough routes. If it proves too taxing, tired participants can hitch a ride with the chase van at any time. On numerous tours, you can choose to either save money and get closer to the land by sleeping in a tent and eating campsite style—usually with running water and showers—or staying in comfortable country inns, lodges, or even chateaux—virtually all with private bath. Meals range from gourmet to health food. Although you are within your rights to bring your own bicycle, you are well advised to rent or buy one of BBT's purpose-built bikes. It will not only be cheaper in most instances than bringing your own bike, but BBT has parts and spares for all their bikes if anything goes wrong.

CONTACT: Backroads Bicycle Touring, 1516 5th Street, Suite Q333, Berkeley, CA 94710-1713, tel. (800) 245-3874 or (415) 527-1555. Fax (415) 527-1444.

BUTTERFIELD & ROBINSON

Who says that bicycling, cross-country skiing, or walking tours have to be sweaty and spartan? In the same way that luxurious spas first put you through a physical torture test and then treat you to unrelenting pampering, Butterfield & Robinson's tours alternate between vigorous and challenging physical exertion and sybaritic, luxurious relaxation. B & R, a Canadian tour operator, combines interesting and educational programs to beautiful, unspoiled places, led by experienced guides, with the finest equipment available, and then tops it off with accommodations in chateaux and castles that also offer superb cuisine. Besides biking, B & R also has some walking tours through Eastern Europe and hikes in the Canadian Rockies.

B & R is relatively expensive, however. For that reason, it tends to attract the older, more affluent Green Traveler. And although it has a series of excellent student programs that combine biking with study—French language, art in Sienna, in and around Cambridge, Spanish-language homestays—they average three to four weeks in length and over $120 per day, which is out of the economic range of most traditional students.

DESTINATIONS: Quebec, Canadian Rockies, France, Italy, England, Denmark, Austria/Hungary, Ireland, Portugal, Spain, Switzerland, Bali, New Zealand

SEASON: Most programs March to November; New Zealand in January and February

LENGTH OF PROGRAMS: 5 to 10 days; student trips, 24 to 32 days

ENROLLMENT: Average number of participants is 21.

TOTAL COST: $1,440 to $2,955; $3,340 to $3,840 for longer trips

COST PER DIEM: $189 to $353; student trips: $120 to $139

TAX DEDUCTIBLE?: No

COST INCLUSIVE OF: 12- or 18-speed bicycle, accommodations, breakfasts, dinners and some lunches, sightseeing and admissions, all local travel on train, ferry, cable car, etc., gratuities

COST EXCLUSIVE OF: Air transportation, helmets, some meals

AMENITIES, FACILITIES, AND REALITIES: Adult tours are for those age 18 years and older, family tours 13 years and older, and student tours for ages 14 to 21. In Europe and Canada, accommodations are in the finest small inns, chateaux, and castles in the area, and almost all rooms have private bathrooms. Meals are world-class, wine served with dinners. Most accommodations in Bali and New Zealand have private bathrooms. Tours vary in challenge and physical exertion, but most European tours offer alternative routes.

CONTACT: Butterfield & Robinson, 70 Bond Street, Toronto, Ontario M5B 1X3 CANADA, tel. (800) 387-1147 in U.S., (800) 268-8415 in Canada. Fax (416) 864-0541.

CHINA PASSAGE/ASIA PASSAGE
▼ ▼ ▼

When we first visited China more than a decade ago, the government severely restricted foreign tourists to Beijing and a handful of "treaty" ports. Only those with special permission were allowed into the interior. China/Asia Passage was one of the first tour operators to pioneer travel to all parts of the country, and despite the post-Tiananmen Square crackdown, its participants are free to roam almost anywhere they wish. And to make it environmentally sound and physically active, most tours are done at a leisurely pace by bicycle and foot. When the distances are too great, participants may travel by train, riverboat, or airplanes.

This is the China few Westerners have ever seen, and conversely, many of the Chinese whom you meet have never before had an opportunity to speak with outsiders, especially Westerners. Depending on the tour, you'll visit little-known but beautiful animal sanctuaries or preserves, Buddhist monasteries, ancient historical sites, and even bike along part of the famous Silk Road. Tours are accompanied by a guide and translator (as well as a van for luggage and those too tired to pedal), but participants have ample opportunity to wander on their own. China/Asia Passage offers an annual kosher tour through China that visits famous museums, historical sites, and synagogues; all meals are kosher, prepared under supervision by Mashgiach. Also offered is a 16-day elephant safari through the interior of Thailand, which includes foot treks and rafting down the Mae Cham River.

DESTINATIONS: China, Thailand

SEASON: All year

LENGTH OF PROGRAMS: 15 to 24 days

ENROLLMENT: No limit

TOTAL COST: $2,295 to $4,173

COST PER DIEM: $125 to $177

TAX DEDUCTIBLE?: No

COST INCLUSIVE OF: Air transportation from North American West Coast, transfers, transportation within China or Thailand, hotel accommodations, most meals, bicycle (or elephant where appropriate)

COST EXCLUSIVE OF: All meals in Hong Kong, helmet

AMENITIES, FACILITIES, AND REALITIES: In the big cities, the company uses the finest hotels and restaurants available. They may not be quite up to

Western standards, but all rooms are air conditioned and have private baths. Once you are in the countryside, you'll probably stay at guest houses or "rustic shelters." Tourism in China's interior is still very new, so be prepared for primitive, un-Western conditions and facilities. Local bicycles are used, which usually means one-speed bikes in China (although 10- and 15-speed bikes may be available on some tours). Participants are responsible for maintenance, and you are advised to bring your own puncture repair kit. No tipping is accepted in China, but small gifts are appreciated.

CONTACT: China Passage/Asia Passage, 168 State Street, Teaneck, NJ 07666, tel. (201) 837-1400. Fax (201) 837-1378.

ECHO: THE WILDERNESS COMPANY
▼ ▼ ▼

ECHO is one of the older, more established whitewater rafting operations in the United States (established in 1971). ECHO offers a wide range of wilderness river experiences, from 1-day challenges of the north or south fork of the American River in California, to 14-day journeys through the Grand Canyon on the mighty Colorado River. While beginners are welcome, and youths 7 to 17 years old are encouraged on most trips, none of the trips ECHO offers can be considered tame or tepid. (The minimum age for trips on the Tuolumne, Cal Salmon, and the north fork of the American Rivers is 12 years. They're among the most challenging stretches of white water on the continent.)

Participants can choose whether they want to be passengers and spectators or get actively involved in controlling their craft in the face of nature's fury. ECHO captains will permit those who wish an opportunity to paddle and even offer one-man kayaks through the rapids.

ECHO also offers a series of once-a-year trips in the Costa Rican rain forest. Other annual special trips include a trout-fishing seminar, a chamber music concert by the Rogue String Quartet along the Rogue River, river trips for kids, whale watching from kayaks in the Sea of Cortez in the Baja, etc. Because these trips are both limited and popular, it's advisable to book as soon as the new catalog comes out each January.

DESTINATIONS: California, Idaho, Oregon, Arizona, Costa Rica, Baja California

SEASON: Mainly April through September; January in the Baja; some trips are held once a year

LENGTH OF PROGRAMS: 3 to 14 days; some 1- and 2-day programs available

ENROLLMENT: 6 to 8 participants

TOTAL COST: $385 to $1,892 for adults, $332 to $1,347 for youths 7 to 17 years old. One-day trips average $87 to $145 for adults, $77 to $135 for youths 7 to 17.

COST PER DIEM: $116 to $149 for adults, $100 to $129 for youths 7 to 17

TAX DEDUCTIBLE?: $1 per day for California trips is donated to conservation groups such as Friends of the River or Tuolumne River Preservation Trust.

COST INCLUSIVE OF: All meals, rafting or kayak equipment, camp accommodations, some shuttles to and from river

COST EXCLUSIVE OF: Transportation to the assembly point, some shuttles to and from river

AMENITIES, FACILITIES, AND REALITIES: These trips are primarily for purists and adventurers who live for white water, the rougher and wilder, the better. Focusing on remote wilderness areas, conditions tend to be primitive. Participants usually have the option of floating in oar or paddle boats, or sometimes kayaks. They can, if they wish, take turns paddling.

CONTACT: ECHO: The Wilderness Company, 6529 Telegraph Avenue, Oakland, CA 94069, tel. (800) 652-ECHO or (415) 652-1600.

EQUITOUR
▼ ▼ ▼

Every sport has its hard-core loyalists who spend every spare minute and extra dollar pursuing and perfecting their skills. For them, nothing less than the most difficult challenges will do. If you are a serious horseperson and you don't want a tame nose-to-tail trek over well-worn trails, then you might want to consider taking a trip with Equitour.

According to Pam Neary, Equitour is an eight-year-old company that "runs tours for the person who loves quality horseback riding. It allows you to get off the beaten path and really interact with the locals." Equestrians with moderate to expert skills are welcome, and every tour gives them the opportunity for cantering and galloping. Some programs stress endurance riding, or feature advanced instruction in jumping or dressage. Only the best horses available in the area are used: Lucitanos in Portugal, Arabians in Morocco, Irish hunters in Ireland, or quarterhorses in Wyoming. Most trips cover rugged, sometimes virginal paths and trails.

Equitour's centerpiece is a stay at the Bitterroot Ranch in Wyoming.

Participants can join in roundups or Pony Express re-creations, or follow the Outlaw Trail that figures in so many historic and legendary sagas of the Old West. Or you can participate in training seminars, in which you are welcome to bring your own horses.

DESTINATIONS: Wyoming, Kentucky, Arizona, California, New England, Quebec, Australia, Austria, Belize, China, Egypt, England, France, Greece, Italy, Ireland, Iceland, Kenya, Hungary, Morocco, Portugal, Spain, India, U.S.S.R., New Zealand

SEASON: All year

LENGTH OF PROGRAMS: 4 to 16 days; most average 8 days

ENROLLMENT: 10 participants

TOTAL COST: $550 to $3,850

COST PER DIEM: $100 to $241

TAX DEDUCTIBLE?: No

COST INCLUSIVE OF: Camp or hotel accommodations, all meals, some transfers, horse, tack and saddle, guide, some admissions, saddlebags upon request, gratuities (on some trips)

COST EXCLUSIVE OF: Transportation to assembly point, some transfers, sleeping bags, gratuities (on some trips)

AMENITIES, FACILITIES, AND REALITIES: Unlike some horse journeys, the outfitters take care of feeding, grooming, and saddling the horses. The hotels used are all different, but few include private bath. Cabins on Bitterroot Ranch are equipped with private baths. Not recommended for novices, some trips require moderate experience and skill. American saddles used in the U.S., English saddles everywhere else.

CONTACT: Equitour, Bitterroot Ranch, P.O. Box 807, Dubois, WY 85213, tel. (800) 545-3363 or (307) 455-0019. Fax (307) 455-2354.

FITS EQUESTRIAN
▼ ▼ ▼

There's hardly an individual anywhere who hasn't fantasized about playing cowboys and Indians, of riding the range, going on a cattle drive, being a Pony Express rider, or even going on the Outlaw Trail with the likes of Billy the Kid or the James Gang. Although the frontier is closed and those colorful trappings of yesteryear are reserved for movie buffs, FITS Equestrian still offers authentic horse trekking experiences in 26 different countries for those who want to know what it is like to sit tall in the saddle for hours and days on end.

FITS Equestrian has an incredibly varied range of programs for those who have fantasized about journeying by horse through beautiful, wild, and remote nontouristy places. Some of its tours are eminently civilized, such as jaunts through the English or Irish countryside that end up each evening in friendly pubs and rustic inns, or outings past medieval castles and Roman ruins in the Scottish Highlands. Others echo back to antiquity, like following the trade routes across the Sahara Desert or through the Holy Land in Israel. And then there are those of pure adventure, such as safaris along the vast animal-rich plains of Kenya or across the mountain-rimmed pampas of Argentina.

Horse journeys are unexpectedly hard for those who have never ridden a horse for more than an hour or two at a stable or dude ranch. It can be downright miserable in a driving rain or raging sandstorm, or if the terrain is hilly or rocky. But it's one of the best possible ways to explore a region as well as experience what it was like for our ancestors to cross the plains or tame a continent.

According to FITS Equestrian president Wolfgang Hallauer, "it is an active, sportive vacation that offers the creature comforts of sleeping in bed, except in wilderness areas where it's more rugged." Asked whether they are environmentally conscious, and if hard-core ecotourists approve of horse treks through the countryside and wilderness, an amused Hallauer responded, "We try not to do any damage. But Sierra Club members do not ride. Hard-core environmentalists think that riding on horses is horrible." (Actually, Sierra Club does have horseback trips.)

While you don't have to be an experienced rider to join most of FITS Equestrian programs, Hallauer notes that "most require various degrees of horsemanship." Some programs are especially challenging and are for expert riders only. Depending upon the country, you'll pick your horse from among Arabians, thoroughbreds, quarterhorses, etc.

DESTINATIONS: California, Alaska, Colorado, Maine, Utah, Vermont, Wyoming, Canada, U.S.S.R., Belgium, Italy, Greece, Portugal, Spain, Australia, New Zealand, Chile, Argentina, Jamaica, Belize, Iceland, Israel, Egypt, Morocco, Algeria, Kenya, Tanzania, Mexico, England, Scotland, Ireland, France, Germany, Austria, and Hungary

SEASON: All year

LENGTH OF PROGRAMS: 5 to 16 days, but 8 days is most typical

ENROLLMENT: 4 to 12 participants

TOTAL COST: U.S.: $400 to $1,560; Foreign: $800 to $3,850

Cost Per Diem: U.S.: $112 to $171; Foreign: $108 to $220

Tax Deductible?: No

Cost Inclusive Of: Horses, saddles (English, but a few Western saddles may be available), tack, accommodations, most meals (all meals on some tours)

Cost Exclusive Of: Transportation and/or air fare to the assembly point, entry fees

Amenities, Facilities, and Realities: Cowboys should have had it so good. You'll select from the best horses, use excellent saddles and tack, have your meals cooked or prepared, your luggage carried for you by minivan or other means as you ride at a leisurely pace through national parks, nature preserves, private ranches, and farms, on dirt roads or mountain trails. Most tours spend the evenings at rustic hotels, country inns, or farmhouses, some with private bathrooms. A few remote treks make camp in the wild and require sleeping bags. Participants are expected to saddle and groom their mounts, "but help is always available." The level of experience and expertise required for each program is clearly noted; some are suitable for novices, others are only for experienced or even expert riders. *Don't* overestimate your riding ability, because it can jeopardize both you and the group. On many programs, arrangements can be made for non-riding companions to accompany the group by bicycle, minivan, or foot. Some treks can be long, arduous, exhausting, uncomfortable, and even hazardous, especially in bad weather. You have to have a can-do spirit and be willing to put up with physical hardships, particularly in remote areas that require making camp. Tipping the guide is optional, unless he is an owner, in which case it is inappropriate. Tips are usually pooled among the participants—$20 to $25 per participant—and given to the leader to distribute.

Contact: FITS Equestrian, 2011 Alamo Pintado Road, Solvang, CA 93463, tel. (800) 666-FITS, (805) 688-9494. Fax (805) 688-2943.

JIM & TOM'S OFF THE DEEP END
▼ ▼ ▼

"Our philosophy is to have fun and learn a little about what we're doing," says co-founder Tom Sheehan. "We like to immerse ourselves in the environment we're visiting. In Japan it's a cultural thing; we try to learn about what it's like to be Japanese so we can understand their culture better. We eat their food, sleep Japanese style, try to follow their etiquette. In Yellowstone or Teton, we immerse ourselves in nature. We concentrate on the natural features, the plant life, the geology."

Jim (Maurer) and Tom's (Sheehan) Off the Deep End is a tiny company that offers pure, unabashed adventure for anyone "as long as they can peddle a bike or paddle a kayak.'' Both men are active in leading tours themselves. In fact, Jim Maurer, ''more often than not, is away from his desk, deep in the back country, delicately sautéing escargots for our guests,'' and Tom Sheehan ''is usually found in some remote corner of the world in quest of the ultimate journey.''

The tours are rated according to the degree of physical challenge: Ratings of 1 or 2 mean three to four hours' travel daily across flat or hilly territory; 3 or 4 is five to seven hours' travel through hilly or mountainous terrain; and 5 is the most difficult and arduous, for which participants must be experienced and in excellent physical condition. The primary emphasis is placed on biking or kayaking, with ample stops at quiet pools for swimming or spectacular mountain views for photography or communing with nature. In addition, guides instruct participants about local culture or the environment. Participants range in age from 7 to 76 years old.

DESTINATIONS: Colorado, Idaho, Wyoming, the Canadian Rockies, Ireland, France, Japan, Thailand, Nepal, Tahiti, Papua New Guinea, New Zealand

SEASON: All year

LENGTH OF PROGRAMS: 7 to 17 days

ENROLLMENT: 8 to 12 participants

TOTAL COST: $550 to $2,930

COST PER DIEM: $79 to $99 in the U.S. and Canada; $91 to $205 abroad

TAX DEDUCTIBLE?: No

COST INCLUSIVE OF: Domestic programs include all meals; international programs include breakfasts and dinners. Also included in all programs are: accommodations, tours, ''ducks'' (inflatable kayaks), park fees

COST EXCLUSIVE OF: Transportation to assembly point, bike rental, taxes

AMENITIES, FACILITIES, AND REALITIES: There are three types of tours offered: safaris, which involve camping outdoors; Inn Tours, which make use of country inns, chateaux, castles, or other semiluxurious accommodations; and an unnamed middle category, with accommodations in guesthouses and home stays. The safari tours are about as comfortable as you can get in camping. About the only thing participants are asked to do is help put up the tents. In the Inn Tours, basically everything is taken care of. All hotel accommodations (with the exception of one or two nights in Japan) have private rooms with baths.

CONTACT: Jim & Tom's Off the Deep End, P.O. Box 7511, Jackson, WY 83001, tel. (800) 223-6833 or (307) 733-8707.

JOURNEYS

▼ ▼ ▼

This is perhaps the only U.S.-based adventure travel company that has a native Nepalese as a founding partner, Pemba Sherpa, a remarkable man who speaks six languages and joined his first Himalayan expedition at 12 years of age. In addition, Journeys' co-directors (also original founders) Will and Joan Weber, both have Ph.D.'s in natural resources and education. Will also spent four years in Nepal with the Peace Corps. Not surprisingly, although Journeys has programs in more than a score of countries, it specializes in unusual, challenging trips and treks to Nepal.

Another unusual Green component is that after 14 years in business, most of the original staff is still with the company. All of Journeys' 100 or so guides are either natives or residents of the countries they work in, and when they're not working, most volunteer their time and talent to the various environmental or cultural projects established and funded by Journeys' nonprofit Earth Preservation Fund. Among the preservation efforts Journeys has supported is buying rain forest land in Costa Rica and Belize, planting trees in Nepal, restoring monasteries in Ladakh, and supporting antipoaching campaigns in Tanzania. Incidentally, their brochures are printed on environmentally correct wood-free paper.

No, you're not going to be forced to eat vegetarian food only or sleep out in the open. In fact, in order to please its clients, Journeys does some things that may seen very unGreen to purists, such as offering exciting options like helicopter rides in some of its Nepalese trips and hot-air ballooning with African safaris. But the company's choice of hotels, trails, and campsites is predicated not only on what offers the best views but what best displays and preserves the local culture or environment.

"Journeys are not 'tours.' Your fellow travelers consist of people who often travel alone and don't need the security of luxury accommodations and a large group with a mother hen tour conductor. Our groups allow like-minded independent travelers to combine resources in completing a trip unavailable to most individuals. We do our best to help you find a group that is complementary with your interests, age, and abilities, or we will help recruit compatible colleagues for the departure you wish to schedule."

DESTINATIONS: Alaska, Hawaii, Mexico, Belize, Costa Rica, Argentina, Peru, Ecuador, Kenya, Rwanda, Tanzania, Madagascar, Zimbabwe, Botswana, Nepal, India, China, Tibet, Hong Kong, Burma, Thailand, Japan, Papua New Guinea

SEASON: All year

LENGTH OF PROGRAMS: 4 to 21 days

ENROLLMENT: No more than 12 participants; some programs have as few as 4 to 6 people.

TOTAL COST: $395 to $3,225

COST PER DIEM: $97 to $179

TAX DEDUCTIBLE?: No. Journeys dedicates a portion of the money it receives from each Green Traveler to a nonprofit foundation called the Earth Preservation Fund. Staff and participants are encouraged to volunteer time and money to the Fund's projects in various countries. However, EPF is not recognized by the IRS.

COST INCLUSIVE OF: Accommodations, most meals, in-country transfers, park fees, sightseeing

COST EXCLUSIVE OF: Air Transportation to the assembly point, optional helicopter trekking, optional hot-air ballooning, some outdoor gear

AMENITIES, FACILITIES, AND REALITIES: Trips are rated according to grades of difficulty. Also, they are divided according to type: Trekking—walking four to eight hours a day in mountainous terrain and camping out at night; Odysseys—less strenuous hiking with most nights in hotels or lodges; Safaris— combinations of camping, hiking, rafting, or animal riding; Exploratory Trips— first-time visits to new places with unknown conditions and accommodations; and Family Trips—tours with less physical exertion and more interaction with local children scheduled. All hotels have private baths, most are air conditioned.

CONTACT: Journeys, 4011 Jackson Road, Ann Arbor, MI 48103, tel. (800) 255-8735 or (313) 665-4407.

MOUNTAIN TRAVEL
▼ ▼ ▼

Mountain Travel, as its name implies, specializes in mountain trekking and climbing. They bring a lot of superlatives to their programs: It's one of the oldest, Greenest, biggest, most successful, and most experienced adventure tour operators in the business. And judging by the quality, inventiveness, and diversity of its programs—not to mention the high number of repeaters who travel with the company year after year—it's also one of the best. As we go to press, a merger with the other big adventure tour operator, Sobek, is imminent, which is something like Hertz and Avis getting together. But until it happens, we'll continue to review them separately.

Mountain Travel owns an impressive record of firsts: first to offer group treks in Nepal, walking safaris in East Africa, and even a cross-country skiing expedition to the South Pole. And its international staff reads like a Who's Who of adventure expeditions, including the first Latin American to scale Mt. Everest, the only man to climb Mt. Everest *twice*, medical doctors, former park rangers, well-known authors, professional mountaineers, scientists, former professors, etc. And while Mountain Travel is a for-profit company, it donates a portion of its profits to worthwhile environmental charities, such as the American Himalayan Foundation, East Africa Wildlife Society, Darwin Foundation, and AREA (Association for Research and Environmental Aid).

While some of its tours are soft adventure programs suitable for most people, regardless of fitness or experience, other trips are the hardest of hardcore adventure. These extraordinary journeys are not for the timid, weak, or those not in excellent physical condition. However, these rigorous trips provide the ultimate challenge to anyone with serious trekking experience who wants to have an old-fashioned adventure without pulling punches but still desires as much comfort as possible in the field. You can, for example, journey across the roof of the world past Mt. Everest from Nepal to China, along the ancient Silk Trail. Or you can trek through a 15,000-foot pass to the mysterious Incan stronghold of Machu Picchu, climb 17,000-foot Mt. Kenya in Africa, or take high mountain passes through the Swiss Alps, to name but a few.

DESTINATIONS: Hawaii, Alaska, Kenya, Tanzania, Rwanda, Botswana, Zimbabwe, Namibia, Morocco, Madagascar, Mali, Egypt, Algeria, Nepal, India, Kashmir, Bhutan, Sikkim, Pakistan, China, Thailand, Papua New Guinea, Bali, Indonesia, Australia, Chile, Peru, Ecuador, Guatemala, Argentina, Galapagos, Costa Rica, Venezuela, Mexico, Antarctica, Switzerland, Italy, France, Spain, Austria, Czechoslovakia, Turkey, Poland, England, Scotland, Wales, Norway, U.S.S.R.

SEASON: All year

LENGTH OF PROGRAMS: 8 to 26 days

ENROLLMENT: Usually fewer than 15 people

TOTAL COST: $1,890 to $5,000. Physicians may qualify for 20 percent to 50 percent reductions if they will take care of medical emergencies.

COST PER DIEM: $68 to $290

TAX DEDUCTIBLE?: No, but part of the Wilderness Medical Seminars are tax deductible to participating doctors.

COST INCLUSIVE OF: Land transportation and transfers, intercountry flights on some programs, all meals in the field, breakfasts when staying in hotels, accommodations, sightseeing fees, and entrance fees

Cost Exclusive Of: Air transportation, some in-country transportation, most lunches and dinners when staying in hotels

Amenities, Facilities, and Realities: Most of the company's tours and treks are far from civilization and require a moderate to high degree of physical stamina. Some also require mountain-climbing experience. Accommodations on most trips are tents; some trips offer showers, while other more remote ones provide only hot water in the morning for washing and shaving. Portable latrines are dug at each site, and tents are erected around them. Porters carry luggage and supplies from place to place, as well as handle cooking, setting up, etc. Mountain Travel says that all rubbish is disposed of properly in an ecologically responsible manner.

Contact: Mountain Travel, 6420 Fairmount Avenue, El Cerrito, CA 94530-3606, tel. (800) 227-2384 or (415) 527-8100. Fax (415) 525-7710.

Nantahala Outdoor Center
▼ ▼ ▼

It's one thing to go on a fully escorted whitewater rafting trip, in which the leader does all the work and makes all the decisions. It's entirely different when you become a knowledgeable and experienced paddler yourself. Then, you are no longer a spectator but a partner in the great adventure of living close to nature.

Set in the Southern Appalachians, Nantahala Outdoor Center is highly regarded as a premier school for paddling. Beginners and experts come here to learn in canoes, kayaks, and in what they call "decked canoes." Some of the skills developed include: how to read the river, personal and group safety, planning out a river run, playing waves, and holes in the river. If you are ready to go all the way, NOC provides training for raft guides and teachers. One important course they offer is "River Rescue," plus, naturally, CPR and first aid. NOC also gives instruction in backpacking, hiking, rock climbing, and other outdoor skills. Schools, corporations, and other organizations come to NOC as a group.

If you are serious about your outdoor adventure, we can't imagine anything more sensible or more fun than to learn how to do it like an expert.

Destinations: North Carolina

Season: March through October

Length of Programs: 2 to 7 days, with some weekend programs

ENROLLMENT: Classes are usually no larger than 10 students, with 2 instructors. (A minimum class has at least 3 students)

TOTAL COST: $260 to $860; discounts are available if you provide your own boat, lodging, and/or meals.

COST PER DIEM: $123 to $130

TAX DEDUCTIBLE?: No

COST INCLUSIVE OF: Instruction, transportation during the program, lodging, meals, boats

COST EXCLUSIVE OF: Transportation to assembly point

AMENITIES, FACILITIES, AND REALITIES: Most students stay in ''shared lodging,'' with two or three people in a room and approximately one bathroom per two or three rooms. Private accommodations may be reserved for an additional fee at a motel or bunkhouse. Vegetarian or sugar-free meals (for diabetics) are available. Daycare for children is available while you are in the course, but they also recommend bringing another adult to care for the children. Be sure you are physically fit and ready to test yourself against the outdoors before you sign up for any of their programs. They also have a weight limit. ''Sampler'' courses are available for those who want to try a taste of a course without making more than a single day's commitment. Price is about $64.

OTHER COMMENTS: When you are ready to go further afield, Nantahala has rafting, kayaking, canoeing, trekking, and bicycling trips to Georgia, Texas, West Virginia, Idaho, Alaska, Tennessee, Minnesota, the Grand Canyon, Florida, Blue Ridge Mountains, Mississippi, Maine, Chile, Mexico, New Zealand, Baja California, England, Scotland, Costa Rica, Nepal.

CONTACT: Nantahala Outdoor Center, 41 US 19 West, Bryson City, NC 28713, tel. (704) 488-6737.

OUTWARD BOUND

At nearly a half-century old, Outward Bound is the granddaddy of adventure organizations. And with over 200,000 alumni—more than 25,000 people successfully complete its programs each year—it is far and away the largest. Despite its importance and popularity among a select group of insiders, few people who are not part of Outward Bound really understand what this non-profit organization is or does.

As city and suburban life becomes more civilized, regimented, and compartmentalized, we begin to lose the sense of what it is like to struggle, survive, and triumph against nature, the elements, and our own fears or inhibitions. Outward Bound gives individuals an unparalleled opportunity to recapture what it is like to be out in the wilds, both as a group and totally on your own, pushing yourself right to the edge of your physical and emotional limits, and then going beyond that point. While you survive and grow, you will learn new skills, how to work and interact with a group (so much so that your life can depend upon teamwork), and how to develop leadership skills. Hopefully, what you learn and experience will stay with you long after you return home.

Outward Bound programs are widely varied, according to the region, season, and student interest. No experience or specific outdoors skills are necessary; nor must you be in prime condition, especially since part of the purpose of these programs is to build up physical fitness and confidence. Your program could consist of canoeing, backpacking, mountaineering, sea kayaking or sailing, whitewater rafting, canyoneering, skiing, dog sledding, winter camping, or combinations that incorporate two or more of the above-mentioned activities. Outward Bound also offers special courses for executives and corporations, troubled youth, Vietnam vets, the blind and others with physical disabilities, and women who need to renew their own sense of self-worth.

DESTINATIONS: Alaska, Maine, Massachusetts, Maryland, North Carolina, Florida, Texas, Minnesota, Colorado, Arizona, Utah, California, Montana, and Washington in the U.S.; Canada, Mexico, Tanzania, Nepal, U.S.S.R.

SEASON: All year

LENGTH OF PROGRAMS: 3 to 30 days

ENROLLMENT: 8 to 12 students

TOTAL COST: $375 to $2,500. Some scholarships or financial assistance available.

COST PER DIEM: $60 to $167

TAX DEDUCTIBLE?: No, though executive or corporate courses may be partially deductible.

COST INCLUSIVE OF: All equipment, meals, camping accommodations, transportation costs while on the course

COST EXCLUSIVE OF: Transportation to and from assembly point, physical examination (required)

AMENITIES, FACILITIES, AND REALITIES: Since some of the purposes of Outward Bound programs are to toughen up participants, develop group intradependency, as well as teach greater self-reliance, conditions are not only primitive but downright spartan. You'll sleep out under the stars or in a small tent in your sleeping bag, carry your own pack, cook your own meals, and use the outdoors as your toilet. (On the sailing programs, going to the bathroom means leaning backwards over the side of the boat, just as sailors thousands of years ago did.) You will also handle your own equipment, and no one will clean up after you. All Outward Bound programs are physically demanding, even exhausting, so take care not to select one that is above your fitness ability, or lasts longer than your stamina can endure. The minimum age is 14 years old; some programs are for adults 18 or older. An attempt is made to select groups according to age. Specific programs are available for executives, teenagers, women, and other special-interest groups. High school, college, or teaching credits may be earned on many courses.

CONTACT: Outward Bound USA, 384 Field Point Road, Greenwich, CT 06830, tel. (800) 243-8520 or (203) 661-0797.

OVERSEAS ADVENTURE TRAVEL
▼ ▼ ▼

When you call Overseas Adventure Travel's toll-free number for information and are put on hold, you quickly discover that they're different. Instead of bubble gum music, you hear the sounds of animals in the wild. OAT is like that: a first-class operation that does almost everything right, including being one of the Greenest midsized for-profit tour operators. In fact, we understand that it's the only adventure travel company endorsed by the African Wildlife Foundation. It was one of the first to produce a written code of ethics for its participants. And when you book for a tour and receive OAT's pre-departure information pack, enclosed with it are such Green endeavors as a membership solicitation for the Jane Goodall Institute for Wildlife Research, Education & Conservation, an appeal for support by the African Wildlife Foundation, plus a U.S. Customs brochure on guidelines for avoiding buying endangered species souvenirs (see pages 42–43).

"OAT has been one of the forerunners of ecology-minded, low-impact tourism over the past decade," says company spokesperson Catherine Gibson. "We credit our success with our dedication to responsible adventure travel and the importance we place on feedback from OAT past passengers." While running programs in many countries, OAT's specialty is safaris in Tanzania.

OAT tours hire local guides, buy most supplies locally, and when accommodations are in hotels rather than tents, they book into locally owned or managed hotels. It offers tours in over 28 countries, ranging from mountain bikes in Ecuador to Elephant walks in Thailand, river rafting in Costa Rica to trekking in Nepal. There are specific programs for families available. Most tours are at least 10 days in duration, because "great adventures don't happen overnight. We know, firsthand, that it takes time to participate in adventure and not just view it as a spectator."

DESTINATIONS: Hawaii, Mexico, Ecuador, Nepal, U.S.S.R., Mali, Galapagos, Peru, Costa Rica, Thailand, Borneo, Indonesia, Papua New Guinea, Rwanda, Zaire, Burundi, Chile, Bolivia, Bhutan, Togo, Tanzania, Kenya, Morocco, Turkey, Tibet, Pakistan, India, Egypt

SEASON: All year

LENGTH OF PROGRAMS: 1 to 3 weeks; longer programs up to 15 weeks available.

ENROLLMENT: 5 to 16 participants

TOTAL COST: $1,790 to $4,290

COST PER DIEM: $89 to $204 for adults, $49 to $105 for children on family adventures

TAX DEDUCTIBLE?: $200 of the Endangered Species Safari is donated to the Rhino Ark in Kenya; some other trips in Africa and Nepal include donations that may be tax deductible.

COST INCLUSIVE OF: All meals, accommodations, in-country travel, bicycles (when appropriate), admissions to parks, tee shirts, duffel bags (on East African safaris), predeparture information pack

COST EXCLUSIVE OF: International transportation, taxes

AMENITIES, FACILITIES, AND REALITIES: Some trips are very physically demanding, requiring strenuous walking or trekking. Each trip is clearly rated according to difficulty: Easy Hiking, Easy Trekking, Moderate Trekking, Demanding Trekking, etc. On outdoors adventure trips, porters and pack animals are used to carry luggage. Three-person tents are used to accommodate two people at a time; shower and toilet tents are always available. All camp work is done by staff. Programs provide, in addition to a rousing physical challenge, opportunities to explore and learn about the local culture and environment. On its cultural-type tours, local hotels are used in preference to U.S.-style hotels. Most are air conditioned, and all include private bath.

CONTACT: Overseas Adventure Travel, 349 Broadway, Cambridge, MA 02139, tel. (800) 221-0814 or (617) 876-0533. Fax (617) 876-0455.

SIERRA CLUB
▼ ▼ ▼

In 1892, John Muir, the great naturalist and wilderness advocate, established the Sierra Club to protect the magnificent Sierra Nevada range. Over the decades, his poetic diaries and other writings have inspired millions to seek and preserve the natural, awe-inspiring beauty that is America at its best. Today, the Sierra Club is a nationwide, membership-based organization that is actively involved in conservation (including the establishment and maintenance of national parks and wilderness areas). Their books and magazines are world renown for majestic photography and memorable writing.

The Sierra Club's travel programs include naturalist-led adventure trips into the wilderness, service projects, and volunteer programs.

One noteworthy volunteer program is Sierra Club's Inner City Outings, which is designed to "provide wilderness adventures for people who wouldn't otherwise have them—including urban youth of diverse cultural and ethnic backgrounds, seniors, hearing or visually impaired individuals, and the physically disabled."

Many of their adventure trips are domestic, focusing on regions that are or should be protected wilderness areas, through which you may hike, backpack, bicycle, ski, raft, or otherwise wander. But not all programs are physically challenging; Sierra Club also offers more extensive, faraway travel. You may find yourself kayaking in Baja California among the great whales, riding a burro through the Sierra Nevada Mountains, following the migration of caribou through the Alaskan Arctic Wildlife Refuge, or backpacking through the Himalayas. The aim of these trips is to experience the wonders of nature on a very personal basis, so you may learn to better protect it.

Service trips involve working hard on rewarding projects, such as swinging sledgehammers to break up rocks to make trails through wilderness areas, or assisting in an archeological survey.

Membership in the Sierra Club is quite reasonable, with sizeable discounts for senior citizens, students, and people with limited incomes. Once you're a member of Sierra Club, your local chapter will also keep you informed about outings to nearby wilderness areas, which are usually quite inexpensive and tend to be short (as little as a day or a weekend).

DESTINATIONS: Alaska, Arizona, California, Grand Canyon, the Everglades, Florida, Georgia, Louisiana, Mississippi, New Mexico, North Carolina, Texas,

Utah, Baja California, Virgin Islands National Park, Belize, Costa Rica, Guatemala, Galapagos, Amazon Jungle, Argentina, Brazil, Peru, Austria, England, Scotland, Germany, Switzerland, Greece, Czechoslovakia, U.S.S.R., India, Nepal, China, Tanzania, Egypt, Kenya, Botswana, Zimbabwe, Thailand, Singapore, Malaysia, New Zealand

SEASON: All year

LENGTH OF PROGRAMS: 6 to 14 days, though there are longer and shorter programs.

ENROLLMENT: 6 to 25 participants, depending on the program

TOTAL COST: Domestic: $210 to $1,555; Foreign: $1,095 to $3,700; Service: $120 to $290

COST PER DIEM: Domestic: $42 to $150; Foreign: $85 to $325; Service: $20 to $30

TAX DEDUCTIBLE?: No, because Sierra Club is an advocacy group that lobbies for conservation.

COST INCLUSIVE OF: Most meals, lodging (or accommodations at camp sites), guides

COST EXCLUSIVE OF: Transportation to the program, some hotel accommodations just before or after the group trip, any camping or other specialized gear (if your program calls for it), fishing licenses (if appropriate), some admission costs and, possibly, some transportation during the program

AMENITIES, FACILITIES, AND REALITIES: The Sierra Club has more than 300 outings every year. So, it is quite difficult to generalize about the amenities and facilities. While many Sierra Club trips are rugged and very suited to those who are interested in living close to nature and the great outdoors, the level of physical activity varies with each program. A number of trips are available for those individuals who aren't able to or don't desire to strain themselves beyond a normal walking pace. If you are uncertain about whether or not the trip you are interested in joining is appropriate to your abilities or interests, you are welcome to call or write the trip leader to discuss it in more detail; his or her address and phone number are given in the trip brochures. If the trip you pick involves indoor accommodations, it may or may not have private bathrooms. If your trip involves a horse or burro, you will probably be responsible for currying, saddling, and generally caring for your own animal. Participants on some trips may also be required to share in the cooking and cleaning. The Galapagos trip is, of course, by boat.

OTHER COMMENTS: If you are very experienced, Sierra Club may consider you for a position as an outing leader. Usually, you have to take a few trips with them first as a participant to demonstrate your abilities.

CONTACT: Sierra Club Outing Department, 730 Polk St., San Francisco, CA 94109, tel. (415) 776-2211.

SOBEK EXPEDITIONS
▼ ▼ ▼

In every field, there are a couple of names that always spring to mind as the best available. These are the Mercedes or Rolls Royces when talking of cars, the Leicas and Nikons of cameras, or Rolexes and Philippes Patek among watches. Similarly, two of the top names in adventure travel are Sobek and Mountain Travel. As we go to press, these two giants are on the verge of merging, which would create the world's largest, most experienced adventure travel company. (However, they will continue to be marketed separately, since Sobek specializes in river rafting, and Mountain Travel's strong suit is trekking and mountaineering.)

David Ripley, Sobek's director of marketing and sales, explained to us, "What distinguishes one adventure company from another is its origins, and ours was the first to offer international river rafting. Most adventure companies hire someone else to run their international trips. Because we do our trips ourselves, no one does international river rafting like us. We give them safety, experience, reliability, and 17 years of having dealt with the cultures on the rivers."

Ripley believes that what attracts certain people to its style of whitewater rafting is the unpredictability, a small element of danger, a sense of the unknown. Together, they give participants a trickle of adrenaline. But, as Ripley proudly points out, "We have never lost anybody on a trip, however."

DESTINATIONS: Alaska, Colorado, Nevada, Utah, Wyoming, and Hawaii in the U.S., Canadian Rockies, British Columbia, Northwest Territories, Labrador, Quebec, Nova Scotia, and Newfoundland in Canada, U.S.S.R., Yugoslavia, Czechoslovakia, Switzerland, Italy, France, England, Scotland, Ireland, Greece, Iceland, Greenland, Tanzania, Kenya, Ethiopia, Zambia, Zimbabwe, Rwanda, Egypt, Zaire, Botswana, South Africa, Australia, New Zealand, Papua New Guinea, Vanuatu, Fiji, Thailand, China, Japan, Indonesia, Nepal, Pakistan, Kashmir, Turkey, Mongolia, Argentina, Chile, Brazil, Belize, Venezuela, Ecuador, Peru, Belize, Guatemala, India, Costa Rica

SEASON: All year

LENGTH OF PROGRAMS: 6 to 28 days

ENROLLMENT: 8 to 16 participants

TOTAL COST: $595 to $6,975

COST PER DIEM: $125 to $150

TAX DEDUCTIBLE?: A portion may be deductible. A $250 donation is made on ecological trips. On adventure tours, $2 per day is apportioned to Sobek's Fund for Conservation.

COST INCLUSIVE OF: Accommodations, most meals, guide services, most transfers, park fees and entrances, hip bag

COST EXCLUSIVE OF: Air transportation, taxes, sleeping bags

AMENITIES, FACILITIES, AND REALITIES: Accommodations range from first-class (locally owned) hotels or inns with private baths to tents and lodges. On most outdoors trips, participants are expected, but not required, to put up their own tents.

CONTACT: Sobek Expeditions, P.O. Box 1089, Angels Camp, CA 95222, tel. (800) 777-7939 or (209) 736-4524.

WILDERNESS TRAVEL
▼ ▼ ▼

One statistic expresses the popularity and satisfaction quotient of Wilderness Travel's 87 different adventure trips in more than 40 countries: Almost 80 percent of its participants are either repeaters or are first-timers referred by repeaters. Obviously, they must be doing something right to win that kind of loyalty. For one thing, unlike many tour operators, Wilderness Travel doesn't broker its trips with sub-contractors but uses its own staff to plan, conduct, maintain, and improve all land and adventure aspects. That insures consistent quality control. Also, it listens to the complaints and comments of participants, which it treats more as partners than merely paying clients.

Wilderness Travel offers a range of experiences, from pure trekking across tortuous Himalayan mountain passes to sailboats along the Adriatic, from elephant walks through the Nepalese jungles to camel safaris in the south Indian desert, four-wheel-drive jeeps in the Serengeti to an *African Queen*-like riverboat down the mighty Congo. The company specializes in tours to remote and infrequently visited areas of the world. As a result, although conditions may be relatively primitive, there's an exhilarating sense of being among the first to visit places that have been hidden from tourists for years or even generations. For instance, Wilderness is the first tour operator to feature a river and cultural tour through the just-opened People's Republic of Congo.

Wilderness, too, promotes responsible Green Travel. "As the world turns 'Green,' you'll find that, at Wilderness Travel, it's not a new color. We believe that adventure travel demands responsibility and sensitivity at both local and global levels. . . . Our adventures actively promote cultural preservation, conservation, and environmental protection. Today, we contribute by supporting a number of environmental and cultural projects and organizations, promoting minimum-impact camping and travel in the field, and actively encouraging cross-cultural ties."

DESTINATIONS: Hawaii, England, Scotland, France, Norway, Italy, Greece, Poland, Bulgaria, Spain, Switzerland, Yugoslavia, U.S.S.R., Turkey, Nepal, India, Pakistan, Tibet, Thailand, People's Republic of Congo, Rwanda, Zaire, Kenya, Tanzania, Botswana, Malawi, Zambia, Namibia, Madagascar, Peru, Amazon, Argentina, Bolivia, Chile, Costa Rica, Venezuela, Galapagos, Indonesia, Borneo, Papua New Guinea, Fiji, Japan

SEASON: All year

LENGTH OF PROGRAMS: 8 to 36 days

ENROLLMENT: 5 to 15 participants

TOTAL COST: $1,050 to $4,990; 25 percent to 50 percent discount to medical doctors on some tours

COST PER DIEM: $74 to $293

TAX DEDUCTIBLE?: No, but Wilderness supports a number of environmental and cultural projects.

COST INCLUSIVE OF: Most meals, accommodations, sleeping bags, some mountaineering equipment, transfers, some in-country transportation

COST EXCLUSIVE OF: Air transportation, some in-country transportation, some mountaineering equipment (rentals available), park fees and permits, taxes

AMENITIES, FACILITIES, AND REALITIES: Unlike most tour operators, permit fees and admission costs are not included in the basic price. Many interesting optional side or supplementary trips and programs are available. Three-person walk-in or dome tents are used for couples. Locally owned or operated hotels and inns are used whenever possible, most with private baths. Meals combine local dishes with Western cuisine. Tips are paid through the group leader; Sherpas would appreciate donations of clothing or equipment you don't want to bring back with you.

CONTACT: Wilderness Travel, 801 Allston Way, Berkeley, CA 94710, tel. (800) 247-6700 or (415) 548-0420.

FURTHER POSSIBILITIES
▼ ▼ ▼

ADVENTURE CENTRE SOLOMON ISLANDS, 44B Alpin Street, Cairns, Australia, tel. 011-61-70-51-0622, fax 011-61-70-52-1127. Adventure Center is an Australian-owned company that offers very reasonably priced one or two-week scuba diving packages in the Solomon Islands. This is one of the premier places for serious divers, not only because of the astonishing diversity of marine life but for wreck diving: There are lots of Japanese ships sunk in shallow water during World War II that can be explored. Above the water, you'll be staying in a resort on the edge of an untouched rain forest.

BACKPACKER, Box 118, Emmaus, PA 18099-0118, tel. (215) 967-8154. An entire magazine (8 issues a year) devoted to the pleasures of backpacking, including travel tips. $15/year.

BHUTAN TRAVEL, 120 E. 56th St., Suite 1430, New York, NY 10022, tel. (212) 838-6382. As it's name implies, Bhutan Travel specializes in journeys through the mysterious Himalayan kingdom of Bhutan. The focus is on nature treks and cultural tours.

CANOANDES is a Peruvian company being marketed by Varig Brazilian Airlines that features rafting, kayaking, or ecological safaris at various places throughout the Amazon River Basin, a million-square-mile region that straddles Peru, Bolivia, Ecuador, and Brazil. The programs and tours range from relatively sedate cruises on riverboats to wet and wild rubber rafts down the remote Apurimax River. CanoAndes, founded in 1981 by five Polish adventurers, was the first tour operator whose guides ran the entire length of the Amazon, and maps they drew up were used by the famous 1982 Cousteau expedition to the Amazon's headwaters.

COLORADO DUDE AND GUEST RANCH ASSOCIATION, P.O. Box 300, Tabernash, CO 80478, tel. (303) 887-3128. As its latest press release begins, "white water enthusiasts can have their horse and water too," because 34 of the 39 ranches that make up this statewide organization have both horseback riding and whitewater rafting. One also features hot air ballooning. All of the ranches offer all-inclusive packages for tenderfeet that includes riding instruction, all meals, entertainment, and programs for the kids. Accommodations are in western-style cabins, and amenities may include hot tubs, swimming pools, and tennis courts. If you have a hankering, the ranch you select from among the Association's members may feature trail rides, cattle roundups, photography workshops, overnight camping, even hunting and fishing.

ELDERHOSTEL, 75 Federal St., Suite 400, Boston, MA 02110, tel. (617) 426-7788; or, for Canadian residents: Elderhostel Canada, 33 Prince Arthur Ave., Suite 300, Toronto, ON M5R 1B2, tel. (416) 964-2260. A program developed to provide student travel opportunities and privileges for senior citizens, Elderhostel also offers bicycle tours, treks, cross-country skiing, and other active trips. But you have to be at least 60 years old to participate. (See pages 152–154.)

HAWAIIAN EXPERIENCE, P.O. Box 1874, Kihei, HI 96753, tel. (800) 344-8496 or (808) 874-1929. Bypass Waikiki and downtown Honolulu for the *real* Hawaii, Old Hawaii, which you can see and experience while bicycling, hiking, or sailing by. Depending upon the program, you'll explore Maui or the Big Island on mountain bike, with ample opportunity to swim and snorkel in cool, clear pools, as well as relax on the perfect beaches. Accommodations are according to your budget, from bed and breakfast houses to luxury hotels, and all meals and snacks are included.

THE NATURE CONSERVANCY, 1815 N. Lynn St., Arlington, VA 22209, tel. (703) 841-5300, fax (703) 841-1283 or (703) 841-4880. In addition to its wildlife and wilderness programs (see pages 96–98), The Nature Conservancy has physically challenging trips by dog sled, raft, sea kayak, etc.

NEW ENGLAND BICYCLE TOURS, Box D, Randolph, VT 05060, tel. (800) 233-2128, offers cycling and canoeing holidays from May through September to Cape Cod and the Islands, Prince Edward Island, the Maine coast, or backroads Vermont. Most trips are leisurely paced—though more difficult and challenging routes are available—and allow you to combine biking with canoeing. There are also walking tours, cycle and sail programs, sea kayaking, and whitewater canoeing. Trips range from weekenders to seven-day journeys. Accommodations and meals are at classic, charming country inns.

NEW ZEALAND ADVENTURES, 11701 Meridian Avenue N., Seattle, WA 98133, tel. (206) 364-0160. Mark Hutson liked living and growing up in Hawaii, but he absolutely fell in love with New Zealand. So much so that he runs a one-man operation out of his house in Seattle that guides small groups in unusual adventure treks and kayak journeys that run between December and April. Most kayak journeys are down river or over lakes, but Hutson has an unusual trip that island-hops in the Tasman Sea through the 100-square-mile Marine Park, stopping at aboriginal Maori archeological sites, old lighthouses, or beautiful bays. You can bathe at the campsite's shower, or you can wash yourself in crystal-clear streams or even waterfalls. The food is all locally bought, and everyone pitches in with camp chores. You can bring or rent a sleeping bag, tent, or snorkel gear, but New Zealand Adventures provides everything else. And if the prospect of kayaking about the ocean is a little daunting, there's a tamer tour that combines kayaking with a 36-foot yacht.

OXYGEN EXPEDITIONS, Av. Presidente Vargas, no. 482/60 andar Centro, Rio de Janeiro, CEP 20040, Brazil, tel. 011-021-263-0864. Oxygen Tours conducts one-day and overnight tours for small groups to jungle areas near Rio de Janeiro. Most of the walks are easy and slow-paced, and afford opportunities to swim or sunbathe. The star attraction is the jungle itself, and participants are shown a wealth of detail about the flora and fauna by expert guides who speak English. All meals are included, and on the overnight walks, participants stay at simple but clean and comfortable "pousadas."

RASCALS IN PARADISE, 650 Fifth St., Suite 505, San Francisco, CA 94107, tel. (415) 978-9800, fax (415) 442-0289. Rascals, a division of Adventure Travel Express, offers tour packages for families that makes available both adults' and kids' time off on their own adventures and time together. Scuba diving is their specialty, but they also have rafting, kayaking, camping, farm stays, and other programs in the Pacific, Caribbean, United States, Canada, and elsewhere.

SHERI GRIFFITH EXPEDITIONS, P.O. Box 1324, Moab, Utah 84532, tel. (801) 259-8229, fax (801) 259-2226. A small, woman-owned company with a highly commendable commitment to the environment, Griffith Expeditions offers soft adventure whitewater rafting in the United States and abroad. All waste (including human) is brought out of the wilderness and recycled, food is bought locally, and containers are reused. What makes it a soft adventure is that the guides take care of everything, including paddling, cooking, and cleaning. In addition, they have style, such as serving wine with dinner. Prices are very competitive. Trips for women only are available. Sheri Griffith is on the Secretary of the Interior's Bureau of Land Management Advisory Council.

TOUR DE CANA, P.O. Box 7293, Philadelphia, PA 19101, tel. (215) 222-1253. An outgrowth of an organization called "Bikes Not Bombs" (which supplied more than 2,000 bikes to Nicaragua since 1987 in order to break the American trade embargo), Tour de Cana offers bike trekking in Jamaica, Costa Rica, Honduras, Nicaragua, and the U.S.S.R. with a social, cultural, and political spin. Only local hotels, pensiones, and restaurants are patronized; local buses or boats are used to transport bikes long distances or over water; and bilingual natives are used as guides. You can use your own bike or buy one at nearly wholesale prices. Besides the pedal-yourself reality tour, there are lots of opportunities to swim and sightsee.

VERMONT BICYCLE TOURING, Box 711, Bristol, VT 05443, tel. (802) 453-4811. Cycle through the beautiful Vermont countryside and stay at some of the finest New England country inns. The cuisine is superb, with even optional gourmet picnic lunch baskets available for munching on the way. Prices are surprisingly reasonable, and fly/cycle packages are available. There's also a Sail & Cycle program where participants sail and sleep on a 114-foot windjammer schooner on Lake Champlain, as well as comparable tours in California, New Zealand, and England.

VOYAGERS INTERNATIONAL, P.O. Box 915, Ithaca, NY 14851, tel. (800) 633-0299 or (607) 257-3091, fax (607) 257-3699. Among its various wildlife expeditions and nature tours, Voyagers has a very unusual trek through Kenya with Maasai warriors. (See pages 101–104.)

THE WAYFARERS, 166 Thames Street, Newport, RI 02804, tel. (401) 849-5087, fax (401) 848-5818. One of the more endearing British traditions is a walk through the countryside. Writers from Chaucer to Dickens to Hardy have recounted the joys of tramping through moor or field or highland, past historic ruins and ancient abbeys, sleeping villages, and magnificent great houses. The six-night tours offered by The Wayfarers reveal a lovely rural England, far from the madding crowd, that few tourists ever see. You'll meander a leisurely 10 miles a day (all your luggage will be transported from place to place, so you won't have to carry anything but your camera), dine at out-of-the-way inns and pubs, spend your evening in the company of fellow travelers and friendly locals, and sleep in thatched cottages, charming country inns, or small hotels. You'll be accompanied by a guide who will point out places of interest and spin stories related to the land you are passing through. If you ever get tired, there will be a van discreetly out of sight that can drive you to your next stop.

Chapter Nine

THE WORLD IS MY CLASSROOM

Vacations for Which You'll Want to Pack Your Mind

▼ ▼ ▼

A FEW WORDS
▼ ▼ ▼

There was a time—which may now seem far in the distant past for many of us—when we couldn't wait until school was finally out. We lived for weekends and holidays, and it felt like forever before we eventually reached the day they handed out our diplomas or sheepskins. And yet, to our surprise, after we had been out in the real world for a few years, many of us found ourselves aching to go back to school. What happened in the interim that changed us from saying when-does-school-end to how-soon-can-I-go-back-again?

Essentially, we now realize that the very act of learning is in itself a pleasure, something to seek for its own sake. Also, we have discovered that those teachers and professors we knew back then really did have much of value to impart to us. There may even be some specific unanswered questions that we wish we had asked when we had access to so many knowledgeable experts.

So now we sit at our desks or benches, waiting for our weekends and holidays, looking forward to going back to school. But our new classes may be halfway around the world, in some museum, in a wilderness park, or even at a legendary university that was out of range of our scholastic qualifications when we were students.

All Green Travel, by its very nature, is a learning experience. However, some tour organizers focus specifically on the educational aspect of travel. With very few exceptions, you don't have to be a college or high-school graduate to participate. In fact, you don't even have to be intellectually oriented, just curious about learning more about the subject involved. You'll have no exams, papers to prepare, or other homework (though most participants tend to enjoy reading on their own). Don't imagine that it's all work and study, either. Most educational programs are interspliced with liberal doses of field trips, sightseeing tours, museum visits, and other pleasant tourist-oriented activities.

In other words, educational travel is simply a good excuse to experience another brand of fun, while at the same time getting something extra for your efforts.

As is to be expected, many colleges, universities, and museums are involved in educational travel. For some, it's an opportunity to make money, such as filling up empty dormitories during the summer break or providing additional income for financially strapped professors. But mostly, they're run as a service to members, alumni, and other interested persons who wish to travel under the aegis of that particular organization or institution. Why? Because they recognize and appreciate its ability to schedule excellent programs, provide expert instruction, and create an atmosphere of friendship and camaraderie with like-minded people who share common points of reference.

Educational-related Green Travel tours and programs may be divided into two distinct categories. The first type makes limited use of travel; it's usually centered around a particular place or campus to which participants from all over the globe may come to learn, such as Oxford University or a rural retreat in Hawaii. Typically, such adult education programs consist of brief but intensive seminars or sessions that may last from several days to a couple weeks. Or they may be training sessions for a particular skill or discipline, such as photography or outdoors mastery; many are designed for those wishing career advancement or college credits.

The other type involves traveling during the program. Such tours are usually wrapped around a specific theme, such as Regency England or Turkish archeological finds. Most consist of a series of lectures and interpretive field trips given by professors, curators, and other experts. However, other study tours may involve learning more about photography, practicing a foreign language, or even doing a little volunteer work.

Incidentally, just because you see a particular university's or museum's name on a brochure, it doesn't necessarily mean that they're wholly responsible for the program. More often than not, such study tours are created and conducted by independent profit-making tour operators and then marketed by the college or museum to its members. However, in many instances, the university or museum provides considerable assistance in setting up the program, as well as furnishing the lecturers and other staff. So don't be dissuaded from considering a particular program because you have found out that your sponsoring organization is only indirectly involved.

Some tours of this type make use of first-class accommodations, even upscale cruise ships, on the premise that you may as well enjoy a little luxury while you're learning. Other programs are offered at what seems like fire sale prices, because the idea is to make them as cheap as possible so people who might be very interested but don't have a whole lot of money could attend.

Locating the educational programs and tours that strike your fancy isn't simply a matter of luck: You have to look for them. The first place to start is with your local museum or alumni society. It doesn't matter if it's a small, provincial institution, because often they're the ones with the most interesting, affordable, and accessible trips. For instance, the natural history museum in the city (since moving out to the country, we don't think of it as *our* city anymore, just *the* city) is not a large, nationally based institution. However, it does offer scores of weekend field trips, summer student programs in Maine and Florida, as well as international tours that have a naturalist's spin on them. A small college is as likely to be marketing educational tours as a large university. Another reason for checking locally first is because it could quickly plug you into part of the Green Travel network close to home, where you may meet neighbors with similar interests. Also, the small local organization may be able to refer you to other people or larger organizations with their own programs.

If the idea of going back to a university for a few days or weeks is appealing, but no program is available that tempts you, call or write the university anyway and ask if you can rent a dorm room. Often, dormitories are left empty over the summer vacation or between terms, and universities will rent them out, sometimes at ridiculously low sums, in order to defray operating expenses. Not only will staying at a dorm be cheaper than staying at a hotel or motel, but you will then have the run of the campus. True, you won't be able to attend classes, but you probably can use the library, look in on the labs, or visit the local museums. Also, universities always have something going on year-round that you may find interesting: teach-ins, seminars, debates, public lectures, interesting entertainment, or just good socializing with students in the junior common room, student union, or favored pubs or campus hangouts.

BERLITZ STUDY ABROAD
▼ ▼ ▼

Berlitz was and is the first name in language lessons. Over a century ago, Maximilian Berlitz established the method of teaching a second language the way you learned your first—by hearing it and living with it. You don't translate but learn to think in the other language. Berlitz has been at it for quite a long time and continues to be the language school of choice of diplomats, world leaders, and corporations. In fact, among its illustrious students was none other than Czar Nicholas I, and one of its more noteworthy instructors was Leon Trotsky! (History does not record if they took classes together, however.)

What makes Berlitz particularly inviting is that they have 240 schools in 25 countries, so you have a wide choice of destinations where you may study. Then, when you return, there may be a Berlitz school near you to continue the program. In addition, youth programs are available for students 14 to 17 years old.

There are also a variety of instruction methods, ranging from private one-on-one tutorials to group study, semiprivate instruction to business-oriented learning. You may tailor a program—and the price—according to where you wish to study, what method of learning you wish to use, and the kind of accommodation in which you want to stay. Berlitz also offers, in conjunction with a tour operator that specializes in bicycle tours of France (Travant International), a special program that combines language lessons with seeing and biking through the countryside like a native. And, as described on pages 235–237, Berlitz conducts French classes on board the Paquet cruise ship *Mermoz* during its transatlantic crossings.

DESTINATIONS: Quebec, Guadalajara (Mexico), Germany, England, Scotland, Spain, France, Italy, Quebec, Belgium, Finland, Italy, Netherlands, Norway, Portugal, Spain, Sweden, Switzerland, Argentina, Brazil, Chile, Colombia, Venezuela, Japan, Thailand, Egypt

SEASON: All year

LENGTH OF PROGRAMS: 1 to 4 weeks

ENROLLMENT: 3 to 10 students per group class; private and semiprivate instruction is available.

TOTAL COST: $641 to $2,517 per week

COST PER DIEM: $92 to $360

TAX DEDUCTIBLE?: No. However, a portion may be deducted if learning the language directly affects your career

COST INCLUSIVE OF: 5 lessons per day (25 per week), 3 hours' morning instruction on the French bicycle tour, accommodations, meals (breakfast on some programs, all meals on others), course materials, airport pickup/dropoff (on some programs)

COST EXCLUSIVE OF: Air transportation, airport pickup/dropoff (on some programs), some meals, optional instruction cassette tapes, optional sightseeing

AMENITIES, FACILITIES, AND REALITIES: Berlitz will arrange accommodations in homestays, hotels, pensiones, or boarding houses, which may or may not include breakfast and/or other meals. Most rooms include private bath. Don't expect to hear English too often (if at all) when you are studying with a Berlitz instructor. The idea is for you to become immersed in the language you are studying.

CONTACT: Berlitz Study Abroad, 293 Wall St., Princeton, NJ 08540, tel. (609) 924-8500. Fax (609) 528-8908. Or, for the French language bicycle tour of France, contact Travent, P.O. Box 305, Waterbury Center, Vermont, 05677-0305, tel. (800) 325-3009.

CENTRO LINGUISTICO CONVERSA
▼ ▼ ▼

One of the basic problems that anyone has when trying to learn a foreign language is that, while the classroom may provide excellent opportunities to be immersed in the language, the minute you go into the real world there is no reason to remember what you learned. Dave Kaufman, the New York-born director of Conversa, understands these limitations from a very pragmatic background. For six years, he served in the Peace Corps as Language Coordinator for the training programs in Puerto Rico and Costa Rica. Now, he heads a small private school in Costa Rica that teaches Spanish (and English) as a second language—Centro Linguistico Conversa.

Conversa may start out rather traditionally—in classrooms. But that's where any similarity ends. Because when they leave the classroom, participants are surrounded by a beautiful and inviting Spanish-speaking society. Everywhere they turn, for recreation, sightseeing, shopping, etc., they must continue to practice their new language skills. Like the other language schools mentioned in this book, Conversa arranges for the students to stay in private homes, rather than dormitories where the temptation would be great to fall back into their native tongue. Obviously, this also gives students the opportunity to learn about the local culture, firsthand, from their host family. However, it is possible to also stay in the school's lodge, if you prefer.

Conversa has two basic programs: a four-week intensive language course and the two-week "TWIST." TWIST stands for Two-Week Intensive Spanish & Touring. In addition to 25 hours of Spanish classes, TWIST includes two overnight beach trips (to the Atlantic and the Pacific), a yacht cruise, and other excursions. The four-week course provides 110 hours in a classroom, with time off (mostly on weekends and evenings) to explore on your own.

DESTINATIONS: Costa Rica

SEASON: All year

LENGTH OF PROGRAMS: 2 weeks or 4 weeks

ENROLLMENT: 6 to 12 participants

TOTAL COST: For 4-week program: $1,636 (individual), $3,049 (married couple); for the 2-week TWIST program: $2,013 (per person)

COST PER DIEM: $54 TO $144

TAX DEDUCTIBLE?: No, unless you are a teacher seeking to advance your accreditation or in some similar situation in which learning Spanish would be directly related to professional advancement. Then, a portion may be deductible.

COST INCLUSIVE OF: Lodging with a private family, three meals a day, transportation between your host's home and the school, use of the recreational facilities at the school, Spanish language classes, text materials (except dictionary), transfers to and from the airport, laundry. TWIST also includes tours and cultural events.

COST EXCLUSIVE OF: Transportation to Costa Rica, excursions other than those arranged for the group, dictionary

AMENITIES, FACILITIES, AND REALITIES: The small hilltop campus is about 10 miles west of San Jose, the capital of Costa Rica. Among its facilities are a dining hall, lounge, 12 indoor and 4 outdoor classrooms, volleyball court, basketball court, tennis backboard, ping pong tables, solar-heated showers in a bathhouse, library, meeting room (with TV and VCR), swimming pool, and hammocks. During the week, you'll have breakfast and dinner with your host family and lunch at school. On weekends, all three meals may be taken with your family. For an additional $150 per week, you may stay in the school's lodge, rather than with a private family. There are no entrance requirements or age limits, nor do you need to know any Spanish. On your first day, you will be placed in classes according to your current ability (if any) in Spanish. When asked how much a student will learn, Conversa sent us a brochure that stated, "If you come down to Costa Rica as a rank beginner, . . . then by the end of the four-week cycle, you'll be at the 'survival level.' . . . You'll be able to form simple, correct sentences. . . . If you come to Costa Rica already at 'survival level,' we will get you to 'limited conversational level.' . . . If you come in at 'limited conversational level,' we will get you to 'complete conversational level.' "

CONTACT: Centro Linguistico Conversa, Apartado No 17 Centro Colon, San Jose, Costa Rica, tel. directly 011-506-21-7649. Fax 011-506-33-2418. Or, contact their U.S. rep, Dr. Brian Adams, tel. (800) 292-9872.

CUERNAVACA CENTER FOR BILINGUAL MULTICULTURAL STUDIES
▼ ▼ ▼

Cuernavaca is a Mexican suburban town that is very popular among Americans and Europeans. So, it should come as no surprise that the town has become known for its various schools that specialize in teaching Spanish as a second language.

Like the Centra Linguistico Conversa in Costa Rica, the Center for Bilingual Multicultural Studies (CBM) teaches Spanish by total immersion in the language. In addition, classes are held on Latin American history and culture in Spanish. The subjects include: History of Mexico, Basic Concepts for Studying Latin America, the Mexican Political System, Understanding the Mexican Mystique, Mural Art in Mexico, and Two Mexicos: Urban and Rural. For the sake of Spanish beginners, the teachers attempt to speak slowly and take the time to explain difficult phrases. The Spanish language is taught in formal classes for three hours a day. Five more hours may be devoted to other classes, private tutorials, or recreational activities and touring. College credit is available.

DESTINATIONS: Mexico

SEASON: All year

LENGTH OF PROGRAMS: A minimum of 2 weeks, with some beginner students enrolling for as long as 12 weeks

ENROLLMENT: 100 to 350 students in the school, no more than 5 students per class

TOTAL COST: $100 registration fee plus tuition of $140 per week

COST PER DIEM: $27 for a 2-week program

TAX DEDUCTIBLE?: No, unless you are a teacher or other professional furthering your career

COST INCLUSIVE OF: Classes, biweekly fiesta, attending physician, daily transportation between your host's home and the school

COST EXCLUSIVE OF: Transportation to the school (a taxi from the Mexico City airport costs about $50), lodging, meals, excursions, textbooks

AMENITIES, FACILITIES, AND REALITIES: Housing is not included in the price that you pay to CBM, but they do offer a variety of reasonably priced options that include meals. For $10 a day, you can stay with a lower-middle-class Mexican family, at two to a room, sharing a bathroom with the entire family. For $15 a day, you can stay with an upper-middle-class Mexican family, have a private room and a semi-private bathroom. These upper-middle-class families usually have servants; some have swimming pools and washing machines. The mothers of the household have to take classes in grammar, conversation, and culture, so that they can add to your experience. That means that they also tend to be intellectually alert and not just renting out rooms for the money. You can choose, instead, to stay in a one- or two-bedroom private apartment or bungalow for $450 to $600 a month. Students must be at least 15 years old, but if they are younger than 18, they must have a letter indicating their parents' written consent for them to go to Mexico. There is no upper age limit. CBM has 27 classrooms, a language lab, swimming pools, an outdoor cafe, a doctor on the premises, and a library. Each session of classes starts on Monday, with an orientation program the previous Saturday. CBM requests that students arrange to arrive on Thursday or Friday. In conjunction with the Experiment in International Living (see page 198), a post-study plan is offered. After your time at the school, you can spend a week or two with a Mexican family somewhere else in Mexico for about $100 a week.

CONTACT: Center for Bilingual Studies, 3133 Lake Hollywood Dr., P.O. Box 1860, Los Angeles, CA 90078, tel. (800) 426-4660 or (213) 851-3403.

ELDERHOSTEL
▼ ▼ ▼

Elderhostel began back in 1975, with the idea that the young shouldn't be the only ones to enjoy the advantages of student life and student travel. So, universities, colleges, research institutes, and museums throughout the United States and Canada were convinced to offer one-week courses for senior citizens. Participants usually stay in dormitories or similar student housing, eat student cafeteria-type food, enjoy the privileges of campus extracurricular activities, and study three subjects daily. Of course, you can take as few as one class a day, but up to three classes daily are available.

Courses are wide-ranging: the cultural history of the early people of the Athabasca River valley in Alberta's Rocky Mountains; the geology of the Grand Canyon; creative writing workshops; Native Americans of Arizona; nature photography; astronomy; women in art history; cross-country skiing; war and culture; birds of the Berkshires; computers; understanding tidal wetlands; Tai Chi; anthropology; Yiddish; etc. In other words, just about any subject that can be taught is available somewhere among the hundreds of Elderhostel classes. What's more, all you have to do is enjoy learning. There are no papers to write, no exams to study for, and no homework (though most Elderhostel students do tend to do a lot of reading). Nor are there entrance requirements; you can even be a high-school dropout.

A variation on the typical Elderhostel programs are the Intensive Study programs. They offer a more in-depth approach to the classroom experience, usually concentrating on a single subject, involving homework and/or the completion of some project, and generally providing less time for recreational activities. Another type of program is the RV Elderhostel, for which you must bring your own housing: a recreational vehicle, a trailer, or a tent.

In addition, Elderhostel offers programs in conjunction with educational institutions throughout the world. The international programs are more expensive, longer, and include more sightseeing. But the basic concept is the same— to give mature people who love to learn a chance to return to school, if only during their vacation.

DESTINATIONS: Universities, colleges, and museums in all 50 of the United States, the 10 Canadian Provinces, plus Australia, Austria, Bahamas, Bermuda, Belgium, Brazil, China, Costa Rica, Denmark, England, Egypt, Finland, France, Galapagos, Germany, Great Britain, Greece, Hungary, Iceland, India, Israel, Italy, Jamaica, Japan, Kenya, Mexico, Nepal, the Netherlands, New Zealand, Norway, Polynesia, Spain, Sweden, Switzerland, Thailand, Turkey, Uruguay, U.S.S.R.

SEASON: All year

LENGTH OF PROGRAMS: U.S. and Canada: 1 week; International: 3 to 4 weeks

ENROLLMENT: 8 to 45 participants; average is about 30.

TOTAL COST: U.S. and Canadian programs: $230 to $315; Alaska and Hawaii: $325 to $807; International: $1,057 to $5,789; some financial assistance is available.

COST PER DIEM: U.S. and Canadian programs: $33 to $45; Alaska and Hawaii: $46 to $115; International: $55 to $357

TAX DEDUCTIBLE?: No

COST INCLUSIVE OF: Meals, lodging, five days of classes each week, course-related field trips, extracurricular activities. Plus, on the international trips, air transportation (except to Mexico, Jamaica, and Bermuda), course-related excursions, admission fees, some evening entertainment, limited insurance.

COST EXCLUSIVE OF: Transportation to the U.S., Canada, Mexico, Jamaica, and Bermuda programs; airport or departure taxes; additional excursions

AMENITIES, FACILITIES, AND REALITIES: As with any student travel, Elderhostel's purpose is to make educational travel inexpensive and accessible. Therefore, don't look for luxury. Though some programs do offer private bathrooms and other amenities, most involve staying in dormitories, sharing bathrooms and showers, eating communally, and generally returning to the life of a college student. Access for the disabled varies with each host institute. Some classrooms are outfitted with equipment for the hearing-impaired. (Full descriptions of each facility are available, so you know exactly what you are getting into.) Of course, you also have the use of other student facilities on campus, including social activities, recreational facilities, and cultural events. Depending upon the campus, that could mean tennis courts, swimming pools, film festivals, dances, etc. Some host institutes allow participants to sign up for consecutive weeks, but that may mean paying a small additional fee for any extra days between the sessions during which you would want to stay in the provided accommodations. Participants must be at least 60 years old, though a companion of an eligible individual may be as young as 50. Large tabloid-type catalogs are printed several times a year and are available free for the first year. If you don't go on an Elderhostel trip in that first year, then the catalogs cost $15 per year in the U.S., slightly more outside the U.S.

CONTACT: Elderhostel, 75 Federal St., Suite 400, Boston, MA 02110, tel. (617) 426-7788. Or, for Canadian residents: Elderhostel Canada, 33 Prince Arthur Ave., Suite 300, Toronto, ON M5R 1B2, tel. (416) 964-2260.

INSTITUTE OF NOETIC SCIENCES
▼ ▼ ▼

According to the *Oxford English Dictionary*, noetic refers to those phenomena that are "pertaining to the mind or intellect, . . . purely intellectual or abstract." The Institute of Noetic Sciences is a research and education foundation that explores those esoteric questions that relate to the power of the mind and, by extension, the human spirit.

The trips they sponsor seek answers to age-old problems, as well as to the modern ones, in ancient arts, religions, and traditions. For instance, their trip to the Himalayan kingdoms of Bhutan, Sikkim, and Ladakh is a study tour that focuses on Buddhism. But it also visits with a Swedish anthropologist who is working with local people to blend their traditional culture with modern education, "so that people can work on solutions to their economic and environmental problems that offer a model for other developing countries."

Similarly, the INS trip to Kenya includes visiting healers and herbalists, studying the relationship of traditional and modern medicine, exploring how music affects healing, etc. Of course, it also includes safari wildlife excursions.

Other tours include: "Shamanic Journeys of the Southwest" (Native Americans in New Mexico), "Swimming with Dolphins in the Wild" (Bahamas), "A Journey for Buddhist Women" (Thailand), "Healing & Earth Energies" (Mexico), "Music, Dance, Trance, Healers & Orangutans" (Indonesia), etc.

DESTINATIONS: Brazil, Egypt, Kenya, Mexico, Indonesia, Turkey, Brittany, England, Wales, New Mexico, Bahamas, Himalayas, Bhutan, India, Japan, Thailand

SEASON: Throughout the year

LENGTH OF PROGRAMS: 7 to 26 days

ENROLLMENT: 15 to 30 participants

TOTAL COST: $1,675 to $5,250

COST PER DIEM: $155 to $309

TAX DEDUCTIBLE?: No

COST INCLUSIVE OF: Air transportation from a U.S. gateway airport, accommodations, most meals, entrance fees, transportation during the tour to group activities, lectures, membership in Flying Doctors Society (during Kenyan trip, see page 79), transfers

COST EXCLUSIVE OF: Transportation to the U.S. gateway airport, some meals, tips for guides and drivers, departure and airport taxes

AMENITIES, FACILITIES, AND REALITIES: Generally speaking, INS attempts to provide the best facilities available in a destination. This will usually (but not always) include private bathrooms. "I tend to go very top first-class, but not luxury," Marguerite Craig of INS told us. "Since we're mostly in Third World countries, I don't want to get into the inexpensive places, because people could get sick." Most tours are essentially bus-based, with a limited amount of walking.

CONTACT: Institute of Noetic Sciences, 475 Gate Five Rd., Suite 300, Sausalito, CA 94965, tel. (415) 331-5650.

InterHostel

InterHostel was designed in the mold of Elderhostel, at a time when the latter had no international programs. Today, Elderhostel has both domestic and international tours, while InterHostel remains only international. Also, InterHostel's lower age limit is younger.

InterHostel is a university-sponsored travel/study program designed for intellectually curious and active adults over 50 years old. The trips are thought-provoking, challenging, and inspiring, covering a wide range of subjects, including the region's history, politics, natural environment, economics, literature, arts, and music. Classroom lectures are interspersed with relevant excursions to places of historic, cultural, or contemporary interest. In addition, you will participate in other events, such as going to the theater, local festivals, and opportunities to meet with residents. While this program is designed for senior citizens, expect to be mingling with young-at-heart individuals who plan to never stop learning.

DESTINATIONS: Mexico, Puerto Rico, Costa Rica, Austria, Czechoslovakia, England, France, Germany, Greece, Hungary, Ireland, Italy, the Netherlands, Norway, Poland, Portugal, Scotland, Spain, Sweden, Switzerland, U.S.S.R., Wales, China, Thailand, Kenya, Australia, New Zealand

SEASON: All year, though specific programs are available for only a few weeks a year.

LENGTH OF PROGRAMS: 2 to 3 weeks

ENROLLMENT: No more than 40 participants per program

TOTAL COST: $1,145 to $1,895

COST PER DIEM: $71 to $126

TAX DEDUCTIBLE?: According to InterHostel, they aren't sure and won't advise about the tax deductibility of their programs. "That's between you and IRS."

COST INCLUSIVE OF: All group educational activities (such as lectures, admission to museums, and performances), ground transportation for group events, tuition, lodging, three meals daily, transfers (for those on group flights)

COST EXCLUSIVE OF: Air transportation (though InterHostel expects that participants will travel to the program on specified flights), personal excursions, arrival and departure taxes, gratuities

AMENITIES, FACILITIES, AND REALITIES: Participants must be at least 50 years old (or over 40, if accompanying someone over 50) and in good health. Programs are strenuous and involve being able to walk at least a mile at a time, to carry your own baggage, and to climb stairs, even several flights, without assistance. However, some programs are less strenuous than others. No provisions can be made for special diets. Accommodations may be in college dormitories or in a hotel. Some programs offer private baths, but others involve shared facilities. Remember, this is a back to school experience, which means that accommodations will usually be spartan and far from luxurious. Sometimes, there isn't even maid service. Their catalogs fully explain what to expect on each program, so there should be no surprises. The basic rule of thumb is if a service or amenity is not specifically listed, then it isn't offered. If you wish to stay in the host country after the program, your airport transfer will not be valid, and InterHostel will not involve itself with any such personal plans, even when you use their travel agent to arrange them. Some programs fill up within a short time after being announced, but registrations are taken until a program is full or up to 30 days prior to departure. Catalogs of travel programs come out four times a year and are free. The University of New Hampshire puts the InterHostel programs together in cooperation with an overseas university or educational institute.

CONTACT: InterHostel, University of New Hampshire, 6 Garrison Ave., Durham, NH 03824-3529, tel. (800) 733-9753 or (603) 862-1147. Fax (603) 862-1113.

THE MAINE PHOTOGRAPHIC WORKSHOPS
▼ ▼ ▼

There is a point at which even the best photographer, amateur or professional, reaches an artistic plateau. Perhaps it's because you need to acquire a new skill like color printing or studio lighting, want more guidance and experience in shooting still lifes or landscapes, or have a desire to break into *National Geographic* or travel magazines. Whatever your reason for wanting to get more out of photography, there's probably a program for you at the Maine Photographic Workshops that will help you grow as a photographer, and perhaps help you turn a serious hobby into a money-making career. And it's fun, too, learning and living in a beautiful, rustic Maine city, and communing and comparing work with fellow photographers.

The Maine Photographic Workshop is universally respected and praised within the photo industry as offering among the best photo and film workshops in the country. Most of the instructors are well-known, successful photographers and photojournalists, and in fact, many of your fellow students may also be working pros. You get to use state-of-the-art or exotic equipment, have access to studios and models, learn tips and tricks that you can't get out of a book or photo magazine, and receive vital, constructive criticism about what's good and what's bad about your photography, and how to make it the best. Incidentally, if you simply are a novice interested in learning how to shoot or get around the darkroom, don't worry, there are classes for beginners, too. On the other hand, there are master classes for established, experienced photographers who wish to move to the top of their field. There are also classes and workshops for film and videotape students who want to become more creative in cinema or television.

DESTINATIONS: Maine

SEASON: Spring to Autumn

LENGTH OF PROGRAMS: 1 to 12 weeks

ENROLLMENT: 12 to 20 students in still photography workshops; 16–40 students in film workshops. Half the programs are designed for working professionals, half for beginners and advanced amateurs. Some workshops and all 12-week programs require portfolio review.

TOTAL COST: Workshops range from $450 to $900 per week, lab fees average $85 per week, accommodations and meals are about $300 to $600 per week. The 12-week programs average $250–$300 per week, lab fees $42–$58 per week. Partial scholarships, financial aid, discounts, extended payments available.

COST PER DIEM: $119 to $226 for workshops, $85 to $137 for 12-week programs

TAX DEDUCTIBLE?: No, unless you are a professional photographer and the purpose is to expand or sharpen your skills. College credits may be arranged.

COST INCLUSIVE OF: Instruction, room and board, most materials, equipment, studio and darkroom use

COST EXCLUSIVE OF: Transfers from airport ($55 round trip), film over amount provided, 35mm camera equipment

AMENITIES, FACILITIES, AND REALITIES: Depending upon cost, accommodations range from motel rooms with private baths to period rooms in Victorian houses with shared baths, bed and breakfasts to three-to-a-room dorms. Because dining is an excellent opportunity to exchange ideas, all students and staff are required to take meals together at The Homestead, a nineteenth-century farmhouse. The campus is scattered about Rockport, but most buildings are within walking distance.

CONTACT: The Workshops, 2 Central Street, Rockport, ME 04856, tel. (800) 356-2618 or (207) 236-8581. Fax (207) 633-6740.

NATIONAL SCIENCE FOUNDATION'S YOUNG SCHOLARS PROGRAM
▼ ▼ ▼

According to Bassam Shakhashiri of the National Science Foundation, "There is an urgent need in the United States to provide opportunities for youngsters with an interest in science, mathematics, and engineering to develop the necessary skills to prepare them for careers in these fields." To this end, the NSF sponsors programs throughout the U.S. in which highly intelligent students entering grades 8 through 12 are able to study and work with scientists in university classrooms, laboratories, and in the field. It's something of an apprentice program, involving the kids in original research while also opening their minds to just what is involved in a scientific career. Heavy emphasis is placed on formal discussions of the ethical issues associated with scientific research.

For instance, Idaho's Foundation for Glacier and Environmental Research has an "expeditionary field sciences program, implemented through research participation [at the Juneau Icefield in Alaska], lectures and seminars and guided by an international faculty and staff. Students are in the field the entire period. Training provided in techniques of field safety and group living in an expedition setting in physically hostile arctic environments." Other programs are much tamer, involving advanced mathematics, chemistry, biology, computer sciences, etc. In 1990, a 15-year-old participant in an NSF program uncovered the first fossil skull of a shatasaur, a prehistoric marine reptile in Oregon.

While some of the programs accept participants from certain regional areas only, most are open to students from anywhere in the United States. Application requirements include: (1) a letter of recommendation from current or recent science or math teacher or counselor; (2) an original short essay by the student; and (3) other personal and educational information. A well-rounded, highly motivated personality is as important as being a good student, according to an NSF spokesperson. But the individual schools set their own requirements for enrollment.

After high-school graduation, NSF Young Scholars may be eligible for other unusual programs. For instance, four are invited to do original research in Antarctica under NSF's auspices during the Austral summer (November to February).

DESTINATIONS: Colleges and universities throughout the United States, including Puerto Rico

SEASON: Mostly summer, some academic year programs, others are year round.

LENGTH OF PROGRAMS: Varies widely, depending upon the specific program. Ranges from a week to a couple of months to seven months.

ENROLLMENT: About 7,500 throughout the country

TOTAL COST: $0 to $1,500; some financial assistance and stipends available, even when there is no program cost.

COST PER DIEM: $0 to $47

TAX DEDUCTIBLE?: No

COST INCLUSIVE OF: Usually only participation in the program

COST EXCLUSIVE OF: Usually registration fees, transportation, room, meals, books, personal expenses, but some programs offer stipends or grants to help to defray these costs.

AMENITIES, FACILITIES, AND REALITIES: The facilities vary extensively depending upon the school, but you can usually expect the type of amenities that are to be found on any university or college campus. Of course, field work such as that which is done in archeology, glaciology, and other such programs may involve much rougher facilities. As a government-sponsored program, the Young Scholars Projects do not allow any discrimination based upon race, color, age, sex, national origins, or physical disabilities. In fact, certain programs have grants specifically designated for physically handicapped students. On the other hand, some programs do place some emphasis on applications from women or minority groups. One limitation established by NSF is that no one secondary school should have greater representation than others within the enrollment balance. So, if a certain secondary school already has a few students in a specific program, it will be harder for another student from that school to get into that program. The application deadline for the summer programs are generally in March, April, or May. For the academic year programs, deadlines are usually September or October. If you are late getting in an application, call the project director; it might be worth your while to apply anyway.

CONTACT: NSF Forms and Publications, National Science Foundation, Washington, DC 20550, tel. (202) 357-7861. Ask for the Directory of Young Scholars Projects. Then, when you have picked a couple that interest you, contact the specific college or university involved in them.

SCHOOL FOR FIELD STUDIES

The SFS offers unusual in-field, hands-on learning opportunities for high-school and college students (16 to 25 years old) who are concerned about the environment. While all the participants aren't necessarily planning careers in ecology, they all want to make some difference about the way the world manages our natural resources.

SFS's classrooms are the very environment being studied. In fact, some of the areas are protected wildernesses that are inaccessible to anyone but scientists, naturalists, and SFS students. Students learn from personal experience about the diversity and complexity of the ecosystem and just how difficult it is to develop and implement plans for saving it. They also learn to work as a member of a team, exploring an exotic locale in unfamiliar surroundings, while developing and testing a scientific hypothesis. Such analytical training can be valuable in just about any career they may choose to follow. (If a student has problems adjusting to this new kind of situation—team studies and scientific inquiry—instructors will work with him or her on a one-to-one basis to help the youngster better integrate into the group.) Finally, when their work is done, they share in the satisfaction of achieving a better understanding of important, highly relevant problems. In fact, data from the students' projects is used by research professionals in their ongoing studies.

SFS offers 13 to 14-week semester programs or 1-month summer courses. Some of their courses include: Humpback Whale Ecology; Tropical Deforestation; Threats to Biological Diversity; Coral Reef Management; Biology and Behavior of Bottlenose Dolphins; Ecology of Bald Eagles; and Primate Ecology and Conservation. All courses are accredited by Northeastern University.

SFS programs stress academic accomplishments as well as research. There are reading assignments and personal projects that must be completed. The work is interesting, even exciting, but it is work that requires each member of the team to do his or her share.

DESTINATIONS: Colorado, Puget Sound (Washington State), Alaska, North Carolina, Baja California, Belize, Ecuador, Costa Rica, Australia, Turks and Caicos, Kenya, North Atlantic Ocean

SEASON: Summer or spring and fall semesters

LENGTH OF PROGRAMS: Summer programs: 4 to 6 weeks; semester programs: 13 to 14 weeks

ENROLLMENT: Summer programs: 15 students per team; semester programs: 24 to 30 students per course

TOTAL COST: Summer programs: $1,990 to $2,980; Semester programs: $8,550. Scholarships or interest-free loans are available, based on need.

COST PER DIEM: Summer programs: $71 to $91; semester programs: $87 to $94

TAX DEDUCTIBLE?: No

COST INCLUSIVE OF: Tuition, food, cooking equipment, tents, all research and scientific equipment, ground transportation during the program

COST EXCLUSIVE OF: Transportation, sleeping bags, backpack, scuba gear (if appropriate), medical insurance (required for acceptance)

AMENITIES, FACILITIES, AND REALITIES: Summer course students must be at least 16 years old, having finished at least grade 11. The semester students must be at least 18 years old and have taken at least one college-level biology or ecology course. A medical form must be filled out and signed by the student's physician. The facilities vary with each project. For instance, at the Center for Rainforest Studies in Australia, where you might study Patterns of Ecological Diversity, students stay in dormitory cabins. The Center for Marine Resource Studies in Turks and Caicos, where you might study Coral Reef Management, has rather comfortable accommodations with private bathrooms and ceiling fans. And The Center for Wildlife Management Studies in Kenya offers walled tents with thatched roofs, where students sleep on foam mattresses. Students may be required to camp out for some programs.

CONTACT: The School for Field Studies, 16 Broadway, Beverly, MA 01915-4499, tel. (508) 927-7777.

SHOALS MARINE LABORATORY
▼ ▼ ▼

The New England shoreline has long been recognized for its powerful, untamed beauty. In the midst of this dramatic seascape, with its profusion of marine life, is Shoals Marine Laboratory, an educational research station cosponsored by Cornell University and the University of New Hampshire. Shoals is on 95-acre Appledore Island, a stark spit of land that's six miles off the Maine and New Hampshire shore. As a Registered Historic Site, as well as a State of Maine Critical Natural Area, Appledore remains a pristine, valuable refuge for a wide variety of wildlife. Among the many critters that congregate on and around Appledore are: gulls, herons and more than 125 species of pelagic and inland birds, harbor seals, whales, porpoises and dolphins, and the fascinating microscopic inhabitants of innumerable tidal pools.

But what makes Shoals really exciting are the opportunities for students, adults, and even children to study marine science at one of the premier facilities in the country. Imagine classes with some of the top experts in the field. Class may mean taking off with them on research trips to bird rookeries, to study tidal pools, on boats that head out to sea or to other islands, or underwater to scuba dive or snorkel among the very life you just learned about.

There are two categories of classes: those designed for college credit and the noncredit adult education programs. You need no previous experience or academic standing to sign up for noncredit courses. All they require is a curiosity about the marine environment and a desire to learn. On the other hand, it is possible for a college student to take as much as a full semester of credits in one summer, which represents a bargain in education costs. Students seeking college credit are screened according to their academic background. Adults who wish to audit the credit courses are accepted without screening if space is available.

Noncredit courses include: Nature Photography; Birds, Islands, and the Sea; Sperm Whales and Oceanic Dolphins; and Ecology of the Gulf of Maine.

Credit courses include: Adaptations of Marine Organisms; Field Marine Science; Ecology of Animal Behavior; Coastal and Oceanic Law and Policy; Archaeology Underwater; Marine and Coastal Geology; Underwater Research; and Marine Biology for Teachers.

DESTINATIONS: Appledore Island, off the New England coast

SEASON: Summer

LENGTH OF PROGRAMS: Noncredit courses: 2 to 6 days; credit courses: 7 to 28 days

ENROLLMENT: Limited to 60 participants on the island at any one time. Classes range in size, depending on the subject, from 10 to 40, with the largest class being an introductory program. The average class has 15 to 20 students. However, if Dr. John Heiser, the director, feels that a credit program is too important not to run, he may allow it to be subsidized for as few as 4 to 6 students.

TOTAL COST: Noncredit courses: $115 to $725; Credit courses: $550 to $1,895; 10% discount available to students for credit courses over the second course. Also, some financial aid is available to students taking credit courses.

COST PER DIEM: Noncredit courses: $58 to $149; credit courses: $32 to $98

TAX DEDUCTIBLE?: No, unless the course(s) may be shown to be directly related to possible professional advancement, such as for biology teachers.

COST INCLUSIVE OF: Tuition, lodging, 3 meals a day (2 meals on Sunday), all required field trips, 1 round-trip ferry ticket

COST EXCLUSIVE OF: Transportation to the ferry (at Portsmouth, New Hampshire), texts, extra trips to the mainland (about $8 round trip), optional whale watch and fishing trips (about $15 to $25 per person)

AMENITIES, FACILITIES, AND REALITIES: The island is an isolated, somewhat self-sufficient facility. It generates its own electricity, processes its sewage, and has a limited amount of fresh water. Access to the mainland is by scheduled ferry, in the summer only. Participants stay in double-occupancy rooms in dormitories, with shared toilets. Showers are in another building. (But given the limited supply of fresh water, saltwater bathing is encouraged as a substitute for frequent showers.) A grant that was received recently may soon provide for housing with private toilets. Dining is communal, prepared by the kitchen staff. Other facilities on the island include: three laboratories, lecture halls, photographic darkroom, library, and infirmary. Several research vessels and inflatable boats are used. Participants should be fit enough to walk about on rugged terrain and may be asked to assist in portering supplies and luggage between the ferry dock and a vehicle. The noncredit programs are open to anyone over the age of 12, though students under 18 years old must be accompanied by an adult. Any course involving scuba diving requires that you be a certified diver.

CONTACT: Shoals Marine Laboratory, G-14Y Stimson Hall, Cornell University, Ithaca, NY 14853, tel. (607) 255-3717. For other adult programs of interest, contact Cornell Adult University, 626B Thurston Ave., Ithaca, NY 14850, tel. (607) 255-6260.

SMITHSONIAN INSTITUTION

The number one tourist attraction in Washington, DC, isn't a White House tour or the Visitors Gallery in the Capitol Building. Instead, it's an hour, an afternoon, a week, a lifetime exploring what is unquestionably the biggest, best, and most diverse museum in the entire world: the Smithsonian. Sprawled over the Mall in Washington, DC, the Smithsonian's buildings offer an incredible diversity of exhibits ranging from natural history to aviation and space. But more than being merely a gigantic collection of sterile exhibits, the Smithsonian is a living, growing organization with more than a million members, a first-rate monthly magazine, scores of research projects, numerous educational programs, and a division that offers its associate members incredibly interesting Green Travel trips and tours.

Basically, there are four different types of educational trips that the Smithsonian features. The first kind, called Smithsonian Seminars, are relatively inexpensive, short four to six-day programs that make use of the awesome governmental and cultural resources in and around Washington, DC. For example, one program, Carrier Warfare in the Pacific, is held at the Navy Museum and includes lectures by prominent military historians and professors, question-and-answer sessions with actual veterans, lunches at the officers' clubs, plus a visit to the Marine Air-Ground Museum. Other seminars cover such subjects as Venetian art, broadcast journalism, animal behavior, and twentieth-century furniture.

The second kind, which also are four to six-day programs, is called a study tour. Depending upon the subject being studied—Civil War battles, astronomy, American prehistory, U.S.A.F. air power, etc.—the programs may be situated near Civil War battlefields, famous observatories, national parks, Indian reservations, active volcanos, or even an air force base. It is similar to the seminars in that academics and other experts intersplice lectures and discussions with field trips, museum visits, and other cultural fare.

The third kind is called a research expedition, in which participants volunteer to assist scientists on Smithsonian-sponsored research projects. This might include things like netting and banding birds in Mexico, taking seismic readings from a Costa Rican volcano, prospecting for prehistoric fossils in rural Maryland, collecting data on a Hindu festival in Jamaica, etc. (For further information, see Field Research on page 188.)

Odyssey Tours is the name that Smithsonian gives its fourth type of tour. Often arranged and furnished by a museum-approved third-party tour operator, but designed and marketed by Smithsonian to its members, Odyssey Tours combine comfortable, conventional travel—first-rate accommodations, excellent restaurants, motor coaches, private receptions, etc.—with generous doses of culture and history. Odyssey Tours may offer brief academic-type programs at famous European universities, insightful on-site surveys of national parks, in-the-footsteps literary tramps of famous English or Irish authors, or tracing the steps of the Moorish legacy in Spain.

Almost without exception, a Smithsonian Tour leaves its participants with extraordinary memories, greater appreciation, and increased understanding of the place visited or the subject studied. They offer some of the best educational programs available anywhere, designed and led by top experts and experienced staff.

DESTINATIONS: Washington, DC, Massachusetts, Vermont, New Hampshire, Virginia, West Virginia, Maryland, Pennsylvania, New York, Illinois, South Dakota, Utah, Arizona, New Mexico, Colorado, Washington, Montana, and Wyoming in the U.S., British Columbia, Alberta, Ontario and Quebec in

Canada, Bermuda, Baja, Mexico, Costa Rica, Jamaica, St. Kitts, Panama, Panama Canal, Brazil, Argentina, Paraguay, Chile, Bolivia, Peru, Ecuador, England, Ireland, Hungary, Belgium, Netherlands, Poland, Norway, Scotland, Wales, France, Italy, Greece, Spain, Portugal, Finland, Switzerland, Germany, Yugoslavia, Czechoslovakia, Austria, Lithuania, Latvia, Estonia, U.S.S.R., Turkey, Egypt, Morocco, India, Thailand, China, Hong Kong, Malaysia, Singapore, Bali, Indonesia, Japan, Zimbabwe, Botswana, Kenya

SEASON: All year

LENGTH OF PROGRAMS: 4 days to 22 days

ENROLLMENT: Numbers vary widely according to type and program, but most groups have a minimum of 20 to 25 members.

TOTAL COST: $415 to $7,730. No reductions for children in those programs that permit them.

COST PER DIEM: $83 to $351

TAX DEDUCTIBLE?: Some programs may be partially or wholly tax deductible, especially research expeditions in which participants do some scientific volunteer work. College credits also may be available.

COST INCLUSIVE OF: Seminar or program, tours or field trips, admission fees, accommodations, some or all meals, local transportation or in-country transportation. Some programs also include all air transportation and transfers.

COST EXCLUSIVE OF: Transportation to assembly point, some meals, some transfers

AMENITIES, FACILITIES, AND REALITIES: Smithsonian Tours are available to all associate members ($20 annual fee, which also gets you a subscription to the magazine) on a first-come, first-served basis. Because the most popular ones fill up quickly, early booking is advised. Accommodations range from dormitories (on some research expeditions) to first-class hotels. Often, participants can either upgrade or request more modest quarters than those offered at the standard price. What's included or not included varies widely, so check each individual program for details.

CONTACT: Smithsonian Study Tours and Seminars, Dept. 0049, Washington, DC 20073-0049, tel. (202) 357-4700; or Smithsonian Associates Research Expedition Program, Smithsonian Institution, Dept. 0577, Washington, DC 20073-0577, tel. (202) 287-3210; or Smithsonian Odyssey Tours, Saga International Holidays, 120 Boylston St., Boston, MA 02116, tel. (800) 258-5885.

UNITED STATES SPACE ACADEMY
▼ ▼ ▼

Space Camp for kids is so famous that you probably know almost as much about it as we do. However, did you know that they also have a Space Academy for adults?

Adults can spend a weekend at the U.S. Space and Rocket Center in Huntsville. Activities include astronaut training, such as space walk simulation, experiencing triple gravity in a centrifuge, shuttle takeoff simulation, hands-on mission control, etc. But more than the adventure and the almost-theme-park aspect of this program is the unparalleled opportunity to learn from personal experience about the space program, the men and women behind it, and the equipment and computers that power it.

DESTINATIONS: Alabama

SEASON: All year but January

LENGTH OF PROGRAMS: 3 days

ENROLLMENT: 20 participants per team

TOTAL COST: $450

COST PER DIEM: $150

TAX DEDUCTIBLE?: No

COST INCLUSIVE OF: Lodging, meals, classes, activities, and simulations

COST EXCLUSIVE OF: Transportation

AMENITIES, FACILITIES, AND REALITIES: Participants stay in a dormitory with shared bathrooms. A health form must be completed satisfactorily and sent to the Space Academy before they will accept you into the program. Delta Airlines is the Space Academy's official airline, which is supposed to mean that if you make your reservation through them, you should get a discount. But we suggest comparison shopping before booking your flight.

OTHER COMMENTS: The Space Camp program for kids may be taken in Alabama or Florida. It lasts 5 to 8 days and costs $450 to $675. There is also a program for teachers, plus one for parents with their children.

CONTACT: U.S. Space Academy, One Tranquility Base, Huntsville, AL 35807-0680, tel. (800) 637-7223 or (205) 837-3400. Fax (205) 837-6137.

FURTHER POSSIBILITIES
▼ ▼ ▼

ABERCROMBIE & KENT, 1520 Kensington Rd., Oak Brook, IL 60521-2106, tel. (800) 323-7308 or (708) 954-2944. Famous for their luxurious African safaris, A & K has branched out all over the world to offer tours that focus on human and natural history. Especially noteworthy are their Asian tours. (See pages 81–82 and 221–224.)

THE ARCHEOLOGICAL CONSERVANCY, 415 Orchard Drive, Santa Fe, NM 87501, tel. (505) 982-3278. Archeology doesn't just mean digs in Biblical lands or excavations of ancient Egyptian pyramids. Native American cultures flourished long before the white man ever arrived, and while those peoples have all but disappeared, they left behind a rich legacy of art and architecture, especially in the American Southwest. You can explore those cliff dwellings, petroglyphs, and Spanish missions on educational tours arranged by The Archeological Conservancy. And along the way, you'll have an opportunity to experience the physical beauty of the land that inspired Georgia O'Keeffe and other artists and writers.

ARCHAEOLOGICAL INSTITUTE OF AMERICA, 675 Commonwealth Ave., Boston, MA 02215, tel. (617) 353-9361, fax (617) 353-6550. A large and venerable organization, chartered under the Smithsonian by the U.S. Congress, AIA offers its members a handful of intriguing, thought-provoking "Art Treasures" study tours to places like South India and Algeria. This year's destinations had not yet been determined at the time we went to press. AIA also provides entrée for those individuals who wish to get dirty working on archeological digs around the world. Becoming a member means that they will also keep you informed about some very interesting projects and plug you into a rather intriguing network of individuals. (See also pages 178–180 for a full description of field work opportunities.)

BENNINGTON WRITING WORKSHOPS, P.O. Box W, Bennington College, Bennington, VT 05201, tel. (802) 442-5401. For closet writers who are about to tackle the Great American Novel or wish to launch some sort of literary career, these professional workshops, set amidst the beauty of rural New England, will help sharpen language skills and reveal useful information in how best to go about it.

BHUTAN TRAVEL, 120 E. 56th St., Suite 1430, New York, NY 10022, tel. (212) 838-6382. As its name implies, Bhutan Travel specializes in journeys through the mysterious Himalayan kingdom of Bhutan. The focus is on nature treks and cultural tours, some of which are scheduled to coincide with important festivals.

BUTTERFIELD & ROBINSON, 70 Bond St., Toronto, ON M5B 1X3, Canada, tel. (800) 387-1147 in U.S., (800) 268-8415 in Canada or (416) 864-1354, fax (416) 864-0541. B & R is best known for its physically active programs throughout the world, including biking, rafting, hiking, cross-country skiing, etc. (See pages 119–120 for a profile of B&R.) But they also have educational tours for students, such as "Art in Siena," "Cambridge Enrichment," "Environmental Studies in the Canadian Rockies," "French Language in Nice," and "Spanish Language Homestay."

CENTER FOR AMERICAN ARCHEOLOGY, Box 366, Kampsville, IL 62053, tel. (618) 653-4316. Archeology summer field school for adults and high-school students, from one to five weeks long, in the lower Illinois River Valley.

COUNCIL ON INTERNATIONAL EDUCATIONAL EXCHANGE, 205 East 42nd Street, New York, NY 10017, tel. (212) 661-1414, fax (215) 972-3231. You say that school's almost out and you don't want the kids loafing around the house all summer? You say that you also want your teenagers to learn something interesting or useful, regardless of where they go or what they do? If those are two of your primary objectives, but you're not certain what's available or where to send them, why not peruse the 200 or so programs for kids described in the Council on International Educational Exchange's (CIEE) 1991–1992 edition of *The Teenager's Guide to Study, Travel, and Adventure Abroad.* This $11.95 book (plus $1 shipping) gives almost everything a parent needs to know about available programs, transportation, housing, costs, etc.

CURTIN UNIVERSITY, North American Office, 2 Appletree Sq., Suite 144, 8011 34th Ave. S., Minneapolis, MN 55425, tel. (800) 245-2575. This Australian university, which is located in Perth on the west coast of Australia, maintains a North American office just to assist students who are considering taking a semester or a year of college abroad. They also have study tours in the summer that are rather intriguing.

FOUR WINDS CIRCLE, 7 Annie Lane, Mill Valley, CA 94941, tel. (415) 381-2373. Four Winds Circle is a nonprofit organization that sponsors "Apprentice Programs & Sacred Journeys" to Native American sacred places. These journeys include studying the old arts from the shamans and other elders of the local tribe, sweat lodge ceremonies, and "healing" trips. The organization says that proceeds from the trips go directly to the native people and groups for their participation, plus toward purchasing land to give back to them.

INTERNATIONAL EDUCATION, P.O. Box 9590, Madison, WI 53713, tel. (800) 558-0215 or (608) 274-8574. This private company creates, organizes, and runs many of the marvelous educational and cultural tours sold through colleges, alumni societies, art museums, or other institutions. While they are wholesale packagers and do not sell directly to individual consumers, you may be able to learn from them what colleges or museums may be looking for extra people in order to fill up their minimum quotas. In that way, you may be invited to join a desired tour or program, even if you aren't a member or alumnus.

INTERNATIONAL PEOPLES' COLLEGE, 1 Montebello Alle 1, DK-3000 Helsingor, Denmark, tel. 011-02-21-33-61. In Denmark, the folk high schools are unique campuses designed for the general public to broaden their cultural and intellectual horizons, and to create an environment where people may freely interact with others. In fact, they've become part of the Danish social fabric. What makes this particular folk school different from the others is that everything is conducted in English.

INTRAV, 7711 Bonhomme Ave., St. Louis, MO 63105-1961, tel. (800) 825-2900. Quite a few special-interest groups, museums, and alumni associations use Intrav to design their travel programs. Some of their clients include: the Association of Junior Leagues, Association of Rice Alumni, Norton Gallery & School of Art, the International Oceanographic Foundation, and the Michigan State Medical Society. Though they generally don't market to the public, you can find out from them what organizations are going where. As we've stated before, you don't always have to be a member of an organization to travel with them. Or, if you do, often membership can be easily arranged in some organizations.

JOURNEYS, 4011 Jackson Road, Ann Arbor, MI 48103, tel. (800) 255-8735 or (313) 665-4407. An adventure tour company that specializes in Nepal, among other countries, Journeys has tours that explore cultural traditions and native history. (See pages 128–129.)

KALANI HONUA CONFERENCE & RETREAT CENTER, RR 2, Box 4500, Pahoa, HI 96778, tel. (808) 965-7828. Shamans and kahunas, celestial dances and Dolphin consciousness are all part and parcel of this unusual Hawaiian cultural and spiritual center. Leave your Western preconceptions and prejudices behind. As you stay in simple but comfortable wooden lodges in this remote area surrounded by state and national parks and littered with ancient sacred sites, you'll be able to recharge your spiritual batteries, swim and snorkel in tidal pools or warm springs, bike or walk along scenic coastal roads, or even visit an active volcano. But the high point of a stay at this retreat is the opportunity to learn about and participate in any number of religious, occult, or mystical rites, programs, or happenings.

LEICA/SOCIETY EXPEDITIONS PHOTO TOURS, 3131 Elliott Ave., Suite 700, Seattle, WA 98121, tel. (800) 426-7794 or (206) 285-9400 (ask for the

Leica photo desk). The maker of the finest camera in the world—Leica—sponsors photo classes in some of the most exotic locales on Society Expedition cruise ships. You don't have to own a Leica to participate; just be interested in picking up tips from the experts. Destinations include: New Zealand, Madagascar, China, Korea, U.S.S.R., Indonesia, Greenland, Canadian Arctic, Polynesia, South America, and Antarctica. Not cheap, but superb. (See pages 241–243.)

NATURE EXPEDITIONS INTERNATIONAL, P.O. Box 11496, Eugene, OR 97440, tel. (800) 869-0639 or (503) 484-6529. As mentioned in the write-up on this company on pages 98–99, NEI's tours have a strong focus on education and culture.

NEWFOUND HARBOR MARINE INSTITUTE, Rte. 3, Box 170, Big Pine Key, FL 33043, tel. (305) 872-2331 or (305) 624-0626. Learn about ecology, marine science, biology, and related subjects in the outdoors along wild trails, on the beach, or underwater among the reefs.

NORTHERN LIGHTS STUDIOS, LTD., Box 40, Bonavista Bay, Newfoundland, Canada AOC 1RO. These are two-week workshops in the summer that combine drawing, photography, painting, sculpture, woodworking, rug hooking, or other aspects of fine and craft arts, with ample opportunity to explore the beautiful, rugged Newfoundland coast. The $1,530 cost includes tuition, room and meals with a local family, field trips, boat excursions, and other activities.

OVERSEAS ADVENTURE TRAVEL, 349 Broadway, Cambridge, MA 02139, tel. (800) 221-0814 or (617) 876-0533, fax (617) 876-0455. In addition to its physically active and wildlife tours (see pages 134–136), OAT offers trips that focus on a region's cultural traditions.

OXBRIDGE ACADEMIC PROGRAMS, P.O. Box 250328, Columbia University Station, New York, NY 10025, tel. (800) 828-8349 or (212) 932-3049. Summer school programs for high-school students at Oxford University, as well as in Paris.

PALM BEACH PHOTOGRAPHIC WORKSHOPS, 600 Fairway Drive, Deerfield Beach, FL 33441, tel. (800) 553-2622 has workshops for professionals and novices throughout the year. It's well respected among professional photographers.

PEOPLE TO PEOPLE INTERNATIONAL, 501 E. Armour Blvd., Kansas City, MO 64109, tel. (816) 531-4701, fax (816) 561-7502. In addition to its well-known programs of citizen exchange, PTP has various summer school programs abroad, for college or graduate school credit, which may be audited by nonstudents. (See pages 193–195.)

PHOTOGRAPHY & TRAVEL WORKSHOP DIRECTORY, Serbin Communications, 511 Olive St., Santa Barbara, CA 93101, tel. (805) 963-0430. Sponsored by Eastman Kodak, this annual directory lists hundreds of photography and travel programs that are available in the United States.

POWER PLACES TOURS, 285 Boat Canyon Drive, Laguna Beach, CA 92651, tel. (714) 497-5138, fax (714) 494-7448. Study tours to "places . . . that have proven their power to energize, to heal, to transform the traveler." Destinations include the Great Pyramid, Tibet, Iguassu Falls, Thailand, Peru, and Bali. College credits are available for participants in these tours from the University of Humanistic Studies, San Diego. Also, some of the tours offer "continuing education programs" for health care professionals. Payment plans available to stretch out the cost of the trip over 12 to 36 months.

REDISCOVERY INTERNATIONAL FOUNDATION, P.O. Box 1207, Station E, Victoria, British Columbia, Canada V8W 2T6, tel. (604) 380-1827, fax (604) 380-3999. Your children can experience what it was to live, think, and feel like a Native American by attending one of this nonprofit organization's Rediscovery camps in the U.S. or Canada. There he or she will sleep, eat, play, and work side by side with Native Americans, be taught the old ways and a respect and reverence for nature by village elders, and soak up the folklore and religion. Aside from participating in typical village life, those students who wish will be prepared to undergo the ancient Indian rites of passage from childhood to adulthood. It's a unique learning, growing experience, not only for normal kids but for troubled youth as well.

SCIENCE SERVICE, 1719 N Street NW, Washington, DC 20036, tel. (202) 785-2255. Science Service publishes an annual *Directory of Student Science Training Programs* for high-ability precollege students. The booklet is an important resource for unusual summer, as well as academic year programs.

SENIOR STUDY CENTER, 1301 North Maryland Avenue, Glendale, CA 91207, tel. (818) 242-5263. Learn or improve your Spanish by the total immersion method while staying with an upper-class family in Cuernavaca, Mexico (all meals, private baths, many with swimming pools) upon whom you can practice the language. But it's not all study, since you'll have ample opportunity to visit museums, outlying villages, native markets, even a silver mine, and other interesting sites and attractions.

YALE UNIVERSITY, Association of Yale Alumni, P.O. Box 901-A, New Haven, CT 06520-7407, tel. (203) 432-1952. Like scores of other universities and colleges, Yale has numerous adult seminars on campus and education travel programs that are promoted through the alumni association. However, many of these colleges do not require that you be an alumna or alumnus. In fact, the Yale brochure is addressed to alumni and *friends.* You might wish to contact the college or university in your area (or your alma mater) to find out about their adult education seminars and travel programs. (See listing of other college programs on pages 175–176.)

ZOV Tours, 801 Portola Drive, San Francisco, CA 94127, tel. (415) 641-5689 or (707) 829-3212. ZOV arranges study tours for doctors, nurses, and other health professionals to the U.S.S.R.

OTHER MUSEUMS WITH TRAVEL PROGRAMS
▼ ▼ ▼

ACADEMY OF NATURAL SCIENCES, 19th and the Parkway, Logan Circle, Philadelphia, PA 19103, tel. (215) 299-1054.

ALBRIGHT KNOX ART GALLERY, 1285 Elmwood Ave., Buffalo, NY 14222, tel. (716) 882-8700.

AMERICAN MUSEUM OF NATURAL HISTORY, Central Park West at 79th St., New York, NY 10024-5192, tel. (800) 462-8687.

THE ART INSTITUTE OF CHICAGO, Michigan Ave. at Adams St., Chicago, IL 60603, tel. (312) 443-3616.

BALTIMORE MUSEUM OF ART, Art Museum Dr., Baltimore, MD 21218, tel. (301) 396-6314.

CALIFORNIA ACADEMY OF SCIENCES, Golden Gate Park, San Francisco, CA 94118, tel. (415) 750-7222.

THE CARNEGIE, 4400 Forbes Ave., Pittsburgh, PA 15213, tel. (412) 622-5774.

CHRYSLER MUSEUM, Olney Rd. and Mowbray Arch, Norfolk, VA 23510, tel. (804) 622-1211.

CINCINNATI ART MUSEUM, Eden Park Dr., Cincinnati, OH 45243, tel. (513) 721-5204.

CLEVELAND INSTITUTE OF ART, 11141 East Boulevard, University Circle, Cleveland, OH 44106, tel. (800) 223-6500 or (800) 223-4700 (Ohio only). Summer workshops in art.

COOPER HEWITT MUSEUM, 2 E. 91 St., New York, NY 10128, tel. (212) 860-6868

DALLAS MUSEUM OF ART, 5232 Forest La., Dallas, TX 75244, tel. (214) 987-2772.

DAYTON ART INSTITUTE, P.O. Box 941, Dayton, OH 45401, tel. (513) 223-5277.

DENVER MUSEUM OF NATURAL HISTORY, 2001 Colorado Blvd., Denver, CO 80205, tel. (303) 370-6307.

FIELD MUSEUM OF NATURAL HISTORY, Roosevelt Rd. and Lake Shore Dr., Chicago, IL 60605-2496, tel. (312) 922-9410.

THE FRANKLIN INSTITUTE, 20th and the Parkway, Philadelphia, PA 19103, tel. (215) 448-1200.

HIGH MUSEUM OF ART, 1280 Peachtree St. NE, Atlanta, GA 30309, tel. (404) 898-1152.

METROPOLITAN MUSEUM OF ART, Travel with the Met, 1000 Fifth Ave., New York, NY 10028-0198; or Raymond & Whitcomb, 400 Madison Ave., New York, NY 10017, tel (212) 759-3960.

MINNEAPOLIS INSTITUTE OF ARTS, 2400 Third Ave. South, Minneapolis, MN 55404, tel. (612) 870-3155.

MUSEUM OF COMPARATIVE ZOOLOGY, Harvard University, Cambridge, MA 02138, tel. (617) 589-0364.

MUSEUM OF MODERN ART, 11 W. 53 St., New York, NY 10020, tel. (212) 708-9696.

NATURAL HISTORY MUSEUM OF LOS ANGELES COUNTY, 900 Exposition Blvd., Los Angeles, CA 90007, tel. (213) 744-3350.

NEWARK MUSEUM, 49 Washington St., Newark, NJ 07101, tel. (201) 596-6644.

NEW ORLEANS MUSEUM OF ART, Lelong Ave., City Park, New Orleans, LA 70119, tel. (504) 488-2631.

NORTH CAROLINA MUSEUM OF ART, 2110 Blue Ridge Blvd., Raleigh, NC 27607, tel. (919) 833-1935.

NORTH MUSEUM, P.O. Box 3003, Lancaster, PA 17604, tel. (717) 291-3941.

NORTON GALLERY & SCHOOL OF ART, 1451 S. Olive Ave., West Palm Beach, FL 33401, tel. (407) 832-5194.

ORLANDO MUSEUM OF ART, 2416 N. Mills Ave., Orlando, FL 32803, tel. (407) 896-4231.

PHILADELPHIA MUSEUM OF ART, Box 7646, Philadelphia, PA 19101, tel. (215) 787-5483.

PHOENIX MUSEUM OF ART, 1625 N. Central Ave., Phoenix, AZ 85004, tel. (602) 257-1880.

SAN DIEGO MUSEUM OF ART, Box 2107, San Diego, CA 92112-2107, tel. (619) 232-7931.

SAN FRANCISCO MUSEUM OF MODERN ART, 401 Van Ness Ave., San Francisco, CA 94102, tel. (415) 252-4191.

SANTA BARBARA MUSEUM OF ART, 1130 State St., Santa Barbara, CA 93101, tel. (805) 963-4364.

SCHOOL OF THE ART INSTITUTE OF CHICAGO, 37 South Wabash Avenue, Room 707, Chicago, IL 60603, tel. (312) 899-5120.

THE TEXTILE MUSEUM, 1101 S. Arlington Ridge Rd., Arlington, VA 22202, tel. (703) 920-0228.

TOLEDO MUSEUM OF ART, 2445 Monroe St., Toledo, OH 43620, tel. (419) 255-8000.

UNIVERSITY MUSEUM OF ARCHAEOLOGY & ANTHROPOLOGY, 33rd and Spruce Sts., Philadelphia, PA 19104, tel. (215) 898-9202.

VIRGINIA MUSEUM OF FINE ARTS, 2800 Grove Ave., Richmond, VA 23221, tel. (804) 367-8762.

SOME COLLEGES AND UNIVERSITIES WITH EDUCATIONAL TRAVEL AND ADULT SEMINARS

Scores of universities and colleges have numerous seminars on campus designed for visiting or vacationing adults plus educational travel programs that are usually promoted through the alumni associations. Many of these colleges do not require that you be an alumna or alumnus. For example, the Yale brochure of programs is addressed to alumni and *friends*. San Jose State University is more direct, stating on the cover of their brochure that their programs are "Open to All Adults."

You might wish to contact the college or university in your area (or your alma mater) to find out about their adult education seminars and travel programs. Or, if there is a school you've always dreamed of attending, just call them and ask them to send you their adult education and travel seminar brochures. A good place to check for phone numbers and addresses is your public library.

The following are just a handful of samples of the many colleges and universities that have such programs.

BROWN UNIVERSITY, Summer College, Brown Box 1920, Providence, RI 02912, tel. (401) 863-2474.

CORNELL'S ADULT UNIVERSITY, 626 Thurston Ave., Ithaca, NY 14850, tel. (607) 255-6260.

DARTMOUTH ALUMNI CONTINUING EDUCATION, 309 Blunt Alumni Center, Hanover, NJ 03755, tel. (603) 646-2454.

HARVARD ALUMNI ASSOCIATION, Wadsworth House, Cambridge, MA 02138, tel. (617) 495-5342.

NORTHWESTERN UNIVERSITY ALUMNI COLLEGE, 2003 Sheridan Rd., Evanston, IL 60208, tel. (800) 346-3768 or (708) 491-5250.

PENN STATE ALUMNI VACATION COLLEGE, 409 Keller Conference Center, Pennsylvania State University, University Park, PA 16802, tel. (814) 863-1743.

SAN JOSE STATE UNIVERSITY, Office of Continuing Education, One Washington Square, San Jose, CA 95192-0135, tel. (408) 924-2680.

Chapter Ten

FIELD RESEARCH

Vacation Ideas for the Archeologist or Explorer Within You

▼ ▼ ▼

A FEW WORDS

▼ ▼ ▼

Have you ever fantasized what your life might have been like if only you had gone into archeology? Perhaps, you would have been the one to finally answer the mystery of why the Mayans left Chichen Itza so suddenly. When you watch Jane Goodall's TV documentaries, do you say to yourself, yes, I would love to work with wild animals, quietly, patiently, furthering my own and the world's understanding of the animal kingdom? Do you ever wonder why certain basic rituals evolved independently in just about every human culture? Or is there a mad scientist inside you aching to spend countless hours in a laboratory in search of the unknown?

If you feel that the idea of real adventure has to do with the possibility of finding something that no one has ever seen, or doing something that just might change how the world thinks, then you might be ready to volunteer for some very hard work as a field researcher. There are countless programs that depend on volunteers not only to get their work done but also to finance the projects. And there are thousands of volunteers who have had such a rewarding time giving of themselves during their vacations to such endeavors, they are more than willing to foot the bills.

Of course, you have to be prepared to get dirty, really dirty. And on some of these projects, there are no hot showers nearby. (Though on others, you may have all modern conveniences.) But you will be working side by side with eminent naturalists, scientists, and other researchers, helping them further their work. These are not programs created to teach but ones that are seeking to learn that which is not yet known.

No experience is necessary. Don't worry if you can't tell a shark from a dolphin, or have no idea how to sort pottery shards. All you need is a willingness to learn and a good sense of humor, because field research is not an easy life, regardless of how rewarding it can be.

As Kara Bettigole of Earthwatch said to us, "I would like to emphasize that we are not a travel organization, nor are we part of this new 'ecotour' industry. While most people work on Earthwatch expeditions during their vacation time, Earthwatch is not a vacation, for the volunteers are working each day from dawn 'til dusk."

In the Foundation for Field Research's agreement to volunteer, it is explained, "The volunteer understands that this is a true expedition setting out into the unknown with all the inherent dangers and physical risks that must be associated with and overcome to achieve scientific goals, and that in signing this document accepts full personal responsibility. It is understood that the Foundation for Field Research is not a travel or tour company, but rather a nonprofit public benefit corporation whose purpose is to fund scientific field research through the use of volunteers donating a share of costs and labor."

In other words, you join these programs with the full understanding that anything can and may happen. And you have to accept the risks, just as the explorers of the past did. And just like those explorers, you will be a member of a team that depends on each other. They become closer than family, working together for a common end that could, just possibly, benefit mankind.

ARCHAEOLOGICAL INSTITUTE OF AMERICA
▼ ▼ ▼

The oldest archeological organization in North America (est. 1879) and one of the largest in the world, AIA is chartered through the Smithsonian Institute by the U.S. Congress. "It is dedicated to the encouragement and support of archaeological research and publication, to informing the public about archaeology, and to the protection of the world's cultural heritage." Among its many activities and publications, AIA produces an annual publication called *Archaeological Fieldwork Opportunities Bulletin*.

The *Bulletin* lists literally hundreds of programs, excavations, and field schools throughout the world that have openings for volunteers, students, staff, and other personnel. For many of the programs, no experience is needed. It's not easy work. Nor is there any of the glamour and adventure of Indiana Jones kind of archeology. However, you will participate in a hands-on history lesson such as working at the Anglo-Saxon find at Sutton Hoo in Suffolk, England, or a protohistoric Aleut site in Alaska. Academic credit may be earned.

Also listed in the *Bulletin* are the names, addresses, and phone numbers of various contacts from whom you can learn about additional programs. These include: state archeologists and state historic preservation officers, AIA regional contacts, and other affiliated institutions and related organizations. AIA is one of those large organizations that can connect you to a wide network of individuals and institutions that offer even more opportunities for Green Travel.

For those travelers who don't want to get quite so dirty but want to learn about archeology from the experts, AIA also conducts a series of study tours to historically important areas.

DESTINATIONS: A large percentage of the programs listed are in the United States, but there are also quite a few in Canada, Bermuda, Caribbean, Central America, Mexico, South America, United Kingdom, Europe, Israel and Africa.

SEASON: Most are in the summer, but some are all year.

LENGTH OF PROGRAMS: A couple of days to a couple of months

ENROLLMENT: Varies widely with each program. But if the program you are interested in is filled up, be persistent and keep in touch with the director. Space may open up.

TOTAL COST: Given the large number of different programs in the *Bulletin*, it is not possible to quote specific prices. Some financial aid may be available, especially for students. This kind of Green Travel can be quite inexpensive compared to traditional travel to the same region.

COST PER DIEM: See Total Cost above.

TAX DEDUCTIBLE?: Probably not, according to AIA.

COST INCLUSIVE OF: Varies, but they provide very little other than instruction and tools. Sometimes some meals are provided. Depending upon who is behind the program, insurance may be included.

COST EXCLUSIVE OF: Probably all your living and travel expenses. But you won't be in a situation in which you would tend to spend much money. Generally, in addition to whatever financial contribution to the program that is required, you will have to pay for your own transportation, lodging, and meals, though small per diems are paid a few committed volunteers. If dormitories or other room and board are available through the program, it tends to be quite reasonably priced. Some programs provide free space in nearby campgrounds, but you have to bring your own sleeping bag, etc. Also, if you are going for academic credit, you will have to pay tuition. If they don't provide insurance, it is highly recommended that you purchase some.

AMENITIES, FACILITIES, AND REALITIES: The hours are long and exhausting, and the amenities are few and far between. The luxury programs are those that are close to bed and board lodges. The comfortable ones are near a hot shower. You must be physically fit, intellectually sharp, and emotionally ready to be flexible. If you have all that going for you, you'll learn about the lives of historic or, even, ancient people with an intimacy born of unearthing and putting together the artifacts of their everyday lives.

OTHER COMMENTS: The *Archaeological Fieldwork Opportunities Bulletin* is published annually. At the time this book went to press, the price wasn't set for the 1992 edition of the *Bulletin*. Currently, it is $10.50 for AIA members or $12.50 for nonmembers, including postage.

CONTACT: Archaeological Institute of America, 675 Commonwealth Ave., Boston, MA 02215, tel. (617) 353-9361. Fax (617) 353-6550.

CEDAM INTERNATIONAL
▼ ▼ ▼

CEDAM is a nonprofit field research organization that supports *C*onservation, *E*ducation, *D*iving, *A*rcheology, and *M*useums. All programs involve scuba diving, which means you must be a certified diver. But they will train you for the other skills that you may need. Programs involve collecting exotic fish specimens for aquariums, conducting research and collecting data about specific marine species, working on reef conservation activities (such as installing mooring buoys to keep anchors from tearing up the reefs), taking underwater photographs for guides and documentation, exploring and mapping underwater archeological sites, etc.

For divers, there is probably no more exciting program available, because it transforms you from a leisure-oriented outsider to a member of the elite fraternity of underwater adventurers and researchers. In fact, CEDAM's programs offer up a good argument for learning how to scuba dive—just so you can participate in the on-going research and conservation work.

DESTINATIONS: Belize, Cayman Islands, Galapagos, Australia, the Red Sea and Palau

SEASON: Various programs at different times of year

LENGTH OF PROGRAMS: 1 to 2 weeks

ENROLLMENT: 16 to 20 participants

TOTAL COST: $1,100 to $4,200

COST PER DIEM: $183 to $300

TAX DEDUCTIBLE?: Probably, but be sure to keep a daily journal, and be prepared to be disallowed the expenses for that portion of time that was spent in leisure activities as opposed to research.

COST INCLUSIVE OF: International air transportation from a U.S. gateway airport on some programs, accommodations, transfers, diving, lectures and presentations, most meals (all meals on some programs)

COST EXCLUSIVE OF: International air transportation from a U.S. gateway airport on some programs, domestic transportation to the gateway, tips to dive masters or boat crews, departure and/or cruising taxes, some meals

AMENITIES, FACILITIES, AND REALITIES: Beyond the enjoyable experience of participating in research, CEDAM actually can represent a value-priced diving vacation. To participate, you must be a member, which costs $20 for an initiation fee plus annual dues of $25. Membership privileges include being kept informed about upcoming expeditions and the progress of the various on-going programs. In Belize, you stay on a boat that carries 16 people and has 3 heads (toilets). Australia's boat accommodates 20 people, with 4 heads. In Curacao and the Caymans, you stay in a resort with all the comforts of private rooms with their own bathrooms. The Palau expedition is conducted on a scuba live-a-board boat, which means that the amenities and space are limited. And the Galapagos boat carries 16 people with 3 heads.

CONTACT: CEDAM International, One Fox Road, Croton NY 10520, tel. (914) 271-5365.

EARTHWATCH
▼ ▼ ▼

Can dolphins be taught a language for communicating with humans? Why did the dinosaurs disappear? How can we save the rain forests? How well can ex-captive orangutans be reintegrated back into the wild? Will the first fossil adult australopithicus be found in southern Africa soon, or was the child found a while back a fluke? What is the relationship of traditional Greek costume to social habits and customs? Researchers all over the world devote their careers to finding answers to intriguing questions. But the work is expensive and can't be done alone. Enter Earthwatch.

For the past two decades, Earthwatch has sponsored hundreds of important field research programs by providing vacationing volunteers (15 to 80 years old) with the unique opportunity of being working members of the research teams. These volunteers pay their own way plus share in the cost of the research itself. No experience is necessary, just a good sense of humor and enthusiasm for the project.

The projects cover the following fields: "Rain Forest Conservation & Ecology," "Threatened Habitats," "Art & Archaeology," "Geosciences," "Life Sciences," "Marine Studies," and "Social Sciences." Quite a few of the projects involve direct interaction with and study of wild creatures, such as black bears, Alaskan muskox, koalas, dolphins, red-billed gulls, orcas (a.k.a. killer whales), orangutans, etc. A few programs require scuba diving. Or if you're not interested in wildlife, Earthwatch also has programs that study the cultural or archaeological history of a region, or how to improve the human condition where there is drought or poverty, etc. It is possible to get academic credit through your school or university under the guidance of the Earthwatch researchers.

DESTINATIONS: Earthwatch programs can be found just about anywhere in the world where there are valid questions to be answered and qualified researchers capable of finding the answers.

SEASON: Varies. Something is going on with Earthwatch just about any time of year. The highest percentage of programs are conducted May through August, for the simple reason that many of the researchers are connected to universities where they teach and work during the school year.

LENGTH OF PROGRAMS: 2 to 3 weeks

ENROLLMENT: 2 to 20 volunteers depending on the program's needs, but the groups are usually small. The wildlife programs tend to be smaller (2 to 8) so that the animals aren't scared away, while the archeology programs need more hands (12 to 20).

TOTAL COST: $700 to $2,750; some grants are available for teachers and students.

COST PER DIEM: $57 to $170

TAX DEDUCTIBLE?: According to Earthwatch, yes, or at least a portion of your costs should be, under Section 170 of the Internal Revenue Code, because the organization is a public charity under Section 509(a) of the U.S. tax code. It is also possible that some of your transportation expenses, to and from the project, may be deductible.

COST INCLUSIVE OF: Food, accommodations, equipment and tools

COST EXCLUSIVE OF: Transportation to and from the project site, airport taxes, any side trips

AMENITIES, FACILITIES, AND REALITIES: Of course, accommodations vary, depending upon the location and needs of each project. However, Earthwatch's descriptions of field conditions in its magazine are quite clear on what you can expect. With some programs, you may be camping out for the entire time, sharing cooking responsibilities with the rest of the team. Others offer dormitory-type arrangements with a cook and family-style eating. A few even stay in very comfortable farmhouses, hotels, or modern condos. On a program that is studying medieval sociology, the group stays in the "seventeenth-century manorhouse of Count Cinelli, who presides over dinner most evenings." Projects may or may not have running water, toilets, privacy, etc. But if your criterion for an enjoyable experience is a hot shower or a comfortable dry bed every evening, you will still have quite a few Earthwatch expeditions from which to choose. Earthwatch is a membership-based organization. It costs $25 to join, for which you receive six issues a year of their magazine, in which all their projects are described, plus articles about what various programs have uncovered.

OTHER COMMENTS: Earthwatch is very forthright in disclosing whatever you may wish to know about their programs and your involvement with them. For instance, where does your money go? "Depending on the size and needs of your team, roughly 55 percent goes to field costs; 33 percent to advance costs, reconnaissance, team recruitment, and logistical support; and 12 percent is used for administrative back-up, communications, and post-expedition follow-up." If a specific program catches your interest, you may order a 25 to 75-page Expedition Briefing for $25, which covers "the history of the project, its research mission, background of the principal investigators and staff, expedition goals, field logistics, reference maps, in-country information, and a bibliography of reading materials." Even if you don't want to go on a project, you might enjoy reading a briefing. But if you do eventually sign up, the $25 fee can be applied to your share of the expedition costs.

CONTACT: Earthwatch, 680 Mount Auburn St., Box 403, Watertown, MA 02272, tel. (617) 926-8200. Fax (617) 926-8532.

FOUNDATION FOR FIELD RESEARCH
▼ ▼ ▼

Like Earthwatch, the Foundation for Field Research helps scientists and other researchers fund their projects by finding volunteers who are willing to work as field labor and pay for the privilege. Subjects include: archeology, botany, entomology, folklore, herpetology, marine archeology, historic architecture, marine biology, ornithology, paleontology, prehistoric rock art, primate studies, sea turtle research, wild mammal research.

Unlike many similar programs, all of the Foundation's projects are accompanied by a field manager who handles all the logistics, so that the researchers and volunteers are free to get the real work done. In the same spirit, volunteers are not involved in the cooking or the washing of dishes.

The minimum age of participants is 14; however, those under 18 must supply a work permit from their school, so that the program can comply with labor laws and cover the child under their insurance. There is no maximum age. According to their newspaper, "Your age, lack of formal education, or nonexistent camping experience doesn't matter, because we will have a meaningful job on the project for you. We need you." On the other hand, if you are a scuba diver, skilled photographer or draftsman, or have other talents, certain projects may be specifically looking for you. Academic credit for participation may be arranged through your school or through the San Diego State University, College of Extended Studies.

DESTINATIONS: Arizona, California, Colorado, Connecticut, Montana, New York, Oregon, Texas, Canada, Grenada, Baja California, Africa, Spain, Mexico, Wales, Italy, Germany

SEASON: All year in the United States and various times of year for the other projects

LENGTH OF PROGRAMS: 2 days to 2 months

ENROLLMENT: 5 to 25 volunteers per project, average about 10

TOTAL COST: $170 to $2,433

COST PER DIEM: $48 to $214

TAX DEDUCTIBLE?: According to the Foundation, "The IRS has ruled that reasonable out-of-pocket expenditures for meals, lodging, and transportation incurred incidental to the rendition of your services can be tax-deductible."

COST INCLUSIVE OF: Accommodations, meals (prepared by a cook), ground and water transportation during expedition, most field gear, insurance for work-related injuries, preparatory book, instruction

COST EXCLUSIVE OF: Travel expenses to and from the expedition site, personal items such as sleeping bag or flashlight, recreational activities or side trips, archeological dig kit (for excavations, available from the Foundation for $42)

AMENITIES, FACILITIES, AND REALITIES: Depending upon the project and its location, you may be camping out in the wild, staying in hostels or other dormitory-style accommodations, or even enjoying modern motels. You will be expected to work hard and give your all to completing the project. Specific tasks will be assigned to you by the head investigator, and it will be your responsibility to get them done. On the other hand, some locations have more than one project going on at the same time. You can arrange to move from one to another if you are seeking a variety of experiences.

OTHER COMMENTS: Your share of the expedition costs are spent in generally the following manner: 76 percent in the field; 14 percent booking, advertising, and other expenses involved in finding volunteers; 10 percent administration. You may order a 50 to 75-page preparatory booklet for $18, which describes all that you can expect on a certain expedition. Then, if you join the expedition, you will receive $18 credit toward your cost. In addition, if you subscribe to the Foundation's *Explorer News* ($10/year), which comes out four times a year and describes all upcoming expeditions, you will receive a $75 discount on your expedition. A 50% discount is offered to licensed medical doctors who are willing to work as the expedition doctor; 25 percent for registered nurses. Scholarships are available for students and for teachers (grades 6 to 12). Also, the Foundation is willing to accept volunteer work in their office near San Diego or the contribution of equipment (such as office machinery, field supplies, or vans) in exchange for credit toward participation in expeditions. In other words, if you are in the right place at the right time with the right skills or excess materials, you could conceivably become part of a field research team for little or no money.

CONTACT: Foundation for Field Research, 787 South Grade Rd., P.O. Box 2010, Alpine, CA 92001-0020, tel. (619) 445-9264.

UNIVERSITY RESEARCH EXPEDITIONS PROGRAM

UREP organizes research teams, headed by University of California scientists and teachers, to "investigate issues of human and environmental concern around the world." With labor and money provided by students and other volunteers, they study and try to solve problems in marine biology (scuba), archeology, resource conservation, anthropology, sociology, botany, music, arts, humanities, animal behavior, geology, etc.

For instance, you could join a group in Bali that is studying the cultural context of ceremonial masks. Another is working in the Pakistan Himalayas, to better understand mountain marmots. In East Africa, the Impala displays some unusual grooming habits. And in New Mexico, the Anasazi Indians somehow survived where there is only eight inches of rain per year.

Some of the projects—known as SHARE projects (Science Serving Humanity and Research for the Environment)—are in collaboration with scientists from the host country, especially where the local resources for funding and training are limited. While no experience is necessary, the group leader may select individuals with certain skills over others. Depending on the project, they may be looking for wilderness experience, photography, scuba diving, observational skills, or drawing.

DESTINATIONS: California, Montana, New Mexico, Baja California, Belize, Costa Rica, Ecuador, Galapagos, Bolivia, Colombia, Portugal, Indonesia, Polynesia, Pakistan, East Africa, Mongolia

SEASON: Summer, with some spring programs

LENGTH OF PROGRAMS: 2 to 3 weeks

ENROLLMENT: 6 to 10 participants per project

TOTAL COST: $835 to $1,630

COST PER DIEM: $73 to $136

TAX DEDUCTIBLE?: A portion of your expenses of volunteering may be deductible.

COST INCLUSIVE OF: Meals, lodging, transportation during the expedition, camping and field gear (except for personal items, such as sleeping bags), research equipment and supplies (except diving gear), preparatory information, recommended reading list

COST EXCLUSIVE OF: Transportation to the project assembly point

AMENITIES, FACILITIES, AND REALITIES: Accommodations vary, depending upon the project and its location, from camping in the wilds to staying in cabins, up to the comparative comfort of modest motels. The researchers studying the ruins of a Mayan community in Belize stay in a modern Benedictine monastery retreat. Team members may be required to share in group responsibilities, such as cooking and cleaning. Also, some projects involve challenging hikes on a daily basis, getting up before dawn to work before the midday rains, or other physical inconveniences or challenges. It is strongly suggested that you have a doctor's examination before signing up. In fact, it is required for some programs, especially the underwater ones. For diving projects, you must also be able to prove diving proficiency by being a certified diver, providing a copy of your dive log, and being checked out in a water and equipment evaluation. If you have special dietary needs, you may have to bring your own supplies.

OTHER COMMENTS: UREP offers grants for teachers (kindergarten through grade 12) that may cover a large part of their expedition fee, as well as some of their transportation. Afterward, during the school year, these teachers are assisted in integrating their personal experience into their curriculum. Priority is given to California teachers, but others are considered. Some student scholarships are also available.

CONTACT: University Research Expedition Program, Desk L-02, University of California, Berkeley, CA 94720, tel. (415) 642-6586.

FURTHER POSSIBILITIES
▼ ▼ ▼

APPALACHIAN MOUNTAIN CLUB, Trails Program, Pinkham Notch Camp, Box 298, Gorham, NH 03581, tel. (603) 466-2727. AMC's important and constructive work toward maintaining and creating trails in the Appalachian Mountains depends on volunteer workers. Caretakers are also needed to maintain their unusual cabins and campsites. Volunteers may work on a weekly basis. (See pages 116–118 for further information on AMC nonvolunteer trips into the mountains.)

DIRECTORY OF YOUNG SCHOLARS PROJECTS, NSF Forms & Publications, National Science Foundation, Washington, DC 20550, tel. (202) 357-7861. Universities and colleges around the United States and Puerto Rico offer summer programs (as well as some academic year programs) to highly intelligent high-school students interested in the sciences. Some of these programs involve field research. The prices tend to be very reasonable and grants are available. (See pages 159–160.)

DIVE INTO HISTORY, National Center for Shipwreck Research, 631 Greene St, Key West, FL 33040, tel. (800) 468-3255. Marine archeology expeditions and coral reef conservation workshops in the Florida Keys, Grand Cayman, Jamaica, and Cancun.

EUROPE CONSERVATION, Via Fusetti, 14-20143 Milano, Italy, tel. 39 (2) 5810-3135. Fax 39 (2) 8940-0649. Focusing on the Alps and Mediterranean, Europe Conservation uses paying volunteers on projects studying wildlife, conservation, archeology, and the environment.

SCRIPPS AQUARIUM, Institute of Oceanography, 8602 La Jolla Shores Drive, La Jolla, CA 92093-0207, tel. (619) 534-6933 or (619) 534-3474. Join Scripps in diving expeditions for collecting exotic fish for study at the Aquarium. They also conduct whale-watching trips.

SIERRA CLUB, Outing Department, 730 Polk St., San Francisco, CA 94109, tel. (415) 776-2211. In addition to Sierra Club's adventure trips, they offer service programs. Service trips involve working on hard but rewarding projects, such as swinging sledge hammers to break up rocks to make trails through wilderness areas, or assisting in an archeological survey. (See pages 136–138 for more information on Sierra Club.)

SMITHSONIAN RESEARCH EXPEDITIONS, Smithsonian Institute, Dept. 0577, Washington, DC 20073-0577, tel. (202) 287-3210. Set out on field research expeditions, assisting scientists, historians, anthropologists, curators, and other investigators from the largest and foremost museum in the world. (See pages 164–166 for a full description of all of the Smithsonian's travel programs.)

Chapter Eleven

PEOPLE-TO-PEOPLE PROGRAMS

Meeting Your Neighbors in the Global Village

▼ ▼ ▼

A FEW WORDS

▼ ▼ ▼

Of all the adventures we have had around the world, what we remember most vividly are the people we have met. The thatch roofer in Ireland who invited us in for tea when we stopped to watch him work; the young man in Istanbul who insisted on showing us the way when we asked him for directions to the Blue Mosque; the two young Chinese girls who sat with us at a banquet, surprised to learn that in our country you choose your own career rather than obey the orders of your government-appointed supervisor; the Bora Indian boy in the Peruvian Amazon Jungle who tried to show us how to use a blowgun. On every trip, we seek to meet new people, find new friends, and thus enrich our lives.

For many, people are more than the spice of travel, they are the reason to travel—to better understand our distant neighbors, to help shrink the world just a bit more toward a global village, to promote peace.

It doesn't really matter if you want to meet people when you travel just for the pleasure of discovering new friends, or if you seek to build bridges between nations through your own personal involvement with former strangers. People-to-people travel programs are rewarding experiences.

People-to-people programs require a bit more of you than typical travel. In addition to preparing yourself by learning as much as you can about the other country, you have to be ready to let go of your everyday expectations and unconscious prejudices. Sometimes, you are even required to put on the outer trappings of another culture, if only for a few days, so that you may understand its people better.

But once you have eaten the same foods, shared a daily routine, tried to use a few words in another's language, your perspective of those people and their country will be irrevocably changed. That is why so many peace organizations promote "people-to-people" programs. As The Friendship Force's motto says, "A world of friends is a world of peace."

If you are traveling to another country (or another region of your own country) independently, it is still possible to arrange to meet people. Many government agencies (such as the Jamaican Tourist Board) will try to arrange an introduction to a local who may be in the same profession as you. Of course, one of the easiest ways to make sure you meet people when you travel is to stay in bed and breakfasts or home stays instead of tourist-only hotels. Other suggestions of how to meet local people when you travel may be found on pages 55–57.

THE FRIENDSHIP FORCE
▼ ▼ ▼

As Wayne Smith told Mikhail Gorbachev in 1987 on the occasion of the Soviet leader's first visit to the United States, "The problem isn't armaments; the problem is fear." Smith knows what he is talking about. In 1977, he founded The Friendship Force in the attempt to make the world a bit smaller, friendlier, and, therefore, safer. Two of his first avid supporters were President and Mrs. Jimmy Carter. (Mrs. Carter is still on the board of directors.)

The Friendship Force has three different types of programs: Exchanges, Missions, and Festivals.

On a Friendship Exchange, a group of people (known as ambassadors) from all over the world visit another country, where they split up to stay in the homes of private citizens (called hosts). The experience is a very personal one of exploring and learning and, eventually, loving strangers.

Friendship Missions were established for those countries that were unable to provide overnight accommodations in private homes. Instead, ambassadors stay as a group in a hotel but have daily interactions with the local citizens.

And Friendship Festivals are convocations of people from all over the world who gather to celebrate their differences and similarities in a central place (such as a hotel) for several days before dispersing into private homes for about a week.

There is also ARMS, an exchange program specifically designed so U.S. and Soviet citizens may stay in each other's homes.

The Friendship Force evolves around local clubs that work all year toward their upcoming Exchange, Mission, or Festival, keeping informed, raising money for scholarships, and preparing themselves for their trip. So far, The Friendship Force has been involved in over 1,500,000 friendship contacts, has 110 U.S. clubs in 40 states and 160 international clubs in 39 countries, and has proven that individuals can make a difference in building bridges of international understanding.

DESTINATIONS: Throughout the United States and the world

SEASON: Various times throughout the year

LENGTH OF PROGRAMS: 1 to 2 weeks

ENROLLMENT: 20 to 80 participants

TOTAL COST: $395 to $2,500, which they call an induction fee

COST PER DIEM: $54 to $179, with the vast majority of programs in the very lower range, including trips to exotic places like Thailand

TAX DEDUCTIBLE?: No

COST INCLUSIVE OF: International transportation from a gateway airport, transportation during the program, lodging, meals

COST EXCLUSIVE OF: Gifts for your hosts, domestic transportation to the gateway airport, sightseeing excursions that you take on your own

AMENITIES, FACILITIES, AND REALITIES: To become a host or ambassador of The Friendship Force, you must be screened by a local committee. They want to be sure that your commitment to goodwill and overcoming cultural differences for the sake of friendship is well founded. You need to be flexible, willing to try new things, caring, and have a healthy sense of humor. If you do pass the screening and are scheduled for a program, you will attend orientation sessions to prepare you for what to expect, plus some rudimentary language lessons. Your hosts will go out of their way to make you feel comfortable and show you their home area, so much so that they may try to stretch their personal (and financial) resources farther than they should. They receive no money for hosting you, so, it would be appropriate to take them out to dinner, perhaps help with the food shopping, or otherwise share in the responsibilities they have taken on to make your visit memorable. Of course, your stay in a home involves becoming a member of the family for a while, probably sharing a bathroom and other common areas. All the rules of being a well-mannered guest apply even more strongly here, where cultural differences can lead to misunderstandings. You may not speak the same language, but trying to communicate with a few words in the local tongue is appreciated. By the way, if you are chosen to be a Friendship host or ambassador, you might wish to contact local businesses to solicit gifts. One teenager who went to Soviet Georgia from Atlanta, Georgia, got several big businesss to contribute tee shirts, mugs, pens, pencils, etc., to give away.

CONTACT: The Friendship Force, Suite 575 South Tower, One CNN Center, Atlanta, GA 30303, tel. (404) 522-9490. Fax (404) 688-6148.

INTERNATIONAL PEACE WORKS
▼ ▼ ▼

International Peace WORKS used to be called International Peace WALK, under which name it won worldwide recognition. But now that the organization does more than walks, it has decided to change its name.

The walks are large-scale demonstrations of international solidarity among ordinary people who seek to break down the interpersonal barriers to peace. From 100 to 500 people from various countries meet to walk through a countryside, generally where there is a tradition of antagonism between the participants. For instance, the Soviet peace walks have been very successful among Americans. Similarly, 1991 walks are scheduled in Vietnam and Cuba. The entire group lives together in a mobile tent city, walking about eight miles a day, meeting and communicating with the people of the host nation. The outpouring of goodwill and welcome that the walks have traditionally experienced wherever they go has led IPW to claim that it can take four to eight hours to walk through a town or village. That's because everyone wants to feed them, touch them, share their homes with them, and embrace them. (According to IPW, after every walk, there is at least one marriage between two people from different nations.) Activities include town meetings and discussion groups. The ratio is generally one to one of local to foreigner, with at least half of the locals able to speak English.

Other projects that IPW has gotten involved in include: ecological bicycle projects, the first stadium concert with foreign musicians in U.S.S.R., the first commercial radio broadcast from the U.S.S.R., film making, and others.

DESTINATIONS: IPW claims that no project is ever repeated, so who knows where they will go in 1992; however, Soviet walks are their hallmark. Other 1991 walks include Vietnam and Cuba.

SEASON: Various times

LENGTH OF PROGRAMS: 3 weeks

ENROLLMENT: 100 to 500 participants

TOTAL COST: $2,200 to $2,900. Some partial scholarships are available, as well as assistance with fund raising.

COST PER DIEM: $105 to $138

TAX DEDUCTIBLE?: Given the basic IRS rule that only the difference between the value of what you get and the amount you pay is deductible, then approximately $1,000 may be deductible.

COST INCLUSIVE OF: Air transportation to the host country from a gateway airport, all transportation during the program, all meals, housing, site expenses, orientation packet (including information on the host country, suggested reading list, information for working with the media and for fund raising, etc.)

COST EXCLUSIVE OF: Transportation to the gateway city in the U.S., tent, sleeping bag, inflatable mattress

AMENITIES, FACILITIES, AND REALITIES: As one IPW participant, a white-haired grandmother told us, "It's remarkable, so much bonding and hope. Of course, you have to ignore the chorus of snores that surround you at night, and the tent showers aren't for the modest." She hopes to go on another Peace Walk. Living in a tent city is not actually comfortable, but it can be fun, especially considering the fact that you will be surrounded by so many people ready to accept you on your own terms. Besides, it's not forever, but only a vacation-long trip. Your gear will be transported for you, so that you won't be backpacking or otherwise carrying your possessions during the walk. Participants under 18 years old must travel with a responsible adult. Attempts are made to accommodate anyone who wants to join a walk, including individuals in wheelchairs. "If you want to join us, we will find a way." If you don't have the money, they will help you try to find it through fund raising, scholarships, and discounts. A medical crew accompanies the walk, as does a film crew.

CONTACT: International Peace Works, 4521 Campus Drive, Suite 211, Irvine, CA 92713-9553, tel. (714) 856-0200. Fax (714) 856-0201; or P.O. Box 58, Baker, WV 26801, tel. (304) 897-6028.

PEOPLE TO PEOPLE INTERNATIONAL
▼ ▼ ▼

PTP is the venerable organization in this group. Having been founded by President Eisenhower in 1956 under the U.S. Information Agency, it became a private, nonprofit organization in 1961.

When asked how PTP differs from The Friendship Force, Rosanne Kohlman (the public information officer) said, "Well, I think they stay in one place for a week or so, we [People to People] generally travel about, with several stops."

PTP has local chapters throughout the United States and around the world, which are the basis of most of their programs. The Adult International Exchange Program arranges for scientists, teachers, technicians, and other professionals to meet their counterparts in other lands to exchange ideas and share new methods. "Because no one country has a monopoly on talent in any field, communication among specialists working at the forefront of their disciplines is essential to professional and scientific advance." The summer study abroad program provides college (or graduate school) credit learning opportunities for students. On the Ambassador Programs, kids (high-school or college age) travel as a group to another country to learn about the society, government, arts, and people of that country and to share information about themselves.

In addition to the travel opportunities that PTP offers, they also try to match up pen pals, arrange a magazine exchange across borders, ask members of the U.S. chapters to host homestays for visitors from other countries and work at other programs that are all designed to promote better worldwide understanding.

PTP doesn't believe that all you have to do is put ordinary people together and you will automatically have international peace. But, as President Eisenhower said, "This is one of the finest duties a citizen can possibly perform because, while mutual understanding itself will not create peace, no universal and just peace is possible without understanding."

DESTINATIONS: Throughout the world, with more than 70 sponsoring chapters throughout the United States

SEASON: Student programs are during the summer, adult programs are all year.

LENGTH OF PROGRAMS: 2 to 8 weeks

ENROLLMENT: 20 to 35 participants per program

TOTAL COST: $3,000 to $5,000 adult, $2,800 to $3,800 high-school students

COST PER DIEM: Not available

TAX DEDUCTIBLE?: Student programs are not tax deductible, but the adult programs are set up as an educational/business expense, with a journal kept to comply with IRS criteria for deductibility.

COST INCLUSIVE OF: International air transportation from a gateway airport, in-country transportation, lodging, most meals, transfers, porterage, meetings, educational programs, most gratuities

Cost Exclusive Of: Domestic transportation (to catch the international flights), some meals, some gratuities

Amenities, Facilities, and Realities: PTP provides some of the nicer accommodations among these kinds of programs. The adults stay mostly in hotels, with private bathrooms. However, some programs do include homestays. Students stay partially in private homes and partially in hotels. Membership to PTP costs $15 (individual), $25 (family), or $10 (student). And if you are a member, PTP will refer you to chapters wherever you travel. That doesn't mean the local chapter will necessarily arrange homestays for you, but the track record is that you will probably receive a rather warm welcome.

Contact: People to People International, 501 E. Armour Blvd., Kansas City, MO 64109, tel. (816) 531-4701. Fax (816) 561-7502.

WORLDPEACE CAMP

In 1982, Samantha Smith, a 10-year-old from Maine, wrote to Soviet Premier Yuri Andropov, "I have been worrying about the Soviet Union and the United States getting into a nuclear war. Are you going to vote to have a war or not? If you aren't please tell me how you are going to help not have a war." And Premier Andropov answered by inviting Samantha to come visit him. She became a symbol of the youth of the world, trying to prod their elders—especially their leaders—to work toward peace and not war. And after Samantha and her father were killed in a plane crash in Maine, her mother established the Samantha Smith Foundation.

Soon after her death, the Samantha Smith Worldpeace Camp was established in Maine, with the cooperation of the Foundation, to "bring together potential world leaders of the twenty-first century from all nations with nuclear capability." Today, in addition to the camp in Maine, Americans may also attend Soviet youth camps in the U.S.S.R.

The Maine camp provides leadership workshops including: world and environmental issues, group problem solving, conflict resolution, language classes in Russian and English, peace studies, etc. But it is in the atmosphere of a camp, where kids can be kids, enjoying recreational activities. They can swim, play basketball, canoe, learn the guitar or waterskiing, study theater or macrame, sail, learn photography, etc.

The camps in the U.S.S.R., which are on the Black Sea, are international in nature, drawing kids from all over the world. According to Karen Steger (who is codirector with Jay Steger), "There is no environmental and educational component in the U.S.S.R. camps; they're purely recreational.'' Everything is rather informal, with no instruction. But there may be an American Day or German Fest, in which the kids from a certain country will entertain the other campers with foods, skits, and stories about what life is like at home. An American staff from Worldpeace travels with the kids to augment the supervision. ''They are still basically our campers, so we give them supervision and provide a handbook on how to handle themselves in the U.S.S.R., such as how to handle themselves in a television interview.'' In addition to recreational activities, most of the Russian programs also offer a three to four-day homestay and some sightseeing.

Each camper is required to sign an agreement to abide by the Worldpeace Camp guidelines. These state: that alcohol, tobacco, and drugs are outlawed; that sexual contact or harassment is forbidden; that curfew will be strictly enforced; that ''respect for all living things is expected''; that no camper may leave the grounds without a staff member; that no valuables are permitted to be kept in the cabins; and other rules, some of which seem rather strict, but all of which must be obeyed. An offender who has broken some of the more important rules, such as those related to drugs and sex, will be sent home and given no refund.

The campers tend to be interested, concerned individuals, who have already shown some leadership potential and/or concern for world peace. And they return home more mature and more aware.

DESTINATIONS: Maine and U.S.S.R.

SEASON: Summer

LENGTH OF PROGRAMS: 4 to 5 weeks

ENROLLMENT: Maine: 140 Americans, 30 Soviets, and a few from Eastern Europe and the Middle East; U.S.S.R.: 110 Americans plus kids from 20 or 30 other nations

TOTAL COST: $1,500. Some partial scholarships may be available.

COST PER DIEM: $44 to $58

TAX DEDUCTIBLE?: No

COST INCLUSIVE OF: Lodging, meals, activities and programs, insurance, recreational equipment

COST EXCLUSIVE OF: Transportation, spending money (about $75 is recommended)

AMENITIES, FACILITIES, AND REALITIES: The kids live in communal cabins and eat together. Meals are served buffet-style. In Maine, alternatives are available for vegetarians and junk food is limited. There are no official visiting days, but parents may visit once anytime during the summer in Maine. A VHS video of the programs is available. No tipping is permitted.

CONTACT: Jay and Karen Steger, directors, Worldpeace Camp, Rural Rte. 2, Box 81, Lincolnville, ME 04849, tel. (207) 338-5165. Fax (207) 338-5765; or Samantha Smith Center, 9 Union St., Hallowell, ME 04347, tel. (207) 626-3415. Fax (207) 626-3417.

FURTHER POSSIBILITIES
▼ ▼ ▼

BEYOND SAFARIS: A GUIDE TO BUILDING PEOPLE-TO-PEOPLE TIES WITH AFRICA (Global Exchange, 2141 Mission St., San Francisco, CA 94111, tel. (415) 255-7296) is a useful book for anyone who wants to really get to know Africa on a personal level. $6.95.

CENTER FOR BILINGUAL STUDIES (in Cuernavaca, Mexico), 3133 Lake Hollywood Dr., P.O. Box 1860, Los Angeles, CA 90078, tel. (800) 426-4660 or (213) 851-3403. This Spanish-language school arranges homestays for their students at very reasonable cost. In addition, they have a post-study program that places students with Mexican families, while they tour the country. (See pages 151–152 for a profile of the school.)

CENTER FOR U.S.-U.S.S.R. INITIATIVES, 3268 Sacramento Street, San Francisco, CA 94115, tel. (415) 346-1875. Glasnost has led to an unprecedented interest in learning more about the Soviet Union and its peoples, and the Center arranges and sponsors numerous programs, projects, and tours to the U.S.S.R. that specifically set up people-to-people encounters with ordinary Soviets as well as professional or social counterparts.

CENTRO LINGUISTICO CONVERSA, Apartado No 17 Centro Colon, San Jose, Costa Rica, tel. (800) 292-9872 (in the U.S. and Canada); or, directly, 011-506-21-7649, fax 011-506-33-2418. Conversa is a small language school in Costa Rica, where you can learn to speak Spanish while staying with a host family. These homestays become even richer, because you are trying to learn your hosts' language. (See pages 149–150 for a profile of the program.)

CONTINUING THE PEACE DIALOGUE, Box 1710, Camel Valley, CA 93924, tel. (408) 659-3578. What would it be like to be a teacher, engineer, student, or journalist in someplace like the U.S.S.R.? Would you like to have a sister town or city in Israel? How would your family feel about hosting a high-school student from Sweden for a semester? Continuing the Peace is one of various organizations that arranges exchanges between citizens, in order to better promote world peace and fellowship. As its name implies, the exchanges frequently have a philosophical slant, and work often with international peace groups and activists.

EARTHSTEWARDS NETWORK, P.O. Box 10697, Bainbridge Island, WA 98110, tel. (206) 842-7986. Earthstewards offers various programs that are designed to help the world resolve conflict and other problems by bringing people closer together. They focus on diplomacy training, projects for the good of a community, accomplished by international teams, youth exchanges between nations, and other programs. One particular program it does in conjunction with the Holyearth Foundation is bringing together Vietnam and Soviet-Afgani war vets in order to share experiences that will help hasten the healing of emotional wounds left by those conflicts. Annual membership is $18 for which you receive a bimonthly newsletter, invitations to trips and training programs, information on ongoing projects, and "worldwide networking information."

ELDERHOSTEL, 80 Boylston St., Suite 400, Boston, MA 02116, tel. (617) 426-7788; or, for Canadian residents: ElderHostel Canada, 33 Prince Arthur Ave., Suite 300, Toronto, ON M5R 1B2, tel. (416) 964-2260. In addition to their educational programs, ElderHostel arranges homestays in various countries. (See pages 152–154 for a full profile of their educational programs.)

THE EXPERIMENT IN INTERNATIONAL LIVING (THE SCHOOL FOR INTERNATIONAL TRAINING), Kipling Rd., Brattleboro, VT 05301-9988, tel. (802) 257-7751. Among the many programs of this very noteworthy organization are ones that involve arranging homestays—both here (for foreign visitors) and abroad (for North American travelers).

MOBILITY INTERNATIONAL, P.O. Box 3551, Eugene, OR 97403. This organization sets up people-to-people encounters between Americans and Soviets who have common problems with physical disabilities. Some of its tours include camping and hiking.

THE SPACE BETWEEN, Instituto de Asuntos Culturales (Institute of Cultural Affairs), Apartado 110630 Jesus Maria, Lima 11, Peru. In small groups (limited to 10 participants), ICA provides English-speaking programs to Peru, Guatemala, and Mexico that try to explore the "souls" of those countries. Included are homestays in Indian villages, visits to the sacred places of the country, and time in the capital city to meet a wider diversity of citizens, as well as see markets, museums, schools, homes, and businesses.

TRAVELING SHOES, INC., Box 4410, Laguna Beach, CA 92652, tel. (714) 497-6773. Now that the Iron Curtain is history, Traveling Shoes can arrange in-depth homestays, exchange programs, and special tours to Czechoslovakia and Poland.

VOLUNTEERS FOR PEACE, Tiffany Road, Belmont, VT 05730, tel. (802) 259-2759. This is more or less a clearing house for the many dozens of European-style volunteer work camps around the world.

Chapter Twelve

REALITY TOURS

*Travel Ideas
for the Socially Aware*

▼ ▼ ▼

A FEW WORDS

▼ ▼ ▼

If you're the type of person who watches CNN first thing in the morning and last thing at night, belongs or contributes to a host of charitable or social organizations, is active in community causes, church affairs, or politics, or simply has a need to know what's *really* going on in the world, then you're a prime candidate for a reality tour.

A reality tour gives the private citizen an opportunity to visit Third World countries or places in the news in order to get a firsthand, up-close view. Frequently, that means meeting with ordinary citizens and activists, politicians, cabinet ministers, and even heads of state. Or it may involve participating in workshops and seminars, or dividing one's time between observing and volunteering in a clinic, a village project, or the like. Depending on the organization, reality tours often require participants to become members or to promise to follow through at home by giving a report, joining a study group, etc.

Quite candidly, many reality tours can be quite one-sided, designed to convince you of a particular political, religious, or ideological viewpoint. Other reality tours do attempt to be impartial by exposing you to opposing points of view. Also, depending upon where you go, conditions can be quite brutal. For example, if you go on a reality tour of South Africa, you might see some of the internecine tribal or political bloodshed that we see in the news every other day. Or, if you visit a refugee camp in Thailand, you may witness wholesale malnutrition, disease, and even death. Accommodations range from large hotels to homestays with locals to cots in church basements. You may eat in restaurants or hotels, or break bread with natives, or share in communal meals. Depending upon the particular tour, you could be chauffeured about in an old bus, a new van, or a private car.

We know of people who have been invigorated and uplifted by reality tours, because they have a better handle on the problem, had the opportunity to meet some of the prime movers that might create solutions, and got involved with support groups or local movement chapters when they returned home. On the other hand, if you have a queasy stomach or an overly sensitive heart, if you are easily upset by encounters with disease, poverty, or oppression, then some reality tours are definitely not for you. Some acquaintances of ours went into months-long depressions after returning from particularly intense reality tours.

Not all reality tours are grim or spartan. In fact, many also schedule normal sightseeing events, time at the beach or pool, opportunities to buy souvenirs, and other more normal vacation activities. So, you can combine having fun with learning and experiencing something unique.

Also, reality tours tend to be very inexpensive, especially since most include round-trip air fare, food, lodging, and in-country transportation. Almost all are sponsored by nonprofit organizations, with a goal other than making money. Therefore, most organizations and institutions are satisfied if they break even by offering travel without the usual profit markup.

Because some reality tours go to underdeveloped or disease-ridden places, always check well in advance with your doctor and the local public health service to make certain that you have all the necessary inoculations or will be taking proper preventative medicine. Don't wait until the last minute, because some shots are two-parters that must be given weeks apart, and some pills must be taken up to three weeks in advance in order to build up immunity.

If you are staying in a host's home, be polite and undemanding, and always try to bring a small gift. Be discreet and sensitive when taking photographs of strangers. Often, people who have nothing in the world other than their personal dignity are ashamed or nervous about being photographed in an extreme environ-ment of poverty or strife. Also, wear clothing suitable to the climate and the culture. For instance, shorts or halter tops are inappropriate for Moslem or other cultures that value modesty, or a jacket and tie or blouse and skirt should be worn when meeting important government bureaucrats or attending official functions. Conversely, don't wear clothing that you care about when working in a rough and tumble or wild and rugged environment.

Incidentally, while tipping is usually optional or inappropriate on most reality tours, giving small monetary gifts to hosts (in addition to nonmonetary gifts like postcards, photographs, books, etc.) is common. Three to five dollars for a one or two nights' stay is the average amount. A number of organizations pool whatever money they have left over from the trip and donate it to their host organization or some other charity mutually agreed upon.

Remember, you're going on a reality tour to learn and observe and not to change peoples' opinions or tell them how to live.

CENTER FOR GLOBAL EDUCATION
▼ ▼ ▼

As one can surmise from the fact that the Center for Global Education is based at Augsburg College, a Lutheran institute of higher education, most of its reality tours have a religious or church perspective. "But not exclusively," according to Joan Moline, coordinator of Travel Seminars. "You might say that it's not ecumenical but Christian in orientation."

While most tours are open to everyone, specialty tours can be arranged. For example, a tour might include only those who speak fluent Spanish, so face-to-face meetings and social interactions can take place without interpreters. Or, a program may consist only of lawyers, such as an informal commission to delve into a country's civil and human rights violations. Global also offers a spring semester program in Cuernavaca, Mexico, for undergraduates who wish to explore the history, politics, and the role of the church throughout Latin America. College credits may be earned on these tours for undergraduate degrees or continuing education credits for teachers.

Unlike some reality tours that book through another organization, the Center "works with one group from conception through planning through the operation stage. We basically plan and conduct all the travel seminars we do. Various other organizations contract with us to do their programs."

DESTINATIONS: Arizona, Hawaii, Mexico, El Salvador, Costa Rica, Nicaragua, Guatemala, South Africa, Namibia, Israel, Jordan, Philippines

SEASON: All year

LENGTH OF PROGRAMS: 11 days to 4 weeks

ENROLLMENT: 13 to 21, but 15 is average.

TOTAL COST: $1,100 to $2,000

COST PER DIEM: $71 to $100

TAX DEDUCTIBLE?: No

COST INCLUSIVE OF: Air Transportation from Houston, Miami, New York, or other gateway cities; all in-country transportation; all meals; lodging

COST EXCLUSIVE OF: Just about everything but personal expenses are covered.

AMENITIES, FACILITIES, AND REALITIES: Moderate hotels and guest houses are frequently used, most with private baths. In addition, the Center owns several facilities. The meals are "similar to food served in U.S. motels." Because some programs are very intensive in nature with long days and busy schedules, participants should be in reasonably good health. Other programs are less strenuous and demanding. There are few entertainment or sightseeing opportunities, since the focus is primarily on education. Participants must be at least 18 years old.

CONTACT: Center for Global Education, Augsburg College, 731 21st Avenue South, Minneapolis, MI 55454, tel. (612) 330-1159.

GLOBAL EXCHANGE

Global Exchange is a 10-year-old nonprofit, nonreligious research, education, and action-oriented 4,000-member organization that runs a series of intense reality tours to Third World countries, impoverished areas in Appalachia, and along the U.S./Mexican border.

"The people who travel with us aren't going as tourists. There is a large and growing internationalism that we wanted to support," said Global Exchange's administrator, Kirsten Moller. The general purpose of the trips, like most other reality tours, is better international understanding and a desire to infuse participants with a strong motivation to join in grassroots activism back home.

The specific focus of Global's reality tours is to arrange an environment for participants to meet, spend time, and exchange ideas and opinions with ordinary citizens as well as some of the country's important labor, religious, medical, and political leaders (both of the ruling party and the opposition). These are people that individuals on their own are not likely to encounter, much less have the opportunity to discuss, face to face, the important issues and problems that beset the region or country.

DESTINATIONS: Appalachia, the Mexican/U.S. border, South Africa, Zimbabwe, India, Philippines, Brazil, Haiti, Vietnam, Cambodia, Puerto Rico, Cuba

SEASON: All year

LENGTH OF PROGRAMS: 10 to 16 days

ENROLLMENT: 10 to 15 participants

TOTAL COST: $700 to $3,300. Limited number of scholarships available for low-income applicants.

COST PER DIEM: $75 to $225

Tax Deductible?: Membership is tax deductible. Also, "the group decides what happens to the excess money, deciding where to donate it. But it's something we don't require."

Cost Inclusive Of: Round-trip air fare from gateway cities of San Francisco, New York, or Miami (except for Appalachia and U.S./Mexican border trips), lodging, in-country transportation, most meals, preparation materials, organizing costs

Cost Exclusive Of: Domestic transportation to the gateway airport or the assembly point

Amenities, Facilities, and Realities: "Accommodations are clean but modest. Meals are mostly local fare." Groups are very diverse and may include journalists, community organizers, teachers, lawyers, senior citizens, students, doctors, church workers, as well as ordinary people "who are sensitive to Third World realities."

Other Comments: Global Exchange has several books available for $6.95 each, including: *The Peace Corps and More: 109 Ways to Work/Travel/Study in the Third World*; *Beyond Safaris: A Guide to Building People-to-People Ties with Africa*; and *Bridging the Global Gap: A Handbook to Linking Citizens of the First and Third Worlds*.

Contact: Global Exchange/Tours, 2141 Mission Street #202, San Francisco, CA 94111, tel. (415) 255-7296.

Our Developing World
▼ ▼ ▼

During an interview with Barby Ulmer, secretary of Our Developing World (she and her husband Vic draw no salary for leading tours), she described Our Developing World's perspective and programs. "We are a nonprofit educational project designed to bring the realities of the Third World and the richness of multiculture to North Americans through programs and study tours, teacher training, a local lending resource library, and teaching kits.

"Responses to our tours have often included words like 'transforming,' 'changed my life,' 'I'll never be the same,' 'enriched perspective.' The focus of our tours is always on people on development. We try to have it very broad so we will see and talk with people who are involved in health, education, women's organizations, development projects, cooperatives, both urban and rural experiences.

"Where the church plays a prominent role we talk with church people. We focus mostly on grass roots experience, and on seeing what people are doing rather than visiting offices or talking with national leaders.

"The only time we have had to ask for qualifications have been our trips to Cuba [because of the U.S. State Department rules], and we used the broadest category we could think of, human services. Normally, we attract a very diverse group in age, education, and knowledge of the place we are going.

"I think the [other] organizations we know of that lead tours either have a religious base or have leaders that are more politically oriented. We're educators, and we realize that if you give people experiences, you don't have to tell them what they're feeling. They will see it for themselves. The sharing of their experiences is part of the emotional and intellectual process. So we're easier to go with than many other tours."

DESTINATIONS: El Salvador, Nicaragua (Past and future destinations include Hawaii, South Africa, Cuba, Tanzania, Mozambique, Zimbabwe, China.)

SEASON: June and July

LENGTH OF PROGRAMS: 3 weeks

ENROLLMENT: Limited to 16, but 12 is average.

TOTAL COST: $1,094 to $1,359, depending upon your gateway city

COST PER DIEM: $52 to $65

TAX DEDUCTIBLE?: No

COST INCLUSIVE OF: Round-trip air fare from gateway airport, all in-country transportation, two meals a day, lodging, orientation material, follow-up material

COST EXCLUSIVE OF: Transportation to gateway city, some meals

AMENITIES, FACILITIES, AND REALITIES: The accommodations are locally owned, simple, and clean. Usually, they have private bathrooms, but it may vary. In some instances there are homestays. Meals are usually taken at restaurants. Honoraria are given to groups visited, taken from trip cost. They also urge participants to use their 66 pounds of free baggage weight to bring school books and medical supplies. Some free time is provided, but it is limited. The programs tend not to be physically strenuous. But as Barby Ulmer said to us, "Emotionally, it varies with individuals. With people who have never been in a Third World country or experienced what life is like to the poor, it certainly is an eye opener, and can be quite moving."

CONTACT: Our Developing World, 13004 Paseo Presada, Saratoga, CA 95070, tel. (408) 376-0755 or (408) 379-4431.

PLOWSHARES INSTITUTE
▼ ▼ ▼

Maralyn Lipner, program administrator of the 10-year-old nonprofit Plowshares Institute, defines their goals as "service, research, and education towards a lasting, sustainable, peaceful, and just society. We expose people to Third World countries to provide them with a more global outlook so that they will think globally and act locally."

Plowshares takes a somewhat different *modus operandi* than other organizations in that its primary purpose isn't to educate and enlighten participants but rather to have them share their knowledge and experience with Third World colleagues. It is hoped that by discussing issues and problems, solutions might evolve. And that in turn will help bridge the growing gap between the First and Third Worlds.

Many of Plowshares' reality tours are cosponsored by other organizations, which are for the most part church-based. While Plowshares itself is nonsectarian, the basic orientation is very often Christian. However, participants do not have to display any religious affiliation.

The organizations and institutions that offer reality travel very often overlap and share with each other by referring prospective participants to one another's programs. Plowshares is one of the most respected and active of these organizations, which is why it often offers cosponsored trips.

DESTINATIONS: El Salvador, Nicaragua, Brazil, South Africa, Uganda, Kenya, Czechoslovakia, Hungary, Germany, Philippines, China, India, Fiji, Australia

SEASON: All year

LENGTH OF PROGRAMS: 13 to 16 days

ENROLLMENT: 12 to 25 participants

TOTAL COST: $2,100 to $3,200

COST PER DIEM: $161 to $200

TAX DEDUCTIBLE?: A portion may be deductible

COST INCLUSIVE OF: Air Transportation from a gateway airport, in-country transportation, all meals, lodging, sightseeing

COST EXCLUSIVE OF: Plowshares attempts to cover all possible expenses so that participants don't fall into the "tourist" profile of having to spend money.

AMENITIES, FACILITIES, AND REALITIES: "The purpose is to live in the style of our hosts. We go as guests, not as visitors." Depending upon destinations, small hotels, seminary accommodations, YMCAs or private homes may be used. Most do not have private baths. Some of the trips require participants to be physically active. They are asked to make a contribution to a group gift to hosts, usually around $35. People are also asked to bring small gifts to their hosts, like books, postcards, snapshots, etc.

CONTACT: Plowshares Institute, P.O. Box 243, Simsbury, CT 06070, tel. (203) 651-4304.

FURTHER POSSIBILITIES

▼ ▼ ▼

GATE (GLOBAL AWARENESS THROUGH EXPERIENCE), Viterbo College, LaCrosse, WI 54601, tel. (608) 791-0462. GATE is a nine-year-old Christian (Catholic) organization that arranges small reality tours, primarily to Mexico and Nicaragua, but also to Czechoslovakia and the eastern part of Germany. Its purpose is a combination of fostering deeper understanding of Christianity around the world, while at the same time assisting participants in gaining insights about the political and economic realities of the Third World.

GOOD LIFE STUDY TOURS OF THE FOOD FIRST INSTITUTE, 30 El Mirador Court, San Luis Obispo, CA 93401, tel. (805) 541-3101. Supposedly, the people who live in the southern Indian city of Trivandrum may be very poor in material wealth but happy in everything that matters. How can they maintain a high level of peace, harmony, and happiness, not to mention an elevated standard of living that includes good health and longevity? And what lessons from the Trivandrums can we learn that may enrich our own lives? Good Life Study Tours offers month-long homestays. Don't look for luxury, or even convenience; most homes will have Indian toilets (holes in the ground), the food is vegetarian, and the temperature is almost always hot. The cost is a modest $900 per person or $1,600 per couple (however, round-trip air fare from the U.S. will be $2,000 to $2,500 more each), and the group will consist of between six and eight participants. We have no personal knowledge of this organization or their programs. If you do, please contact us.

INSTITUTE FOR INTERNATIONAL COOPERATION AND DEVELOPMENT, P.O. Box 103, Williamstown, MA 01267, tel. (413) 458-9466. The nonprofit, nondenominational Institute for International Cooperation and Development is a little like a nongovernment mini-Peace Corps. Participants volunteer for 9 to 12-month programs in Central America and Asia to study and learn as well as help take surveys that will improve our knowledge of what the local conditions are really like. Each program requires a 2-month orientation session at the Institute's school in Massachusetts, followed by 5 to 6 months abroad as part of the program. After returning back to the U.S., participants are expected to spend a further 2 months at the school decompressing and then sharing what was learned and experienced by making presentations to church groups, civic clubs, schools, prisons, etc. Anyone over 18 is eligible, and the cost to the participants is $7,900.

THE LISLE FELLOWSHIP, 433 West Sterns Road, Temperance, MI 48182, tel. (800) 477-1538 or (313) 847-7126. Founded in 1936, Lisle operates study groups in such diverse places as Toledo, Ohio; Indonesia; and Mexico. The purpose is for participants to meet with their counterparts and exchange ideas, explore social issues like racism, and generally help develop a sense of one-worldism. The program is open to all races, religions, nationalities, and socioeconomic groups. Lisle is primarily for those who want to do off-campus study, but anyone is welcome to apply.

THIRD WORLD OPPORTUNITIES PROGRAM, 1363 Somermont Drive, El Cajon, CA 92021, tel. (619) 449-9381. Third World Opportunities runs short field trips to Mexico in order to introduce participants to the realities of poverty and hunger in the Third World, which is combined with work volunteer opportunities. Although nominally a Lutheran organization, it is open to Christians and non-Christians. Unlike charity-type organizations, TWO is forming long-range development programs that can provide employment, income, and even the pride of ownership to Third World citizens. One of the objectives of the tour is to teach participants how they can get involved in creating their own self-help projects. Anyone over 16 may participate.

Chapter Thirteen

NEEDING TO BE NEEDED

Programs for Those Who Want to Give of Themselves

▼ ▼ ▼

"I don't know what your destiny will be, but one thing I do know: the only ones among you who will be really happy are those who have sought and found how to serve."

—*Albert Schweitzer*

A FEW WORDS

Sometimes you can't help but feel that it simply isn't enough to live a decent life, support the right causes, and keep your mind open to new possibilities. Sometimes, for some people, the only answer to the need to do, to give, to make a positive impact is to just get up and act. In this chapter, we have listed a few organizations that not only provide for intimate contact and interaction with people from other cultures, but, more definitively, offer opportunities for you to volunteer to work and help your new friends.

Like the projects in the Field Research chapter, these programs require a personal dedication and a willingness to work darn hard that transcend any need for physical comfort or material amenities. You won't be a tourist, though this is one of the least expensive ways there is to see the world. Put simply, you are cheap labor donating your muscles and time to further some purpose that is important to you. You may be building homes, bathing the sick, teaching children, planting trees, or just about any other service needed by host communities. Many programs are religious in nature or, at least, religiously inspired. Others are quite secular, but spiritual by the very nature of people working in service for other people. It's only the source of the inspirational spirit that varies—in the name of God, to awaken a new sense of self through selflessness, or to further world peace through human interaction.

In addition, these programs offer another kind of adventure for the individual who wants to explore new cultures and meet different kinds of people. There are none of the protective barriers that traditional travelers experience, so the trip becomes a very intense, personal encounter that can shake up the way you see the world and your own place in it. Emotions can run deep, uncomfortably so, if you aren't prepared for it. But for those individuals who are ready to shake off the everyday myopia of "normal" life, if only for a few weeks of vacation, volunteering in service to the world community is one of the most vivid adventures you can have. Just be sure to budget some time to decompress after you return home before trying to fit back into your daily routine of work or school.

AMIGOS DE LAS AMERICAS

Since 1965, Amigos has been sending North Americans down to Latin America to work hard to help improve the level of public health. They build latrines, give inoculations, vaccinate animals against rabies, teach dental hygiene (and distribute toothbrushes), plant trees, renovate schools, assist in housing improvements, etc.

Most of the volunteers are young people, including 70 percent to 75 percent of whom are high-school students. The rest are college and graduate-school students. To help these youngsters learn, they are given leadership training, as well as taught how to complete the project at hand. The minimum age is 16 years old, but there is no upper age limit. In fact, some parents have become volunteers after their children have returned home praising the experience.

DESTINATIONS: Latin America

SEASON: Summer

LENGTH OF PROGRAMS: 4 to 8 weeks

ENROLLMENT: About 45 volunteers per country, with 2 to 3 volunteers assigned per village

TOTAL COST: $2,300 to $2,900 must be raised to support each volunteer, some scholarships are available to supplement fund raising.

COST PER DIEM: Not applicable

TAX DEDUCTIBLE?: Yes (which is a great help in fund raising)

COST INCLUSIVE OF: International travel, in-country travel to the assigned village and debriefing, lodging, meals, fund raising and training materials, program costs (including the needed supplies, tools, etc.)

COST EXCLUSIVE OF: Domestic travel to Houston or Miami (from where the international flights leave), spending money (most volunteers take about $100 to $150 for soft drinks, souvenirs, etc.), insurance

AMENITIES, FACILITIES, AND REALITIES: The volunteers are responsible for raising the funds needed to support them in their work. Local chapters assist with various programs, such as bicycle marathons, fashion shows, cookie sales, etc. If you don't live near a chapter, Amigos does offer correspondence training for fund raising. Once in Latin America, the volunteers live with families in the primarily rural villages in rather primitive surroundings. Most do not have running water or electricity. (One of the more important things they do is build latrines.)

OTHER COMMENTS: Amigos is affiliated with the Pan American Health Organization of the World Health Organization among many other prestigious groups. It is also a member of the President's Initiative for Youth Exchange and is accepted by the Council on Standards for International Educational Travel.

CONTACT: Amigos de las Americas, 5618 Star Lane, Houston, TX 77057, tel. (800) 231-7796, (800) 392-4580 (in Texas), or (713) 782-5290. Fax (713) 782-9267.

HABITAT FOR HUMANITY
▼ ▼ ▼

Since 1976, Habitat for Humanity (which was made famous by President Jimmy Carter's involvement in it) has been helping the impoverished and the homeless rediscover a sense of dignity and pride by helping them build or renovate their own homes. The concept is based upon the belief that everyone has the inborn right to adequate housing. Once such basic needs are taken care of, then they can begin to pull themselves up out of poverty. In the process, volunteers develop a sense of mutual responsibility and of the world as a single community.

Volunteers converge on a neighborhood for a short time to build or renovate a home or homes. The needy family (who would not be able to get a bank loan) pays the costs of the building over a period of time, with no profit to Habitat and no interest charges. (The money they pay goes to future building projects.) The family must also "contribute an average of 500 hours of 'sweat equity' in the construction of their own new home and to help other prospective homeowners build their homes."

Participants may volunteer as a traveling work camp builder or as an administrative assistant. All kinds of skills or nonskills are needed. Though Habitat is a Christian organization, it provides housing regardless of a family's religion or race. Also, the volunteers are of many religions, races, and nationalities.

This is a direct hands-on, give-something-back program that will provide no rest or relaxation on your vacation. In fact, you will probably return home quite tired and questioning the meaning of your "normal" life. Also, part of the agreement that you make as a Habitat volunteer is to devote some of your time telling people about what you have learned and how important it is for everyone to have at least a roof over their heads.

DESTINATIONS: Throughout the United States and, through Habitat's international partners, around the world (especially the Third World)

SEASON: All year

LENGTH OF PROGRAMS: 1 week to a year

ENROLLMENT: 8 to 20 participants

TOTAL COST: Most projects do not charge any fee unless they need help in the cost of volunteer housing or the services of a translator for the volunteers. Others may ask for a donation, but even those that don't ask for donations could use some financial assistance.

COST PER DIEM: Not applicable

TAX DEDUCTIBLE?: Yes

COST INCLUSIVE OF: Practically nothing is covered by Habitat, because they are a shoe-string, nonprofit organization. However, they usually provide orientation materials, instruction, tools, prayers.

COST EXCLUSIVE OF: Transportation to and from the project or workcamp, food (though sometimes potluck meals are provided), accommodations, sleeping bag, insurance

AMENITIES, FACILITIES, AND REALITIES: Housing is usually in a dormitory-type situation, possibly in the common rooms of a local church, with some showers and toilets available. Comfort is not the object in these kinds of projects. You will work hard, surrounded by giving, devoted individuals. "Each project attempts to transcend the boundaries of culture, status, and race through the sharing of a common goal. By working together as partners, the affluent and the poor become aware of their common heritage as God's children.'' You will be expected to not smoke or drink any alcohol. And the pressure will be great for you to be gentle and loving. In addition, prayer meetings are held on a regular basis.

OTHER COMMENTS: Habitat accepts no money from the government or any other body or organization that tries to control how they function.

CONTACT: Habitat for Humanity, 121 Habitat Street, Americus, GA 31709-3498, tel. (912) 924-6935. Fax (917) 924-6541.

SCI VOLUNTARY SERVICE

SCI is a workcamp-based peace organization that was established by a Swiss pacifist in the 1920s. The original idea was to heal the emotional and social wounds of World War I by promoting understanding between people. In other words, if you know someone from another place, if you have lived and worked side by side with him or her, then you can't consider that person an enemy. Thus, the cause of peace is forwarded.

Projects vary depending upon the needs of the host community. Some of the examples given by SCI are: organize and run daycamps in Ireland, plant city gardens in New York City, restore ruins in Bulgaria, and build a village school in Hungary. They provide social service, manual labor, environmental studies, solidarity workshops, etc. The work is important, but it isn't the focus. Rather it is to become part of a world community by being good neighbors and friends.

DESTINATIONS: Throughout the United States and Europe

SEASON: Mostly in the summer, with a few winter or autumn workcamps

LENGTH OF PROGRAMS: 2 to 4 weeks, with a few programs of 3 to 6 months

ENROLLMENT: 8 to 20 participants

TOTAL COST: $35 to $75 registration fee

COST PER DIEM: Not applicable

TAX DEDUCTIBLE?: The registration fee is not deductible, but your transportation and some other expenses may be.

COST INCLUSIVE OF: Room and board, sometimes accident and illness insurance

COST EXCLUSIVE OF: Transportation, out-of-pocket expenses, travel insurance, personal purchases

AMENITIES, FACILITIES, AND REALITIES: As with all the organizations in this chapter, the material amenities are few, but the emotional ones are rich indeed. Your accommodations and facilities will depend upon the program you sign up for and its location. Workcamp descriptions are available from SCI for $2 each.

CONTACT: SCI Voluntary Service, c/o Innisfree Village, Rte 2, Box 506, Crozet, VA 22932, tel. (804) 823-1826. Office hours are only on Monday, Wednesday, and Thursday, 9 AM to 12 noon and Sunday.

VOLUNTEERS FOR PEACE
▼ ▼ ▼

VFP is a nonprofit membership organization that sees itself as a "short-term Peace Corps." Every April they publish a booklet ($10) called the "International Workcamps Directory," which lists over 800 volunteer workcamps throughout the world. VFP describes workcamps as "places where the power of love and friendship can transform prejudice." But it isn't all sweetness and light, it's also a place to work on very tangible projects such as: construction, restoration, archeological digs, environmental projects, assisting the handicapped, farming, etc. But you won't just be working. The camps are also designed for the free exchange of ideas and thoughts, so there'll be opportunity for discussions on current issues plus time for shared recreational activities. However, the amount of free time will vary depending upon the host organization.

All the workcamps in the booklet are sanctioned by the United Nations. Even more interestingly, other organizations we have written about in this chapter (and others we wish we had room to include individually) are listed in the VFP booklet. This is one field in which competition between organizations seems to be so antithetical to their philosophy that they tend to work together.

By the way, in addition to providing unique, inexpensive travel opportunities, VFP seeks people who are willing to host visitors from other countries who come here. There are also opportunities for former workcamp participants to become workcamp coleaders, with some funding available to help defray personal expenses.

DESTINATIONS: 34 countries in eastern and western Europe, U.S.S.R., Asia, Africa, and North America

SEASON: The great majority are during the summer, but some are other times of year.

LENGTH OF PROGRAMS: 2 to 4 weeks. Some participants enroll in consecutive camps in the same locale or elsewhere.

ENROLLMENT: Approximately 10 to 20 participants in a workcamp at a time

TOTAL COST: $80 to $700; $10 will be refunded to you if you submit a report on the workcamp no later than October 1 (if yours were a summer program). When grants are received by VFP, scholarships are sometimes available.

COST PER DIEM: Not applicable

TAX DEDUCTIBLE?: Yes

COST INCLUSIVE OF: Accommodations, meals, some accident insurance (on some workcamps)

COST EXCLUSIVE OF: Transportation, personal expenses, sleeping bag, passport and visa charges, travel insurance

AMENITIES, FACILITIES, AND REALITIES: Depending upon the workcamp you choose, you may live in a church, school, dormitory, community center, or private home. Cooking, cleaning, and other chores are shared responsibilities. Usually, the participants in any one workcamp come from at least four different countries. You need no experience or foreign language skills; however, you are expected to work according to the schedule set out by the host organization, cooperating with the group to make the experience positive and productive. VFP stresses that you should pack a musical instrument if you play (for evening sing-alongs) and a healthy sense of humor (to keep you going during trying times).

OTHER COMMENTS: Peter Coldwell, the executive director of Volunteers for Peace, has offered to send any of our readers a free copy of their newsletter.

CONTACT: Volunteers for Peace, 43 Tiffany Road, Belmont, VT 05730, tel. (802) 259-2759.

FURTHER POSSIBILITIES
▼ ▼ ▼

AMERICAN FRIENDS SERVICE COMMITTEE, 1501 Cherry St., Philadelphia, PA 19102-1479, tel. (215) 241-7105. Among its many programs, AFSC has various workcamps, including ones in Cuba and Mexico.

CHRISTIAN VOLUNTEER MINISTRIES, CRISPAZ, Christians for Peace in El Salvador, 701 S. Zarzamora St., San Antonio, TX 78207, tel. (512) 433-6185. In addition to their programs that ask volunteers to work for at least one year, CVM offers one-week seminars in El Salvador. Volunteers who have more than a week and less than a year to offer should still call to talk about possibilities. Their programs are an example of Liberation Theology, in which work toward improving literacy, health care, education, and agricultural production is swathed in an ecumenical, nonpartisan, but Christian, aura.

DOCTORS WITHOUT BORDERS, 30 Rockefeller Center, Suite 5425, New York, NY 10112, tel. (212) 649-5961. For physicians who can drop everything on a moment's notice to rush to the aid of disaster victims anywhere in the world. Thoroughly apolitical and nondogmatic, Doctors Without Borders' only reason to exist is to save lives and improve the health conditions of other human beings. At times, it can be dangerous.

INTERNATIONAL WORKCAMPS DIRECTORY is a publication from Volunteers for Peace, Tiffany Road, Belmont, VT 05730, tel. (802) 259-2759, that describes and details most of the European-style volunteer workcamps around the world.

PEACE CORPS, P-301, Washington, DC 20526, tel. (800) 424-8580. Traditionally, the Peace Corps has required a minimum commitment of 2 years. However, some skills are so needed that you may be able to offer 3 to 15 months, if you have certain abilities. The basic requirements are that you have at least 3 to 5 years of work experience and/or a college degree. In addition to the service time, you will be required to attend an intense training program for 8 to 14 weeks.

WORLD TEACH, Harvard Institute for International Development, 1 Eliot St., Cambridge, MA 02138-9611, tel. (617) 495-5527, fax (617) 495-1239. If you have a bachelor's degree (in any subject) and want to spend a summer or a year teaching in a foreign country, then, for a fee, World Teach will place you in a position that includes housing and a modest stipend. You will probably not be able to support yourself completely on that stipend, especially if you want to tour around the country before coming home, but you will have the opportunity to work, one on one, with locals, teaching their children and learning about their culture. In 1991, World Teach placed people in China, Costa Rica, Namibia, Poland, and Thailand. Another program, called Score, sends people interested in sports to South Africa for three months to coach black students.

Chapter Fourteen

GREEN CRUISES

From Small Sloops to
Stately Ships
▼ ▼ ▼

A FEW WORDS
▼ ▼ ▼

Forget about the ads you've seen on TV about cruising. You know the ones, with the bikini-clad woman singing and dancing her way across the Caribbean, or the steward floating along wide teak decks oblivious that a bald eagle might be soaring overhead. Green Cruises are as different from traditional cruises as Green Travel is from the old "If-It's-Tuesday-It-Must-Be-Belgium" tours. It's just that sometimes a ship or boat is the best or only way to get to certain wilderness areas. Or, sometimes, it's the most comfortable way to go. Besides, with more than 70 percent of the earth covered by water, how better to explore, encounter, and learn about the wondrous profusion of sea life?

The great majority of Green vessels are much smaller than traditional cruise ships. Requiring less space in which to move or moor, they can anchor in small, shallow coves and don't need the kind of commercial wharfs that aren't available in the less-developed areas of the world. In other words, they can venture where few tourists have ever been, seeking out the empty, untouched, still beautiful spaces on the map. They maneuver with ease when chasing whales or winding through pack ice. And they carry fewer passengers, which means that when you go ashore, you won't be part of a hoard descending on and potentially destroying the fragile balance of the native culture and ecology.

In the terms of nautical design, small is synonymous with compact. The smaller your boat or ship, the fewer amenities and the less space per passenger you will have. But most Green Travelers tend to prefer ships or boats that don't have casinos, big shows, lots of bars, etc. They have chosen this type of cruise specifically because they want to focus on the sea, their destinations, and the specific program on board. They don't wish to be distracted by the fun and games available on those large floating resorts. On the other hand, there are compromise ships, such as those offered by Paquet and Ocean Cruises (see profiles below), that are Green because of where they go and the lecture series they offer but are more traditional and commercial in terms of accommodations and amenities.

Small, of course, is a relative term. The ships and boats in this chapter range from about 5 tons to 18,100 tons. Yet, even with that wide a spectrum of size, it is possible to make certain generalizations about what it's like to go on a Green Cruise.

Green Cruises, like all Green Travel, are friendly and intimate, with little or no barriers between people. This is a point of necessity, since everything is usually quite close, but it is also a natural outgrowth of the bonding of like-minded people who are setting out together on an adventure.

Given the limitations of size, Green Cruises also tend to be more egalitarian, with most cabins very similar to each other, though there may be a handful of more expensive "suites" on some of the ships. And, as a rule, the smaller the ship or boat, the higher the percentage of outside cabins. (An outside cabin has a view of the sea, though it may be no more than a waterline porthole. It is considered preferable to inside cabins, which are usually priced lower, but which may seem claustrophobic. Just about all the small boats in this chapter offer only outside cabins. Usually, only the larger ships have inside cabins.)

On traditional cruise ships, there are so many passengers that the dining room can't accommodate all of them. So, lunch and dinner are usually served in two seatings, with each passenger rigidly assigned to a specific table and a certain time for the entire trip. On the vast majority of Green Cruises, meals are served in flexible, single, open-seatings, which means you can change tables and dining companions with every meal. The exceptions to this rule are noted in the individual cruise company profiles below.

The navigation bridge (with exceptions) is usually open to passengers at any time of day or night. (For security purposes, and because the number of passengers are simply too large to control, the bridge is almost never opened on traditional ships.) On the very small boats, passengers may actually be invited to help take the helm or man the lines, if they wish. On the larger expedition ships, the captain or mate will be happy to explain the technology of navigation and assist you in reading the charts. Or, you may just want to join your fellow passengers and staff naturalists on the bridge, for the romance of it or for the best view of the sea, land, and far horizon. At least once in your cruise, go up to the bridge at night, when the only light is that of the moon, stars, and luminescent sea. You'll cherish that moment of black radiant silence for the rest of your life.

Since your ship or boat will usually anchor out in a harbor or cove, you will have to take a smaller boat or launch ashore. Most Green vessels use zodiacs for this purpose. Zodiacs are extremely seaworthy, rubber-pontooned boats. You've probably seen them in documentaries about scuba diving. Being somewhat flexible, they bend a bit when they hit a wave rather than thud like typical launches. This makes them quite stable and safe. But you have to be agile enough to climb in and out of them. (We have seen octogenarians scrambling out of zodiacs with ease. It seems to be more a factor of spirit than age.) "Wet" landings are usually made by running the zodiac up onto the beach and jumping out into the surf. That's why so many Green Cruise packing lists recommend bringing knee-high rubber boots and waterproof pants. The zodiac is unsurpassed in providing freedom of movement in the sea when you want to set out to chase a pod of whales or study the strange geological formations of a sea-washed cliff. More than anything else, zodiacs have become the symbol of adventure cruises.

What are the negatives of taking a Green Cruise? Again, the answer is that the vessels are small. Since Green Travel will take you to the remote regions of the world, going there by boat or ship may mean that you will have to cross wide reaches of open sea. In other words, your itinerary may take you into rough waters. The smaller the vessel, the more it will be bounced about by the currents. If this worries you (or your stomach), then the best answer is to stick to the larger ships whenever possible. You'll feel the sea less when there is more ship around you. Or, keep to routes that don't go into the open sea, such as trips on rivers or ones that keep close to protected coastlines. Also, try to book a cabin that is in midships, which is the most stable place on a ship.

ABERCROMBIE & KENT
▼ ▼ ▼

Having made its name in high-quality, nonintrusive, conservation-oriented photo safaris in Africa, A & K has now branched out to tours throughout the world. (See the write-up in the "All Things Wild and Beautiful" section, pages 81–82.) This includes exclusive, interesting cruises on very small but comfortable boats or charter yachts to exotic regions such as the Galapagos, Indonesia, and China.

Abercrombie & Kent is fully aware of its own elite standing, and A & K clients tend to be among the wealthiest and most sophisticated of travelers. Therefore, superb service that takes into consideration all details and possible requests is A & K's hallmark. They couldn't have survived all these years as a leader in this market otherwise. For instance, on most cruise itineraries, most or all of your meals ashore, when you are not with the group or on the ship, are included. And you can dine anywhere you wish, whenever you wish. All cruises include expert lecturers, expedition leaders, and extremely knowledgeable staff that know the region, speak the local language, and have established personal friendships with the local leaders of the community and government. This can lead to unusual invitations for the entire group to private homes or, even, palaces. Of course, it is taken for granted that A & K clients are quite accustomed to familiarity with the upper echelon of any society. It is quite common for passengers to arrange (with or without the assistance of A & K) independent or group land travel to explore the region more intimately, before and after the cruise. They may stay away from home as long as several months, and though they are willing to rough it or trek through difficult terrain for the sake of adventure, they expect and get a certain level of comfort, even luxury, at the end of the day.

In addition to those described below, A & K has other cruises, including their own boat on the Nile River. A & K also markets voyages with Society Expeditions (see pages 241–243).

DESTINATIONS: In China, A & K has cruises along the historic Yangtzi River, which call at Chongqing, Fengdu, Shibaozhai, Wanxian, Yunyang, Fengjie, The Three Small Gorges, and Yichang. According to their Galapagos brochure, "While uncontrollable factors such as weather and water conditions can affect your cruise itinerary in the Galapagos, . . . we ensure that you spend as much time as possible on 'enchanted isles' . . ." Indonesia is so large (over 17,000 islands that spread across thousands of miles of sea) that any cruise can only offer a sampling. One A & K cruise visits Bali, Komodo, Sumbawa, Flores, Timor, and Lembata, while the other stops at Bali, Satonda, Lombok, Komodo, Sumba, Sawu, and Timor. The two alternate, so they may be combined for a longer, more comprehensive cruise.

SEASON: The China cruise is offered April through October. Galapagos and Indonesia cruises are available all year.

LENGTH OF PROGRAMS: The Yangtzi River cruise, which generally lasts 5 days is usually packaged in the middle of a 17-day China tour. But you may purchase the cruise separately. (The prices below reflect a 5-day cruise.) Galapagos programs vary, with an average cruise lasting about 11 days and the charter programs 7 days. The Indonesian cruises are 7 days each, which can be combined for a cruise of 14 days.

ENROLLMENT: On the Yangtzi (China) cruises, there is a limit of 72 passengers. In Indonesia, the MV *Island Explorer* carries 36 passengers on a double-occupancy basis or up to 56 if all cabins carry triple occupancy (which is highly unlikely). Its sister ship, the MV *Spice Islander*, carries 42 passengers, double occupancy, or up to 60, triple occupancy. In the Galapagos, the MV *Isabela II* accommodates up to 40 passengers, and the *Lammer Law* has space for up to 18 passengers.

TOTAL COST: $1,250 to $4,710

COST PER DIEM: $250 to $390

TAX DEDUCTIBLE?: No

COST INCLUSIVE OF: Shore excursions; sightseeing (including entrance fees); most meals ashore and transportation as listed in the itinerary; all meals on board; services of a professional guide and excursion leader; one bottle of mineral water per person per meal (China and Galapagos); free use of the ship's watersports equipment (Indonesia)

COST EXCLUSIVE OF: Gratuities, air transportation, sightseeing or meals other than that which is listed in their catalog as part of the itinerary, airport taxes

AMENITIES, FACILITIES, AND REALITIES: On the Yangtzi, the 2,800-ton MS *Bashan* has 36 cabins (including some larger suites), all double occupancy, with picture windows, lower twin beds, private bathrooms (head, sink, and shower), and air conditioning. It also has a small swimming (or wading) pool, a glassed-in observation deck, a small lecture hall/cinema, a tiny shop, a hairdresser, and a doctor-staffed clinic where Western and traditional Chinese medical care is available.

The sister ships MV *Island Explorer* and the MV *Spice Islander*, which A & K uses in Indonesia, are small motorized catamarans, whose cabins all have outside views, most with twin beds (though some double beds are available), all with private bathrooms, telephone, and piped-in music channels. They also offer a lounge with bar where lectures and briefings are held, a covered patio adjacent to the sun deck, and a library. Watersports equipment available at no extra charge includes: scuba (for certified divers), snorkel, fishing gear, water skis, windsurfers, Hobie Cat sailboat (on the *Explorer*), aluminum skiffs (the *Islander*) and zodiacs (the *Explorer*). The *Islander* also carries its own glass-bottom boat and has a rear swimming ramp. The *Island Explorer* (859 tons) is larger than the *Spice Islander* (884 tons), but the former carries fewer passengers. This means that the *Island Explorer* has more space per passenger. It also has a slightly shallower draft. On the other hand, the *Spice Islander* has one more bar/lounge. Neither carries a doctor, nor is there easily accessible medical assistance ashore. However, a registered nurse may travel with the ship.

In the Galapagos, A & K offers cruises on the motor vessel the MV *Isabela II* and the sailing trimaran *Lammar Law*. The *Isabela II* has 20 cabins and air conditioning. On the *Isabela II*, you may encounter passengers who booked through another agent other than A & K. The *Lammer Law* has 9 air-conditioned cabins whose twin beds may be pushed together to become doubles. The cabins on both boats have private bathrooms (head, shower, and sink). Dinner and lunch are served *al fresco* on the deck of the *Lammer Law*. It's hard to imagine a more romantic way to see the Galapagos than under sail.

A & K can also arrange a crewed charter yacht (sail or motor) for your use in the Galapagos, accompanied by a naturalist. If you get together with 11 friends, your portion of the shared cost can be much less than many Galapagos cruises.

CONTACT: Abercrombie & Kent, 1420 Kensington Rd., Oak Brook, IL 60521, tel. (800) 323-7308, or, in Illinois, (708) 954-2944.

AMERICAN CANADIAN CARIBBEAN LINE
▼ ▼ ▼

ACCL offers highly accessible, relaxed, nonintellectual excursion cruising to unusual but mostly domestic destinations. The design of ACCL's two ships— *New Shoreham II* and *Caribbean Prince*—is what defines the company's style of cruising. Quite small (about 89 tons), carrying comparatively few passengers in very small, no-frills cabins, the vessels are intimate and homey, with few amenities (they suggest you bring your own beach towel), family-style dining, and a BYOB bar (mixers and sodas are free). A ramp opens out from the bow (front) to allow passengers to just walk off onto isolated beaches, and a small platform in the stern (rear) provides direct access to the sea for snorkeling, sailing, and rides on the ship's own glass-bottom boat. Sunfish sailboats (that carry one or two people) and snorkeling equipment are also available at no extra charge. Therefore, the focus of the southern cruises is on the sea, with numerous additional opportunities for beachcombing, sunbathing, and other lazy shoreline activities. Shore excursions further inland tend to be unusual, well-organized tours and are available at very reasonable additional cost (average about $10 per person). In fact, everything is done on ACCL with an eye to keeping the cost down for passengers.

Don't look for the lectures by natural and human history experts that one usually gets on Green Cruises. There are no organized activities of any kind on board and only the optional shore excursions when you approach land. Passengers tend to be independent, intelligent, well-educated individuals who can entertain themselves, appreciate a good price, and care little for luxury. The northern and intracoastal cruises attract a more sedate group than the Caribbean cruises. In fact, other than the watersports and shore excursions, passengers pass the time on board the ship playing cards, reading, and fishing from the rail. (Bring your own fishing gear.) The average age tends to be about 63, but younger travelers who want a relaxing inexpensive cruise to beautiful regions away from the crowds would do well with this company.

DESTINATIONS: In the winter, ACCL sails to out-of-the-ordinary islands in the Caribbean, including the smaller Bahamas and nontouristy Virgin Islands.

Summer and fall foliage cruises sail along Erie Canal (with its locks) and the St. Lawrence Seaway to Montreal, Quebec, and the Saguenay River. (The ships' pilot houses actually retract down into the lower deck so they can clear the bridges on this northern route.) Repositioning cruises in the spring and autumn go along the historic intracoastal waterway of the eastern United States. The Belize Barrier Reef itinerary is especially noteworthy, with its profusion of marine life, lush rain forest, interesting archeological sites, and empty coves. Idyllic waterways and exotic wildlife are the focus of the spring Everglades cruise, which also goes to Lake Okeechobee, Caloosahatchee River, Fort Myers, Indian Key, Shark River, Marquesas Key, the Dry Tortugas, Key West, Marco Island, and other islands and beaches.

SEASON: All year, with seasonal offerings as noted above in "Destinations"

LENGTH OF PROGRAMS: 12 to 15 days

ENROLLMENT: 76 passengers on the *New Shoreham II* and 80 on the *Caribbean Prince*

TOTAL COST: $1,190 to $2,495, depending upon your cabin category and itinerary

COST PER DIEM: $99 to $183

TAX DEDUCTIBLE?: No

COST INCLUSIVE OF: All meals, snacks, cabin, soft drinks, use of snorkeling equipment and sunfish sailboats, rides on glass-bottom boat, parking at Warren (Rhode Island) for the northern cruises, and, on the Caribbean cruises only, transfers from the airport

COST EXCLUSIVE OF: Air transportation to the ship, gratuities, shore excursions, and, on the northern cruises, transfers from the airport

AMENITIES, FACILITIES, AND REALITIES: ACCL's ships are very small, barely larger than yachts. Therefore, if you need space to wander, you may feel cramped or, even, claustrophobic. The cabins are about 8' × 10' each, with private bathrooms (head, sink, and shower) and air conditioning. All cabins have outside views. For an additional $50 per person, you may arrive a day early for the southern cruises and use the ship as your floating hotel, but no meals will be provided during that extra day. There is a minimum cancellation fee of $50 per person (which may be taken in the form of a voucher for a future cruise), but depending upon how close to your cruise you decide not to go, you may forfeit as much as 100 percent of the cruise fee.

CONTACT: American Canadian Caribbean Cruise Line, Box 368, Warren, RI 02885, tel. (800) 556-7450.

BIOLOGICAL JOURNEYS

As its name implies, Biological Journeys specializes in natural history cruises on small yachts that provide up-close educational encounters with wildlife. As Ron Levalley, one of the owner/managers, explained to us, "Our goal is to thoroughly involve people in the subject they came to see." Whales of all kinds—sperm, blue, gray, humpback, killer, Bryde's, fin, etc.—are Biological's specialty. They know where those magnificent creatures tend to be at specific times of year and bring you in close, sometimes to touch one (in the San Ignacio Lagoon, Baja, in February) or even, possibly, swim with them (in the Galapagos in late January or early February). On the Australia trip, whale sightings are rare. They also seek out and study exotic birds, seals and sea lions, dolphins and porpoises, giant tortoises, tropical fish and desert flowers, grizzly bears and bald eagles, etc.

Alaska's Inside Passage has a profusion of wildlife that most large tours only briefly glimpse when a humpback or grizzly or bald eagle happens to cross their paths. Biological Journeys devotes the entire summer in Alaska to yacht cruises designed to seek out these creatures and learn about them.

Each trip has a specific theme, related to the type of wildlife that will be accessible. All programs are lead by expert naturalists, who share their knowledge and understanding freely, enthusiastically, and do not conform to a head-office established itinerary. Instead, each trip's flexibility is designed to increase the frequency and quality of wildlife sightings and encounters. On some trips, you'll have the opportunity to snorkel among hundreds of technicolor fish that inhabit tropical reefs. Others include hikes through land so empty you'd swear you were the first human to step foot there. Of course, the animals you'll see and the activities available will depend upon which Biological Journey you take.

Biological Journeys has been in this business for a while, but they remain a small owner-operated company that has a strong commitment to ecological conservation. You'll not find Styrofoam cups on board, and all attempts are made to control garbage, taking it away from the region and recycling it. The number of participants per cruise is strictly limited to increase the quality of the experience and control the potential of any impact on the environment. Don't expect luxury or even private bathrooms. Informality is the key phrase. Meals are family-style, with local seafood and produce offered whenever possible. Passengers may help themselves to coffee, tea, and snacks in the galley; they are even welcome to start the morning coffee pot if they're the first to get up. Every evening, there is some kind of presentation, such as a lecture, slide show, or informal discussion in which everyone quickly becomes involved. If you weren't an avid conservationist when you started the cruise, you will be by the end of it. In fact, it isn't uncommon for passengers to pool donations for local study and conservation projects, because once they have become so intimate with the natural beauty of a region, they find it hard to remain passive. Passengers are encouraged by the tour naturalists to become involved back home in conservation.

DESTINATIONS: Baja California, Galapagos, Amazon, Alaska, Australia. There is also a tour of Australia and the Great Barrier Reef.

SEASON: Biological Journeys essentially follows the whales, with overlapping seasons. From June to September, Biological Journeys travels to Alaska. Galapagos cruises are offered from January to August. No cruises are offered October through December, other than the single Australia/Great Barrier Reef tour which is in October. However, some land programs are available in Ecuador all year.

LENGTH OF PROGRAMS: 4 to 22 days

ENROLLMENT: In Alaska, Galapagos, and Australia, the limit is 8 to 10 passengers. In Baja California, larger boats are used that accommodate 14 to 26 passengers.

TOTAL COST: $1,195 to $4,595, depending upon your itinerary

COST PER DIEM: $190 to $388

TAX DEDUCTIBLE?: No

COST INCLUSIVE OF: Meals, field trips accompanied by a naturalist, a windbreaker with insignia. In Galapagos, hotel accommodations before and after the cruise and whatever permits are necessary.

COST EXCLUSIVE OF: Air transportation, gratuities

AMENITIES, FACILITIES, AND REALITIES: Biological charters different boats at different times in various parts of the world. So, it is difficult to pin down exactly what you can expect. However, as Ron Levalley says, "You would not call them luxurious. Sometimes the staterooms would be better called closets. But we can promise you a clean, warm, dry place to sleep, hot showers, and good food." Most cabins are sold on a double-occupancy basis, though some can (and may) hold more people. Generally, there's approximately one head for every two cabins. One of the Galapagos boats does offer private bathrooms. On the other hand, another boat that they may use in the Baja has only four heads for 26 passengers. The waters they sail are generally pleasant, but the return trip from San Ignacio to San Diego can be rather rough. By the way, the consumption of hard liquor is discouraged. As the company's guidelines state, "Ordinarily, hard liquor is out of place on a vessel. A ship is simply no place for drunken or disorderly behavior." They also suggest that if you are sensitive to noise, to consider bringing earplugs—which indicates just how close everything tends to be on these boats. On most cruises, there is little opportunity for shopping for souvenirs or any forgotten necessities. Biological does offer patches and tee shirts for sale.

OTHER COMMENTS: Biological Journeys is a member of the Specialty Travel Alliance, which is made up of small owner-operated companies that "offer a broad range of intellectually and physically stimulating involvement with uncommon and rewarding environments." Members are required to have been in business at least 5 years (on average 10 years), limit their groups to 2 to 26 participants, provide useful and interesting pre-trip information, control their impact on the fragile ecologies and cultures they visit, and practice sound "nonconsumptive use of resources."

CONTACT: Biological Journeys, 1696 Ocean Drive, McKinleyville, CA 95521, tel. (800) 548-7555

CLASSICAL CRUISES
▼ ▼ ▼

Classical Cruises is the retail arm of Travel Dynamics, one of the more respected wholesale cruise companies, which specializes in providing programs for university alumni associations, major museums, and other important special-interest groups. Travel Dynamics' rather impressive client list includes the Smithsonian Institute, the American Museum of Natural History, the International Oceanographic Foundation, and the alumni associations of Harvard, Princeton, and Yale. Classical offers the public most of the same itineraries, and sometimes the very same trips as Travel Dynamics, depending upon whether or not the contracting organization releases unsold berths. The cruises focus on the intellectually stimulating aspects of their destinations. Lectures by university professors, museum curators, and other experts are the centerpiece of a Classical cruise, and passengers are avid students who carry on the classroom-inspired discussions through dinner and into the evening. Passengers tend to be rather mature, somewhat sedate, and well educated.

Classical Cruises comes from Greece, so they are very at home in that region and know how to seek out unusual, fun, and interesting attractions and events. A feast at a taverna ends with passengers dancing back to the ship. Other shore activities may include wine tasting in Santorini, a Cretan dance and musical performance in Aghios Nicholaos, etc. Classical claims to spend more time in ports than other cruise lines, giving passengers the time to set out and explore on their own. The Antarctic cruises, by their nature, have no opportunity for similar cultural experiences, but they do carry a larger contingent of lecturers in Antarctica than in Greece. Precruise land tours are included in your cost.

DESTINATIONS: Classical cruises has long specialized in voyages through the Greek Isles in the Aegean Sea and onto Turkey and the Black Sea. A few years ago, they also added trips to the Antarctic Peninsula from South America. Other itineraries may be available, especially during repositioning, shoulder seasons.

SEASON: Antarctica: in January and February, which is the summer down there; Aegean and Black Seas: May through October.

LENGTH OF PROGRAMS: 11 to 22 days

ENROLLMENT: Up to 140 passengers, double occupancy

TOTAL COST: $3,175 to $7,895, depending on your cabin category and destination

COST PER DIEM: $265 to $564

TAX DEDUCTIBLE?: No, unless you book through one of the special-interest groups in which case a small portion of your cost or perhaps whatever membership fee is involved may be tax deductible.

COST INCLUSIVE OF: Air transportation from New York, hotel accommodations, breakfast, and some sightseeing tours for a couple of days before boarding the ship, transfers, all meals on board the ship. Also, in Antarctica, shore excursions, a red expedition parka, a copy of *Natural History of the Antarctic Peninsula*, annotated reading list, map portfolio, wildlife checklists, flight bag, document wallet, port charges, post-cruise log.

COST EXCLUSIVE OF: Transportation to New York, port charges (in the Aegean and Black Seas), shore excursions (Aegean and Black Seas), gratuities

AMENITIES, FACILITIES, AND REALITIES: While Classical Cruises may occasionally charter other vessels, just about all of its voyages are on board the 4,000-ton cruise ship *Illiria*. All 74 cabins have a private bathroom (head, sink, and shower), phone, radio, and air conditioning; ten of them do not have a view of the sea. Services include 24-hour room service and the complimentary use of terry robes and toiletries. The rather popular library is well stocked. Other facilities include a small gym and sauna, a small swimming pool, a beauty salon, a gift shop, a card room, and a main lounge. A band plays in the evening for those who wish to dance. Unlike most ships in this section, the navigation bridge is not open to passengers except by appointment, on special request. In the Aegean and Black Seas, the chef uses local produce, meats, and fish whenever possible. Complimentary house wines are served with lunch and dinner.

OTHER COMMENTS: Some cruises that are contracted exclusively to a certain special-interest group may still be available to the public. In some cases, you will be asked to join an organization, which involves paying a membership fee. Other times, you may just be able to talk your way onto the passenger list. If Classical can't provide you with a berth on the cruise you want to take, ask them for the name of the organization that has booked it and call directly.

CONTACT: Classical Cruises, 132 E. 70th St., New York, NY 10021, tel. (800) 252-7745 in U.S., or (800) 245-7746 in Canada.

CLIPPER CRUISE LINE
▼ ▼ ▼

More upscale than American Canadian Cruise Line, but less adventurous or elite than Abercrombie & Kent's cruises, Clipper is a yachtsman's cruise line that has recently added some very Green destinations. The best description of Clipper's small ships is to say that they feel like a floating country clubhouse. What makes them noteworthy is their destinations, which tend to be domestic, with some forays into the Caribbean and Central America, plus the ability of their small ships to focus on the small ports that other larger, more traditional cruise lines bypass.

In those areas where the natural beauty and wildlife are the point of the cruise (such as Costa Rica, Orinoco River, and Baja California), zodiacs are used to bring passengers in closer. However, along the two U.S. coasts, Clipper pulls right up to the wharf and passengers walk right into the nearby historic areas. Established in 1982, Clipper's philosophy has long been to avoid touristy areas. They cater to mature, well-educated travelers who aren't looking to be entertained and prefer a casual, though stylish, atmosphere. Therefore, the only organized activities on board are lectures by guest experts on the regions visited. In the evenings, passengers entertain themselves with card games, reading, or strolls along the waterfront.

The Audubon Society of New York state and various corporate partners, including Clipper, have formed The Earth Fund, "to provide funding for a wide variety of environmental research, education, and conservation projects in specifically designated areas in the Western Hemisphere." The Earth Fund also participates in several cruises on Clipper's ships including: "The Orinoco Jungle River and Lower Caribbean," "Costa Rica's National Parks and the Darien Jungle," "Wildlife on the Intracoastal Waterway," "A Naturalist's Perspective of Southeast Alaska," and "The Ecology and History of the Chesapeake Bay."

DESTINATIONS: The American coasts from New England down to Florida (including the Intracoastal Waterway) and from Baja California to Alaska are

Clipper's focus. They also offer superb explorations of the lesser-known Virgin Islands, Costa Rica's National Parks and the Panama Canal, plus the lower Caribbean and South America's Orinoco River.

SEASON: December to March: Caribbean. December to January: lower Caribbean and Orinoco River. February to March and November: Costa Rica and the Panama Canal. March to April and November: colonial South. April and November: colonial eastern seaboard. April and November: Pacific Mexico and Sea of Cortez whale watch. April to May and October: San Francisco Bay and Sacramento Delta. May and September: Columbia River and Olympic Peninsula. May to August: Alaska. May and September: British Columbia and Southeast Alaska. June and October: Chesapeake Bay. June and September: northern Intracoastal Waterway. June: New England. July: Maine and the Bay of Fundy. September to October: Chesapeake Bay and Hudson River.

LENGTH OF PROGRAMS: 6 to 15 days

ENROLLMENT: Up to 138 passengers on the *Yorktown Clipper*, 102 on the *Nantucket Clipper*

TOTAL COST: $1,500 to $5,300, depending on your cabin category and itinerary

COST PER DIEM: $212 to $353

TAX DEDUCTIBLE?: No, though if you participate in the Earth Fund cruises, a small portion of your cost may be tax deductible.

COST INCLUSIVE OF: Meals and other services onboard, use of snorkeling equipment

COST EXCLUSIVE OF: Shore excursions, air transportation, port charges, gratuities

AMENITIES, FACILITIES, AND REALITIES: The *Nantucket Clipper* and *Yorktown Clipper* are sleek and elegant but understated twin ships, with the lines of a beautiful yacht. Small (99.5 tons), they provide the kind of comfort one would expect at a country club. The cabins all have views of the sea, private bathrooms (head, sink, and shower), lower beds, and air conditioning. The food is wholesome, the hot chocolate chip cookies in the afternoon are legendary, and some local fish is occasionally served. The staff is solicitous and competent, providing good, unobtrusive service. The one observation lounge is more like a large, comfy living room. In other words, Clipper's "adventures" are thoroughly soft, undemanding experiences.

CONTACT: Clipper Cruise Line, 7711 Bonhomme Ave., St. Louis, MO 63105, tel. (800) 325-0010; or The Earth Fund, c/o The Audubon Society of New York

State, Hollyhock Hollow Sanctuary, Route 2, Box 131, Selkirk, NY 12158, tel.
(518) 767-9051.

OCEAN CRUISE LINES
▼ ▼ ▼

Ocean Cruises (and its sister company, Paquet, which is described below) breaks
the mold of what we have defined as Green Cruises. They use rather traditional
vessels, that even have casinos, dance bands, musical revues every evening, and
all the other activities (such as trivia contests, dance lessons, bingo, etc.) that
one expects from large mainstream ships. However, the destinations they visit
and the team of lecturers that they carry with them does bring them into the Green
sphere. In addition, the famous adventure travel pioneer, Lars-Eric Lindblad, is
now organizing Ocean's cruises to Antarctica, the Chilean fjords (Patagonia),
and the Falkland Islands, which does give these specific itineraries a distinguished
endorsement.

It should be noted that the *Ocean Princess* is the largest ship offering
cruises in the Antarctic and, as such, has been at the center of controversy.
Richard Taylor sailed on the *Princess*'s first Antarctic season as a National
Science Foundation observer to see just what kind of impact so many people
would have on the ecology. According to him, the passengers and the ship's
staff were quite careful to protect the environment. On the other hand, he ac-
knowledged that Ocean's passengers had less time ashore than those who were
on the more typical smaller ships. Take Ocean to Antarctica if you want (1)
more diversion than lectures, wildlife sightings and landings, (2) more creature
comforts, or (3) to minimize the effect of the rough seas of Drakes' Passage. As
stated in the beginning of this chapter, the larger the ship, the less you feel
the sea.

Ocean's passengers are intelligent, stimulating, curious, wanting to learn
from their travels rather than just collect another stamp in their passport. Given
the length and expense of the cruise, they tend to be mature, sophisticated, and
well-off. And, yes, they do dress for dinner every evening. But they also get
excited over sighting a whale or seeing a Balinese Barong ceremonial dance.
And they attend just about every on-board lecture.

By the way, Ocean Cruises is a rather complex company. Its parent company owns Paquet Cruises (see Paquet profile below), and the two lines are
marketed jointly. Also, until a corporate merger a few years ago, the *Ocean
Pearl* was known as the *Pearl of Scandinavia*, under which name it became
famous for its cruises into China. The *Pearl*'s reputation is of such a caliber that
Ocean Cruises continues to use the old name from time to time.

DESTINATIONS: The *Ocean Pearl* stays in the Orient, cruising to China, Indonesia, India, and the South China Sea. The *Ocean Princess* spends half the year in South America and Antarctica, offering Carnival cruises to Rio, voyages on the Amazon River, and explorations of Tierra del Fuego. The other half of the year, she takes off for Europe: the Scandinavian fjords, Baltic Sea, Iberian Peninsula, and the Mediterranean. Transatlantic crossings are available. (On most of the destinations, zodiacs are not used for landings.)

SEASON: May to October: Europe and China. October to May: Indonesia and India. January: Antarctica. January to April: South America.

LENGTH OF PROGRAMS: *Ocean Princess*: 11 to 19 days. *Ocean Pearl*: 18 to 24 days.

ENROLLMENT: *Ocean Princess*: 460 passengers. *Ocean Pearl*: 450 passengers.

TOTAL COST: $2,250 to $8,795, depending on your cabin category and itinerary

COST PER DIEM: $158 to $508

TAX DEDUCTIBLE?: No

COST INCLUSIVE OF: Air transportation, excellent pre- and postcruise hotel and sightseeing package, shore excursions (in China and Antarctica only), all meals on board, some meals ashore, sauna, and, in Antarctica, a red parka

COST EXCLUSIVE OF: Shore excursions (except in Antarctica and China), gratuities, massage, port and airport taxes, and some meals ashore

AMENITIES, FACILITIES, AND REALITIES: While not large compared to traditional cruise ships, the *Ocean Pearl* (12,456 tons) and the *Ocean Princess* (12,200 tons) are quite sizeable compared to the typical Green Travel vessels. Both ships have a number of inside cabins that have no windows. All the cabins have air conditioning, private bathrooms (sink, head, shower, and, in some cases, bathtub), telephone, and piped-in music channels. In addition, the *Pearl* has a number of higher-priced suites that have separate sitting rooms. Other facilities on the *Pearl* include: a fitness center, massage, sauna, one indoor and one outdoor swimming pool, cinema, laundry service, doctor's office, dining room, casino, gift shop, photographer, three bars, three entertainment lounges (including a piano bar and disco), hairdresser, and card room. The *Princess* has three bars, three entertainment lounges (including a piano bar and disco), dining room, one swimming pool, card room, casino, cinema, library, writing room, gift shop, hairdresser, doctor's office, photographer, deck tennis, sauna, massage, gym, and laundry service.

CONTACT: Ocean Cruise Lines, 1510 S.E. 17th St., Fort Lauderdale, FL 33316, fax (305) 764-2888

OCEAN VOYAGES
▼ ▼ ▼

Ocean Voyages offers charter sailing and motor boats all over the world that allow a small group of people to explore exotic regions. Enthusiastic, knowledgeable, personable crews take care of all the workaday problems of running a boat, including cooking, cleaning, unfurling the sails, and taking the wheel, but passengers are welcome to participate. In fact, a high percentage of passengers choose Ocean Voyages specifically because they want to learn how to navigate a small boat. And, according to Mary Crowley, the owner of Ocean Voyages, "By the end of the trip, anybody who wants to learn will be able to pilot a boat on his own."

Ocean makes a distinction between custom charter and adventure sails, which has to do with the way the boat is booked. All programs, which cater to individuals who want to join a small group on a boat, fall into the adventure category, which is the least expensive group of boats. On the other hand, a custom charter is booked whole by a group or individual, with no outsiders allowed, and with the itinerary completely in the hands of the participants (with nautical and sensible advice provided by the captain). Custom charters range through the entire spectrum, from inexpensive adventure boats to ultimately pampering luxury. There are also a few schooners and tall ships.

Certain boats specialize in teaching snorkeling or navigation, others can provide scuba diving. Some can be used for marine research or photo crews. "People have very individualized and personal experiences on our programs," said Crowley during an interview. "Some of our captains are lifelong friends of mine. . . . The captains have to really like people, enjoy teaching and sharing, and they have an environmental awareness and sensitivity. . . . Part of their love of the ocean is wanting to preserve it."

The captain and crew live in the region you will be visiting, so they know the secret hideaways, the perfect cove for snorkeling, where the wildlife can be found, what the best and least expensive restaurants are in port, etc. You quickly feel more like guests than tourists, but be prepared for close quarters.

DESTINATIONS: All over the world, including the Galapagos, Pacific Ocean, Europe, Caribbean, Alaska, Asia, etc.

Season: All year

Length of Programs: 1 week to 8 weeks

Enrollment: 4 to 10 passengers per typical boat, though some will hold more. Also, more than one boat may be chartered together to accommodate larger groups.

Total Cost: $525 to $5,955, depending upon the vessel, the itinerary, and the number of participants

Cost Per Diem: $68 to $168

Tax Deductible?: No

Cost Inclusive Of: Meals and soft drinks on board, instruction

Cost Exclusive Of: Air transportation, shore excursions

Amenities, Facilities, and Realities: As anyone who has ever sailed on a private boat will tell you, such vessels are far from spacious. Everything is fitted together compactly to maximize space, but even so, quarters tend to be cramped. Sailing boats are generally smaller on the inside than motor boats, and they usually take longer to get anywhere. However, on a sailboat, the voyage—just being under sail—is as important or more so than getting anywhere. By the way, when you are under sail, the boat will lean to one side or the other. You don't need experience on the sea to participate or enjoy these boats, but you should be an easygoing individual who doesn't mind being *very* close to other people and who views some discomfort as part of the great adventure. Before your trip, you will be asked to fill out a questionnaire, specifying your food and beverage preferences, including favorites and any that you don't wish to see.

Contact: Ocean Voyages, 1709 Bridgeway, Sausalito, CA 94965-1994, tel. (415) 332-4681. Fax (415) 332-7460.

Paquet French Cruises

▼ ▼ ▼

As with its sister company, Ocean Cruise Lines (see above), Paquet breaks the mold of what we have defined as Green Cruises. Paquet's ship, the *Mermoz*, is a rather traditional vessel that even has a casino, dance bands, musical revues every evening, and all the other activities (such as trivia contests, dance lessons, bingo, etc.) that one expects from large mainstream ships. However, some of the destinations it visits and the team of lecturers that it carries does bring them into the Green sphere. For instance, the *Mermoz* is the only large (13,800-ton) ship that has a permit to visit the Galapagos Islands. (However, the *Ocean Princess* may soon be sailing there, too.)

Also noteworthy are three special theme cruises. The highly acclaimed Music Festival at Sea brings together world-renown performers such as Mstisla Rostropovish, Jean-Pierre Rampal, Isaac Stern, and the Chamber Orchestra of the Berlin Philharmonic. They perform together, with rehearsals open to passengers, and they are available for informal get-togethers, mingling freely with their fellow travelers—all this and a cruise of the Mediterranean. For French-speaking passengers, there is the Theatre Festival at Sea, during which prominent French actors perform French plays while sailing among the Greek Isles. Or if you don't speak French and want to, there is the Berlitz French Immersion Course during a transatlantic crossing.

The biggest difference between Paquet and Ocean is Paquet's essential French character. Everything on board the *Mermoz* is done with a French flair.

DESTINATIONS: The Galapagos, Patagonia (and the Chilean fjords), Norwegian Fjords and Spitsbergen, the Caribbean, the Baltic, France and Iberia, Transatlantic

SEASON: All year, with different itineraries offered at different times

LENGTH OF PROGRAMS: 12 to 22 days, though there are some shorter voyages including a 7-day Caribbean cruise.

ENROLLMENT: 530 passengers, double occupancy

TOTAL COST: $2,650 to $21,395, depending on your cabin category and itinerary

COST PER DIEM: $147 to $1,337

TAX DEDUCTIBLE?: No

COST INCLUSIVE OF: Air transportation from New York (for the European cruises) or from Miami (for the Caribbean and South American cruises). Also, all meals on board, wine with lunch and dinner, transfers, pre- and postcruise hotel and sightseeing package, use of the sauna and exercise equipment, entertainment and daily activities.

COST EXCLUSIVE OF: Gratuities, shore excursions, spa treatments (such as hydrotherapy and massage)

AMENITIES, FACILITIES, AND REALITIES: There are differences between the various categories of cabins, and generally the higher price you pay, the larger cabin you will have. Some of the more expensive rooms even have bathtubs and sitting rooms. About 25 percent of the cabins are inside with no windows.

But all rooms have private bathrooms, air conditioning, multichannel music systems, and telephones. The cuisine is decidedly French, which includes complimentary wine with lunch and dinner. You are assigned to one of the two restaurants, depending upon just how much you spend on your cabin. Other facilities on the *Mermoz* include a cinema, a health club, a casino, a disco, photographer, gift shop, two small swimming pools, a Lido buffet (for informal breakfasts and lunches), barber shop/beauty salon, four bars, two entertainment lounges, library, two piano bars, a doctor, and two elevators. It should be noted that with this large a ship, you will not experience the intimacy with wildlife or your fellow passengers that you will have on smaller vessels. The advantage of larger ships, on the other hand, is that they are more accessible for those individuals who are physically limited or, even, confined to a wheelchair.

CONTACT: Paquet French Cruises, 1510 S.E. 17th St., Fort Lauderdale, FL 33316, tel. (305) 764-3500. Fax (305) 764-2888.

RENAISSANCE CRUISES

Among all the cruise companies listed in this book, Renaissance is the most luxurious, sophisticated, even sybaritic. It is made up of a fleet of eight nearly identical vessels of about 4,500 tons. Designed in the mold of *Sea Goddess*, as a thoroughly gracious, all-suite, white-glove fleet, Renaissance differs from other luxury cruise companies by focusing on the areas it visits with in-depth lectures presented by top experts, leisurely shore visits, pretrip reading lists, and dynamic natural history programs. In fact, many of their voyages are chartered by prestigious special-interest organizations such as the Smithsonian Institute, university alumni associations, etc.

Passengers are intellectual, well-educated, very well-off financially, and intensely curious about the world. According to David Gevanthor, Renaissance's former vice-president of marketing, ''These cruisers want attentive service and wonderful meals, but they also want more out of cruising, or indeed, out of any kind of trip. They want to learn and to grow, to be intellectually and even emotionally stimulated.'' But when the day of adventure is over, they relax in their ultimately comfortable suite, dine in a gourmet restaurant, and sip brandy under the stars. Or, to put it more succinctly, Renaissance caters to a champagne and caviar group that seeks soft adventure, natural beauty, and out-of-the-ordinary destinations.

DESTINATIONS: With such a large fleet of ships, Renaissance is able to cover the world. Among its many cruises are those to Indonesia, Malaysia, the Philippines, South China Sea, Caribbean, Indian Ocean, Japan, Korea, China,

Mediterranean, Adriatic Sea, Aegean, much of the European coastline, Scandinavia, Baltic Sea, Black Sea, Red Sea, the Seychelles, South America, etc. If you want to get somewhere, Renaissance probably goes there.

SEASON: All year, with different itineraries offered at different times

LENGTH OF PROGRAMS: 2 to 3 weeks, though there are longer cruises and consecutive cruises may be booked for a longer voyage

ENROLLMENT: *Renaissance I, II, III,* and *IV* carry up to 100 passengers. The other ships each carries up to 114.

TOTAL COST: $3,799 to $11,681, depending on your cabin, itinerary, and length of cruise

COST PER DIEM: $270 to $480

TAX DEDUCTIBLE?: No, though a very small portion may be deductible if it is booked through a nonprofit organization.

COST INCLUSIVE OF: Pre- and postcruise hotel and sightseeing package, air transportation from U.S. gateway cities, all meals and other services on board, sauna

COST EXCLUSIVE OF: Provisions used from your cabin refrigerator, massage, transportation from your hometown to the gateway airport, port changes, shore excursions

AMENITIES, FACILITIES, AND REALITIES: All cabins are luxury suites with a view of the sea, remote-control color TV and VCR, telephone, separate sitting area, refrigerator, queen-size bed (or two twins, if you wish), 24-hour room service, private bathrooms (sink, head, and shower), hair dryer, and lockable security drawer. The larger suites also have private verandas and walk-in closets. Before the trip, the company sends you a questionnaire on which you may indicate how you want your cabin refrigerator stocked. From the stern platform that opens up to sea level, you may swim, snorkel, or sail. Other facilities include: piano bar, a small swimming pool, jacuzzi, beauty salon, doctor, a main lounge, a library (of books and VCR tapes), massage, sauna, three bars, a blackjack table and slot machines, a small gift shop, and a hairdresser. Given the elegance of these ships, they offer probably the softest adventures in this entire book. If you want to get out and do for yourself, with no pretensions of style, you may wish to save your money and go on a less luxurious trip. However, if you can afford these cruises, they do give you your money's worth in gracious, intellectual stimulation.

CONTACT: Renaissance Cruises, 1800 Eller Drive, Suite 300, Fort Lauderdale, FL 33335-0307, tel. (800) 525-2450.

SALEN LINDBLAD CRUISING
▼ ▼ ▼

Salen Lindblad is a true expeditionary cruise line, with a strong commitment to conservation. Like its direct competitor, Society Expeditions, Salen offers a thorough immersion in the regions it visits. Expert lectures, extensive preparatory material (logs, reading lists, maps, etc.), naturalist-guided shore excursions, and a shared enthusiasm for the cultures and creatures of their destinations add up to a top-quality Green Cruise. (Please refer to the description of a typical Society Expeditions cruise, below, to get a clearer idea of what it is like to cruise with Salen Lindblad.)

More to the point, Salen's involvement with conservation is not just window-dressing but an active, almost proselytizing stance. The newer of their two ships, the *Frontier Spirit*, was the first vessel to be built with environmental safeguards incorporated in the design. Some of these safeguards include state-of-the-art garbage collection and sorting, onboard sewage treatment, oil separator in the bilge, etc. All refuse is held on board, in specially designed refrigerator units, if necessary, until it can be disposed of properly, rather than discharged into the fragile ecosystems that Salen visits (which is the traditional seafaring method). In addition, Salen not only distributes guidelines to their passengers informing them about what is expected from them to help protect the environment, the passengers on both the *Spirit* and the *Caledonian Star* are actually asked to sign an agreement promising not to litter or disturb the wildlife. (A fine may be enforced by Salen if a passenger is discovered littering.) Salen helped to establish and continues to support Oceanities, a nonprofit organization whose ''goal is raising the public's awareness and consciousness about the world's oceans, their inhabitants, and the islands and land masses found within and along their boundaries.'' Oceanities has organized ecotourism conferences on board the *Spirit* in which passengers participate.

DESTINATIONS: The *Frontier Spirit* sails through the Pacific, from New Zealand and Australia, through the many islands of Melanesia, Micronesia, and Polynesia, to Indonesia, Malaysia, Singapore, the South China Sea, up to Hong Kong, Taiwan, China, and Japan. Then, she crosses to the Aleutian Islands and Alaska and heads north through the Arctic Northwest Passage to Greenland, the eastern Canadian Maritimes and New England. Heading back south, she sails to the Bahamas, the Caribbean, South America's Orinoco River, the Amazon River, the South American eastern coast, the Falkland Islands, and Tierra del Fuego. The final destination is Antarctica from where she continues again in this grand annual loop. (This past year, her Arctic Passage was blocked by ice.) The *Caledonian Star* focuses on unusual cruises of coastal Europe, in the north and south, including a circumnavigation of Ireland and trips to the isolated British isles of Scilly, Hebrides, Skye, Orkney, and Shetland. It also cruises to Egypt, Africa, the Canary Islands, the Seychelles, and the Indian Ocean.

SEASON: All year, with different itineraries offered at different times. For instance, the Arctic Northwest Passage is available in the summer, the British Isles in August, etc.

LENGTH OF PROGRAMS: The *Caledonian* cruises (8 to 19 days) tend to be slightly shorter than the *Frontier Spirit*'s (10 to 31 days).

ENROLLMENT: The *Frontier Spirit* carries up to 164 passengers, the *Caledonian Star* carries up to 134.

TOTAL COST: *Caledonian Spirit*: $2,900 to $6,305. *Frontier Spirit*: $3,050 to $26,200.

COST PER DIEM: *Caledonian Spirit*: $221 to $606. *Frontier Spirit*: $218 to $845.

TAX DEDUCTIBLE?: $25 out of every ticket purchased is donated to Oceanities, which may make that small amount tax deductible.

COST INCLUSIVE OF: Air transportation on some itineraries, shore excursions (including entrance fees to any museums, parks, etc.), pre- and postcruise hotel and sightseeing package, sauna, snorkel equipment, scuba gear (for certified divers), transfers, all meals on board and some ashore, medical services on board, postcruise expedition logbook, port charges, and other taxes

COST EXCLUSIVE OF: Air transportation on some itineraries, massage, some meals ashore, gratuities

AMENITIES, FACILITIES, AND REALITIES: While the *Frontier Spirit* was built for Salen Lindblad and was inaugurated in 1990, the *Caledonian Star* previously sailed for the now defunct Exploration Cruise Lines as the *North Star*. On the 3,095-ton *Caledonian Star*, every cabin has an ocean view, air conditioning, and a private bathroom (sink, head, and shower). Other facilities and amenities on the *Caledonian Star* include: swimming pool, observation deck, lecture hall, library, one bar, two lounges, and small shop. Every cabin on the 6,700-ton *Frontier Spirit* has a view of the sea, telephone, TV, sitting area, air conditioning, refrigerator, and private bathroom (head, sink, shower, and, in the most expensive suites, bathtub). The suites also have private verandas. The *Spirit* is a Super Ice Class ship, especially designed for polar expeditions. Other facilities and amenities on the *Spirit* include: a helipad, massage, gymnasium, sauna, small swimming pool, scuba and snorkeling gear, library, one bar, one main lounge, observation lounge, a launderette and full-service laundry, beauty parlor, small shop, and a marine laboratory where specimens are collected, displayed, and explained. The *Frontier Spirit* is the finest expedition ship afloat. And though Salen is expensive, it provides an unsurpassed expeditionary experience.

CONTACT: Salen Lindblad Cruising, 133 East 55th Street, New York, NY 10022, tel. (800) 223-5688, or (212) 751-2300 in New York. For further information on Oceanities, 2378 Route 97, Cooksville, MD 21723, tel. (301) 854-6262.

SOCIETY EXPEDITIONS

Society Expeditions has long been the queen of adventure cruising, setting the standards for top-quality, educational experiences in exotic areas. Known for its dedication to sharing with its passengers its considerable understanding and intimate relationship with wildlife and unusual cultures, Society has been and continues to be a leader in assuming responsibility for controlling its impact on ecologies and societies around the world. Their most direct competitor is Salen Lindblad, and passengers will probably choose between these two companies based upon where they wish to go, and when.

On a Society cruise (as on Salen and Special Expeditions), you will be thoroughly immersed in the natural and social history of the region visited. Landings ashore (via zodiacs) are naturalist-led explorations of wilderness areas or seldom-visited towns and villages, with plenty of opportunity to take off on your own on leisurely walks or rigorous hikes. A full and varied series of lively lectures and beautiful slide shows by top experts is presented every day, whenever a shore landing isn't planned. You'll learn more about birds and conservation than you ever thought would interest you—and you'll be fascinated, because the enthusiasm of Society's naturalists is contagious. Between landings and lectures and informal discussions, all eyes are on the sea, in search of whales, dolphins, and other creatures. Be prepared for early morning announcements of wildlife sightings over the loudspeaker at the head of your bed when you're fast asleep. That's when everybody scrambles in varying stages of dress, with binoculars and cameras, to the outside decks and navigation bridge. The captain may veer off course to follow the animals for a while, giving everyone a chance for exciting views that they wouldn't have wanted to sleep through, even if they could.

Considering Society's standing as a leader in expeditionary cruising (as well as the wonderfully photogenic places they visit), it's no surprise that its ships have been chosen by Leica (the manufacturer of the finest camera in the world) as the site for Leica's photography workshops and seminars. If you are interested in participating in a Leica workshop, be sure to tell Society when you book your cruise. (Not all cruises have a workshop, and you don't need to own a Leica to participate.) Among the many prestigious special-interest groups that work with Society are: Sierra Club, Smithsonian, Audubon Society, California Academy of Sciences, Los Angeles Museum of Natural History, etc. Society is now marketed in the United States by Abercrombie & Kent, which is a rather natural marriage between two elite tour companies.

DESTINATIONS: Society Expeditions specializes in exotic destinations, such as: Antarctica, Falkland Islands, South American jungles, the Chilean fjords, Seychelles and other islands of the Indian Ocean, Indonesia, Papua New Guinea, the Solomon Islands, Polynesia, Easter Island, etc.

SEASON: All year, with different programs offered at different times. Essentially, the tropical itineraries are wedged between the southern summer (December–February) in the Antarctic and, when the cruises are available, the northern summer (July–August) in the Arctic.

LENGTH OF PROGRAMS: 8 to 26 days, with a greater emphasis on the longer cruises

ENROLLMENT: *World Discoverer*: 140 passengers. *Society Explorer*: 100 passengers.

TOTAL COST: $2,350 to $18,490, depending on your cabin category, itinerary, and length of cruise

COST PER DIEM: $168 to $840

TAX DEDUCTIBLE?: No, unless purchased through one of the many nonprofit organizations that charter voyages with Society, in which case a portion may be tax deductible.

COST INCLUSIVE OF: Shore excursions and expedition stops; group transfers and baggage handling; precruise hotel and sightseeing package; gratuities; precruise guidebook, reading list and maps; backpack, flight bag, documentation wallet, postcruise expedition logbook, and, for the Arctic and Antarctic cruises, a red parka with insignia

Cost Exclusive Of: Air transportation, some meals ashore

Amenities, Facilities, and Realities: The baby of the fleet (and the oldest), the *Society Explorer*'s small size (2,500 tons) has made her the favorite of many of the company's repeat passengers. But being smaller, she has fewer amenities and less space per person. The cabins have outside windows, air conditioning, and private bathrooms (sink, head, and shower). A couple of suites have sitting areas, but all the others are quite minuscule. Other facilities include: two bars, two lounges, library, tiny swimming pool, laboratory (for specimens collected during trip), tiny well-stocked gift shop, dining room, doctor's office, hairdresser, tiny gym, and sauna.

Until the launching of Salen Lindblad's *Frontier Spirit*, Society's *World Discoverer* was considered the best, most modern expedition ship. At 3,153 tons, she has room for two bars, two lounges, and an observation lounge, lecture hall, library/card room, a small but very well-stocked gift shop, tiny swimming pool, doctor's office, dining room, closet-sized gym, sauna, and hairdresser. The cabins all have outside views, air conditioning, two music channels, private bathrooms (shower, sink, and head), and offer the complimentary use of terry robes. There are a few suites with a separate sitting room.

Both ships have ice-hardened hulls. They also offer scuba and snorkel equipment (though it is suggested that you bring your own regulator and BC for diving), plus other watersports equipment. After the upcoming December 1991 to February 1992 Antarctica season, the *Explorer* is scheduled to be retired from the fleet. In summer 1991, the company declined delivery of a new ship that was designed and built for them—*Society Adventurer*. It would have rivaled Salen's *Frontier Spirit*.

Contact: Society Expeditions, 3131 Elliot Avenue, Suite 700, Seattle, WA 98121, tel. (800) 426-7794; or Abercrombie & Kent International, 1420 Kensington Road, Oak Brook, IL 60521, tel. (800) 323-7308, or, in Illinois, (708) 954-2944.

Special Expeditions

Another of the big-three adventure cruise lines (along with Society Expeditions and Salen Lindblad), Special Expeditions is a much smaller, less commercially polished operation. And, for many travelers, that is an important distinction. Special Expeditions' ships are homey, friendly, definitely cozier than those of the other two companies. And most of Special's itineraries tend to be closer to home, which makes them less expensive and easier to get to. However, while the names of most of the destinations seem rather familiar, the experience that Special has to offer is entirely different from any other trip you may have taken to the very same regions. Their naturalist and historian viewpoint refocuses our minds to see much more than we ever did.

Despite the differences between Special Expeditions and the other two companies, the description in the Society Expeditions profile above reflects rather closely what you can expect with Special—zodiac landings, naturalist-led excursions, lively lectures, enthusiastic wildlife sightings, attempts to follow whales, etc.

By the way, Special Expeditions is run by Sven-Olof Lindblad, the son of the famous adventure travel pioneer Eric-Lars Lindblad. Sven is a highly respected naturalist and wildlife photographer in his own right and keeps a rather close rein on the quality of Special's cruises (and the few land tours they offer).

DESTINATIONS: Most of Special Expeditions' itineraries are on the North American coasts. Columbia and Snake Rivers (Pacific northwest), Alaska Inside Passage, Baja whale watching, and the eastern Canadian Maritimes are some of their noteworthy routes. By the way, many travelers rate the Canadian Maritimes as highly as Alaska for pristine beauty and wildlife encounters, without the high cost of Alaska's tourist success. In addition, Special has a series of excellent cruises in the Caribbean, Central America, and South America's Orinoco River. For instance, one Central American cruise focuses on the area between the Yucatan Peninsula and Honduras, exploring the reefs, jungles, and ancient archeology of Belize, Tulum (Mexico), Copan (Honduras), etc. Also available are unique cruises of the British Isles and the Iberian Peninsula.

SEASON: All year, with different itineraries offered seasonally. For instance, the Canadian Maritime cruises are generally in late summer or autumn, and the Central American Mayan Coast is available December and/or January.

LENGTH OF PROGRAMS: 8 to 16 days

ENROLLMENT: *Polaris*: 80 passengers. *Sea Lion* and *Sea Bird*: 70 passengers each.

TOTAL COST: $1,860 to $8,670, depending on your cabin category, ship, and itinerary

COST PER DIEM: $223 to $542

TAX DEDUCTIBLE?: No

COST INCLUSIVE OF: All meals and services on board, all meals ashore during the cruise, shore excursions, transfers for those on group flights, informative precruise package, postcruise expedition logbook, free use of snorkeling equipment

COST EXCLUSIVE OF: Air transportation, gratuities

AMENITIES, FACILITIES, AND REALITIES: If you take the time to look at the numbers that dictate size and space per passenger on Special Expeditions' ships, you'll quickly see the difference between their flagship, *Polaris*, and the twins *Sea Lion* and *Sea Bird*. All three carry approximately the same number of passengers, but the *Polaris* is 2,214 tons, and the other two are each 99.7 tons. So while space on board the *Polaris* is close, the *Sea Lion* and *Sea Bird* are *tiny*. But to put that in perspective, they are designed primarily for river cruising, such as on the winding, wonderful Columbia River, where you want small vessels to get into all the nooks and crannies that would ground larger ships. The *Polaris* is more of an oceangoing vessel that is capable of combating the rough north Atlantic seas. The cabins on all three boats have air conditioning and private bathrooms (head, shower, and sink). Other facilities on the *Polaris* include: one lounge/bar, library, sauna, small gift shop, and doctor. The *Sea Bird* and *Sea Lion* have one lounge/bar and a doctor.

CONTACT: Special Expeditions, 720 Fifth Avenue, New York, NY 10019, tel. (800) 762-0003.

WORLD EXPLORER CRUISES

World Explorer Cruises does only one thing—and it does that better than anyone else—highly intellectual, educational, nonexpeditionary cruises of Alaska's Inside Passage.

Essentially, World Explorer's ship, *Universe*, is a floating university campus that becomes available to the adult public during the summer. The rest of the year, it is chartered for two Semesters at Sea, organized by the University of Pittsburgh. College students sail around the world, while taking a full-course load, attending lectures and classes on board, taking exams, and writing papers.

But in the summer, the kids go home, and the adults come to Alaska to attend lectures by professors, naturalists, historians, and other experts while sailing through the dramatic Alaskan scenery. World Explorer's shore excursions follow through with the shipboard philosophy that learning is not only fascinating but downright fun. They offer a large variety of unusual, intriguing, optional (i.e., extra cost) excursions that rank among the best in the state. Add to all that the fact that World Explorer's cruises are among the least expensive of any

Alaska tour. If you never tire of learning, you can't lose with this company. But if you want a more physically challenging or close-to-wildlife experience, you might find it a bit sedentary or aloof. Unlike most Green cruises, the navigation bridge is closed to passengers on the *Universe*, and zodiacs are not used for landings.

DESTINATIONS: An in-depth cruise of Alaska Inside Passage that sees more than any major cruise ship, sailing from Vancouver to visit Wrangell, Juneau, Skagway/Haines, Glacier Bay, Columbia Glacier, Valdez, Seward/Anchorage, Sitka, Ketchikan, and Victoria.

SEASON: May through August

LENGTH OF PROGRAMS: 14 days

ENROLLMENT: 550 passengers

TOTAL COST: $1,895 to $3,795, depending on your cabin category

COST PER DIEM: $135 to $271

TAX DEDUCTIBLE?: No

COST INCLUSIVE OF: All meals and services on board the ship, lectures

COST EXCLUSIVE OF: Air transportation, shore excursions, transfers (unless air is purchased through World Explorer), gratuities

AMENITIES, FACILITIES, AND REALITIES: The *Universe* is a large ship (18,100 tons) compared to all the others in this chapter, which means you have room to roam. But it is still not the *Love Boat*. Rather, the facilities reflect its primary function as a floating university. While all the cabins are air conditioned and have private bathrooms (sink, head, shower, and, in some of the most expensive rooms, bathtubs), space is tight, and fixtures are no more than serviceable. For instance, the closets are metal lockers. Also, a high percentage of the cabins are inside, which means they have no windows. On the other hand, the lecture facilities are excellent, the glassed-in promenade deck wonderful for watching for wildlife while remaining warm and dry, and the inside Mandarin Lounge a cozy, living room-like refuge. Other facilities include: the largest library on any cruise ship (Dewey Decimal-indexed, no less), fitness center, laundromat and full-service laundry, three bars, six lounges (including separate smokers and nonsmokers rooms, in which the lectures in the main lounge are shown on closed-circuit TV), cinema/lecture hall, gift shop, dining room, children's playroom, and beauty shop. But as Dennis Myrick, the vice-president of World Explorer says, "Our passengers come to see Alaska, not the ship." By the way, dinner and lunch are served in two separate seatings, and you are assigned a specific table and the late or early dining time for the entire cruise. For those who are interested, it is possible to arrange for college or tenure credit in conjunction with an Alaskan tour on the *Universe*.

OTHER COMMENTS: University of Pittsburgh's Semester at Sea on the *Universe* is available to college students for credit, with some possible space for auditing adults. For more information, contact: Institute for Shipboard Education, 811 William Pitt Union, Pittsburgh, PA 15260, tel. (412) 648-7490. Fax (412) 648-2298

CONTACT: World Explorer Cruises, 555 Montgomery St., San Francisco, CA 94111-2544, tel. (800) 854-3835. Fax (415) 391-1145.

FURTHER POSSIBILITIES
▼ ▼ ▼

AUDUBON SOCIETY, 950 Third Avenue, New York, NY 10022, tel. (212) 546-9140, fax (212) 832-0242. The National Audubon Society sponsors cruises on Renaissance, Clipper, Society Expeditions, Special Expeditions, and Travel Dynamics (Classical Cruises). In addition, look into the various travel programs that are offered by some local chapters of the Audubon Society that may include trips on small boats. (See also the profile of Audubon's camps and workshops on pages 84–85.)

BIG FIVE EXPEDITIONS, 2151 E. Dublin-Granville Rd., Columbus, OH 43229, tel. (800) 541-2790 or (614) 898-0036, fax (614) 898-0039; or 110 Route 110, S. Huntington, NY 11746, tel. (800) 445-7002 or (516) 424-2036, fax (516) 424-2154. In addition to its nature and photography tours and its Africa wildlife safaris, Big Five offers cruises of the Nile River and the Galapagos Islands. (See pages 86–87 for full profile of the company.)

GEO EXPEDITIONS, P.O. Box 3656, Sonora, CA 95370, tel. (800) 351-4041 or (209) 532-0152. Geo has small yacht cruises of the Galapagos Islands. Among their other programs, they also offer African photo safaris.

INTERNATIONAL EXPEDITIONS, One Environs Park, Helena, AL 35080, tel. (800) 633-4734 or (205) 428-1700, fax (205) 428-1714. Cruises of the Galapagos are among the many wildlife adventures offered by International Expeditions. (See pages 92–94 for a full profile of International Expeditions.)

JOURNEYS, 4011 Jackson, Ann Arbor, MI 48103, tel. (800) 255-8735 or (313) 665-4407. A wilderness company that specializes in treks and other physically challenging adventures, Journeys offers small boat cruises in the Galapagos and Papua New Guinea, as well as various combination sail/treks. (See full profile of Journeys on pages 128–129.)

MAINE WINDJAMMER ASSOCIATION, P.O. Box 317, Rockport, ME 04856, tel. (800) 624-6380. This is an association made up of 12 members that feature two- and three-masted sailing vessels that range in size between 64 feet and 132 feet, some dating to before the 1890s. Depending upon the vessel, they carry between 22 and 44 passengers, and sail on three-day or six-day trips out of Camden or Rockport from Memorial Day to Columbus Day. Although all itineraries and schedules are based upon the weather, the basic plan is to sail during the day and anchor during the evening and morning at tiny fishing villages or deserted islands. The only organized activity is an evening lobster bake. Prices range from $275 to $585.

MARQUEST, Merrill Lynch Building, P.O. Box 2438, Laguna Hills, CA 92654, tel. (800) 854-4080, is handling the bookings on a new ship—the *Columbus Caravelle*—that will be sailing Antarctica and the Arctic. If you have any experience with this company or this ship, please contact us. At the time of going to press, it was too new for us to have full information.

MOUNTAIN TRAVEL, 6420 Fairmont Ave., El Cerrito, CA 94530-3606, tel. (800) 227-2384 or (415) 527-8100, fax (415) 525-7710. Known for its trekking programs and other land adventures, Mountain Travel also offers Green Cruises through wilderness areas around the world including the Galapagos Islands, the Amazon River, the Great Barrier Reef, Antarctica. (Please see the full profile of Mountain Travel on pages 129–131.)

TRANS NIUGINI TOURS, c/o UNIREP, 850 Colorado Blvd., Suite 105, Los Angeles, CA 90041, tel. (213) 256-1991, fax (213) 256-0647; or P.O. Box 371, Mt. Hagen, Papua New Guinea, tel. (675) 52-1438, fax (675) 52-2470. Cruises through the Blackwater and middle Sepik region of Papua New Guinea on the riverboat *Sepik Spirit*, which offers air-conditioned cabins with private bathrooms. Trans Niugini is an environmentally concerned, socially aware, and highly experienced tour operator that also offers land programs and lodges in Papua New Guinea, where the owners of the company live and contribute to the community. (See pages 99–101.)

VESSELS OF WINDJAMMER WHARF, P.O. Box 1050, Rockland, ME 04841, tel. (800) 999-7352. This small company has two sailing vessels that accommodate 20 to 24 passengers and a 12-passenger motor yacht. They offer three-day and six-day cruises up and down the Maine coast that combine traditional sightseeing with hiking. The motor yacht, *The Pauline*, is a former sardine carrier and is described by the company as a "Bed and Breakfast at sea." Prices range from $300 to $900 per passenger.

VOYAGERS INTERNATIONAL, P.O. Box 915, Ithaca, NY 14851, tel. (800) 633-0299 or (607) 257-3091, fax (607) 257-3699. In addition to its extensive natural history and photography tours, Voyagers offers Galapagos cruises. Voyager books a variety of boats and ships, depending upon your budget and preferences. The more expensive yachts all have private bathrooms in every cabin and air conditioning. Some of the economy boats have shared showers. Or, you can choose a "cruise ship" that carries up to 90 passengers. Their Galapagos prices do not reflect a commission for travel agents, so contact them directly or expect to pay a surcharge for using an agent to handle the booking. (See full profile on Voyagers on pages 101–104.)

ZEGRAHM EXPEDITIONS, 1414 Dexter Avenue North, Seattle, WA 98109, tel. (206) 285-4000, fax (206) 285-5037. A new company headed by Werner Zehnder (the former vice-president of Society Expeditions), Zegrahm has scheduled a cruise through the Soviet Arctic Northeast Passage on a Russian icebreaker. They also plan to be the first U.S. organization to offer land excursions into Vietnam as soon as the State Department lifts the current sanctions.

PART THREE

POINTS OF REFERENCE

▼ ▼ ▼

The following are just a few of the many organizations, newsletters, and magazines (other than those mentioned elsewhere in this book) that could provide useful information about Green Travel, conservation, nature, history, social issues, etc. Though the list is not long, you will find that any one of them will plug you into an interesting network of individuals and organizations that will lead to further referrals.

NEWSLETTERS, MAGAZINES, AND BOOKS
▼ ▼ ▼

BUILDING ECONOMIC ALTERNATIVES, Co-op America, 2100 M Street N.W., Suite 403, Washington, DC 20063, tel. (800) 424-2667. While this Co-op America quarterly magazine deals mainly with consumer concerns and news, each issue carries various articles and features on Green Travel, ecotourism, and responsible tourism. It is also a good source for smallish Green Travel tour operators that advertise here and almost no place else. The magazine is distributed free to members but is also available for $1 per issue to nonmembers.

BUZZWORM, P.O. Box 6853, Syracuse, NY 13217-7930. An independent bi-monthly magazine that reports on environmental issues. Heavy on color photography and consumer-related ecotourism articles. $18/year.

CONSUMER REPORTS TRAVEL LETTER, P.O. Box 51366, Boulder, CO 80321-1366, tel. (800) 999-7959. Published monthly, *Consumer Reports Travel Letter* offers no-nonsense advice and tips about how to be an intelligent travel consumer. $37/year.

THE EDUCATED TRAVELER, P.O. Box 220822, Chantilly, VA 22022, tel. (703) 471-1063. A monthly newsletter directed to more intelligent traveling, with various travel tips. $75/year.

THE GREEN CONSUMER, a 250-page book published by Penguin Books, which discusses how consumers' purchase choices can help in the fight to save the world from pollution. Available in bookstores.

JUST GO, 1095 Market St., San Francisco, CA 94103-1613, tel. (415) 255-5951. A glossy, four-color quarterly magazine that is available on newsstands and through subscriptions, *Just Go* is, according to the publisher, Lisa Taub, "dedicated to supporting local cultures and people who are doing responsible things." But it's also a travel magazine designed to make people want to get up and Just Go.

NATIONAL COUNCIL OF CHURCHES, 475 Riverside Drive, Room 851, New York, NY 10115, tel. (212) 870-2044. The Council's newsletter, MIROR, often carries notices and information of people-to-people and reality study tours.

NATIONAL GEOGRAPHIC MAGAZINE, 17th & M Streets. NW, Washington, DC 20007, tel. (202) 944-8530. Certainly, one of the great magazines of all time, *National Geographic* has also promoted Green Travel (as we define it) for longer than any other publication or organization we know. If you get only one magazine a month, this should be it. $18/year.

NATURAL HISTORY, the magazine of the American Museum of Natural History, P.O. Box 5000, Harlan, IA 51537-5000, tel. (800) 234-5252. This is a beautifully written and printed full-color magazine that is filled with fascinating information about nature. Also, the ads are a useful source of Green Travel options. $22/year.

OUTSIDE, 1165 North Clark Street, Chicago, IL 60610, tel. (312) 951-0990, is a magazine dedicated to outdoor adventure travel. Heavy on first-person, I-did-it-myself writing and photography, it is a celebration of hiking, trekking, rafting, skiing, or climbing throughout the world. Of special note is its special February issue that lists literally hundreds of different adventure trips and tours.

SIERRA, 730 Polk Street, San Francisco, CA 94109, tel. (415) 776-2211. One of the oldest, best, and most prestigious nature magazines, *Sierra* is a treasure-trove of stories, articles, and columns on the ecology and environment of our planet. More than that, it is perhaps the primary voice of this country's conservation movement. It also contains a wealth of reviews and advertisements that give numerous names and phone numbers of small, specialized Green Travel tours and trips. The $33 annual Sierra Club membership includes a subscription to this monthly magazine.

SMITHSONIAN MAGAZINE, 900 Jefferson Drive, Washington, DC 20560. For the price of an annual membership ($20), you receive an exciting and varied magazine with stunning photographs and brilliant writing. While it doesn't carry travel articles per se, its eclectic character insures that there's always something in every issue that deals with nature and the wilderness. Incidentally, the membership gives access to Smithsonian's extensive travel, study, and research programs.

TRANSITIONS ABROAD MAGAZINE, P.O. Box 3000, Denville, NJ 07834; or 18 Hulst Rd, P.O. Box 344, Amherst, MA 01002, tel. (413) 256-0373. For only $18 a year, Transitions Abroad will send you bi-monthly magazines about living and traveling in other countries. Designed originally for people who plan to move to another country, *TA* offers quite a bit of information and travel tips that are valuable to the vacationer, too. Don't expect a glossy or even pretty magazine; *TA* is a flimsy newsprint-type book that is filled with truly useful material, such as: meeting locals, how to get a job, becoming an apprentice, homestays, unusual alternatives to traditional travel, etc. Especially noteworthy are their special publications, such as the *Educational Travel Directory* ($6.95), which is updated and printed annually. If you are serious about meaningful and unusual travel, then *Transitions Abroad* is a must.

TRAVEL ALTERNATIVES, 1117 Del Mar Avenue, Santa Barbara, CA 93109, tel. (805) 962-7157. A recently started newsletter, *Travel Alternatives* plans to promote responsible tourism, while providing vacationers with access to alternatives to traditional tourism. Subscription is $12 per year.

ON-LINE DATABASES
▼ ▼ ▼

There's a high-tech, 24-hour-a-day adventure travel service called *Adventure Atlas* that lists basic information on approximately 12,000 adventure and special-interest travel tours and programs. However, it is for computer-smart readers who possess basic communications equipment—computer, modem, and communications software—plus membership in one of two popular on-line database services, *Delphi* or GENIE. To access the *Adventure Atlas*, log on and call up the OAG Electronic Edition Travel Service on *Delphi*, and Travel + Plus on GENIE.

ORGANIZATIONS

▼ ▼ ▼

THE CENTER FOR RESPONSIBLE TOURISM, P.O. Box 827, San Anselmo, CA 94979, tel. (415) 258-6594. One of the most important organizations involved in improving the quality of impact that tourism has on Third World cultures, the Center is at the forefront of the Green Travel movement, making a difference in how tour operators, tourism developers, and tourists behave.

CO-OP AMERICA, 2100 M St. NW, Washington, DC 20063, tel. (800) 424-2667 or (202) 872-5307. Co-op America is one of the largest and best-known environmentally and socially responsible organizations in the country. Based in the cooperative movement of the 1960s, Co-op is essentially a networking clearinghouse among organizations, businesses, and individuals who are making an effort to live and work according to a basic ethic. Among their members are travel companies. Plus, their in-house travel agency, Travel-Links, guarantees to book the least expensive flights available. Also available to members is Diane Brause's thin "Directory of Alternative Travel Resources."

DEFENDERS OF WILDLIFE, 1244 19th St. NW, Washington, DC 20036, tel. (202) 659-9510. Defenders is a highly regarded "national nonprofit citizen's organization working to preserve, enhance, and protect the natural abundance and diversity of wildlife and the habitat critical for its survival." Very active and successful in lobbying for conservation and wildlife protection, Defenders also publishes a beautiful bimonthly glossy magazine for their members. One of their current projects, which will benefit travelers, has been to locate and mark places on public lands where the public may see the wildlife without negatively impacting on the animals or other natural resources. As a result, they are publishing a series of excellent "Wildlife Viewing Guides" and are in the process of placing markers on highways. Also noteworthy is their work to promulgate a "Wildlife-Watching Etiquette." $20 annual membership.

THE ECOTOURISM SOCIETY, 2021 L Street NW, Suite 250, Washington, DC 20036, tel. (202) 234-5465. Among their activities, the Ecotourism Society is attempting to establish standards by which those organizations which claim to be environmentally and socially responsible may be measured.

FRIENDS OF CONSERVATION, 1420 Kensington Rd., Oak Brook, IL 60521-2106, tel. (708) 954-3388, fax (708) 954-1016. Under the royal patronage of H.R.H the Prince of Wales, the internationally prestigious Friends of Conservation sponsor research, education, and conservation through direct measures in East Africa (Kenya, Tanzania, Zimbabwe). Its origins may be found in the

Friends of the Maasai Mara, which was established to prevent and stop the decline of wildlife in Kenya's famous game reserve. The measures FOC implement are having a direct effect on the quality of wildlife preserves in Africa, as well as the understanding of the local populace that such conservation is necessary for their nations' economic welfare. FOC's chairperson is Jorie Kent (of Abercrombie & Kent). Dr. Richard Leakey is the honorary director in Kenya. Membership in FOC not only means that you are promoting important conservation work, it provides entrée into a group of people whose names grace many a social register.

ONE WORLD FAMILY TRAVEL NETWORK, P.O. Box 3417, Berkeley, CA 94701, tel. (415) 841-8747. A member-based organization that is working to network individuals and organizations that believe travel can be meaningful and exciting as well as socially responsible. $15 to $35/year.

RAILS TO TRAILS CONSERVANCY, 1400 16th St. NW, Washington, DC 20036, tel. (202) 797-5400. An organization working at converting old, disused railway corridors into nature trails that would be accessible even to those who are physically handicapped.

TERN: TRAVELER'S EARTH REPAIR NETWORK, Friends of the Trees, P.O. Box 1064, Tonasket, WA 98855, tel. (509) 486-4726. Friends of the Trees is an organization devoted to the reforestation of the earth or "Earth Healing." TERN is a service in which, for a fee, they will refer travelers to individuals and organizations in other countries that are involved in conservation and care about the future of the earth. If you are going to a certain country, they will do a computer search for contacts for you, which may include possible homestays. The Friends of the Trees newsletter also keeps members informed about upcoming seminars.

WORLD RESOURCES INSTITUTE, 1709 New York Ave. NW, Washington, DC 20006, tel. (202) 638-6300, fax (202) 638-0036. World Resources Institute explores through scientific and social research the basic questions of how economic development, improved human welfare, and environmental conservation can coexist side by side as pragmatic objectives of governments, international organizations, and private businesses. They publish the papers that result from this research.

OTHER CONTACTS
▼ ▼ ▼

AFRICAN AMERICAN HERITAGE STUDIES PROGRAM, 120 S. LaSalle St., Suite 1144, Chicago, IL 60603, tel. (312) 443-0929.

AFRICAN WILDLIFE FOUNDATION, 1717 Massachusetts Ave. NW, Washington, DC 20036, tel. (202) 265-8393.

ALLIANCE FOR THE WILD ROCKIES, Box 8731, Missoula, MT 59807, tel. (406) 721-3621.

AMAZON CONSERVATION FOUNDATION, 18328 Gulf Boulevard, Indian Shores, FL 34635, tel. (813) 391-6211.

AMERICAN HIKING SOCIETY, 1015 31st St. NW, Washington, DC 20007, tel. (703) 385-3252.

CENTER FOR ENVIRONMENTAL INFORMATION, 99 Court St., Rochester, NY 14604, tel. (716) 546-3796.

COALITION FOR ENVIRONMENTALLY RESPONSIBLE ECONOMIES, 711 Atlantic Ave., Boston, MA 02111, tel. (617) 451-0927.

CULTURAL SURVIVAL, 11 Divinity Ave., Cambridge, MA 02138, tel. (617) 495-2562.

ECUMENICAL COUNCIL ON THIRD WORLD TOURISM, P.O. Box 24, Chorakhebua, Bangkok, 10230 Thailand.

ENVIRONMENTAL DEFENSE FUND, 257 Park Ave. S., New York, NY 10010, tel. (212) 505-2100.

FORESTRY PRIVATE ENTERPRISE INITIATIVE, P.O. Box 12254, Research Triangle Park, NC 27709, tel. (919) 549-4030.

HAWAIIAN CENTER FOR ECOLOGICAL LIVING, Star Route 13008, Keaau, HI 96749, tel. (808) 966-8592.

INTERNATIONAL WOMEN'S STUDIES INSTITUTE, 1230 Grant Ave., San Francisco, CA 94133, tel. (415) 931-6973.

NATIONAL PARKS & CONSERVATION ASSOCIATION, 1015 31st St. NW, Washington, DC 20036, tel. (202) 857-7000.

RAINFOREST ACTION CENTER, 6321 Roosevelt Way NE, Seattle, WA 98815, tel. (206) 524-0194.

RAINFOREST ACTION NETWORK, 301 Broadway, San Francisco, CA 94133, tel. (415) 398-4404

UNITED NATIONS ENVIRONMENT PROGRAMME/INDUSTRY & ENVIRONMENT OFFICE, Tour Mirabeau, 39-43 quai Andre Citroen, 75739 Paris, France, tel. 011-331-40-58-88-56.

THE WILDERNESS SOCIETY, 1400 I St. NW, Washington, DC, 20005, tel. (202) 842-3400.

WILDLAND JOURNEYS, 3516 NE 155th Street, Seattle, WA 98155, tel. (800) 345-4453 or (206) 365-0686.

ZERO POPULATION GROWTH, 1400 16th St. NW, Washington, DC 20036, tel. (202) 332-2200.

AFTERWORD

▼ ▼ ▼

Networking—the open communication among diverse people and organizations—is at the heart of Green Travel, as a phenomenon and as a book. We would like to hear from you to establish our own network. We are planning to update this book, and we would love to incorporate your input into our future work.

Please write to us c/o our editor, Steve Ross at John Wiley & Sons, Inc., 605 Third Avenue, New York, NY 10158. Tell us about your Green Travel experiences—both positive and negative. Are there organizations or destinations or types of trips that you would like us to look into more fully for you? Do you have any questions or comments about this book or about Green Travel in general? Please tell us what you think.

What we're talking about is an open-ended forum that should provide interesting feedback for all of us. But then, networking always has been a very fertile medium. We'll look forward to hearing from you.

Thank you,

Daniel Grotta & Sally Wiener Grotta

GEOGRAPHIC INDEX OF PROGRAMS

▼ ▼ ▼

The following organizations presently offer Green Travel to the places noted. Please remember that organizations can and often do change their trip plans, and while a group may no longer offer programs to the areas indicated below, other groups probably have added new destinations. Please check with each organization about their trips before setting your heart on going to a certain place with them.

▼ ▼ ▼ AFRICA

▼ ▼ ▼ The Americas

▼ ▼ ▼ ANTARCTICA

▼ ▼ ▼ ARCTIC

NORTHEAST PASSAGE (U.S.S.R. ARCTIC)

NORTHWEST PASSAGE (CANADIAN ARCTIC)

▼ ▼ ▼ ASIA

BHUTAN

BORNEO

▼ ▼ ▼ EUROPE

▼ ▼ ▼ MIDDLE EAST

▼ ▼ ▼ PACIFIC

SUBJECT INDEX

▼ ▼ ▼